Lands
that Hold One
Spellbound

NORTHERN LIGHTS SERIES

WILLIAM BARR, GENERAL EDITOR
COPUBLISHED WITH THE ARCTIC INSTITUTE
OF NORTH AMERICA

ISSN 1701-0004

This series takes up the geographical region of the North (circum-polar regions within the zone of discontinuous permafrost) and publishes works from all areas of northern scholarship, including natural sciences, social sciences, earth sciences, and the humanities.

Lands
that Hold One
Spellbound

A STORY OF EAST GREENLAND

UNIVERSITY OF
CALGARY
PRESS

Spencer Apollonio

University of Calgary Press
2500 University Drive NW
Calgary, Alberta
Canada T2N 1N4
www.uofcpress.com

LIBRARY AND ARCHIVES CANADA CATALOGUING IN PUBLICATION

Apollonio, Spencer
     Lands that hold one spellbound : a story of East Greenland / Spencer
     Apollonio.

(Northern lights series, ISSN 1701-0004 ; 11)
Includes bibliographical references and index.
ISBN 978-1-55238-240-0

1. Greenland–History. I. Title. II. Series.

G760.A66 2008   998.2   C2008-903840-1

The University of Calgary Press acknowledges the support of the Alberta Foundation for the Arts for our publications. We acknowledge the financial support of the Government of Canada through the Book Publishing Industry Development Program (BPIDP) for our publishing activities. We acknowledge the financial support of the Canada Council for the Arts for our publishing program.

Printed and bound in Canada by Marquis Printing Inc.
∞ This book is printed on FSC Silva Enviro Edition paper

Cover background photo of southeast Greenland courtesy of Douglas Bart
Cover design, page design and typesetting by Melina Cusano

Table of Contents

List of Illustrations

List of Maps

List of Graphs

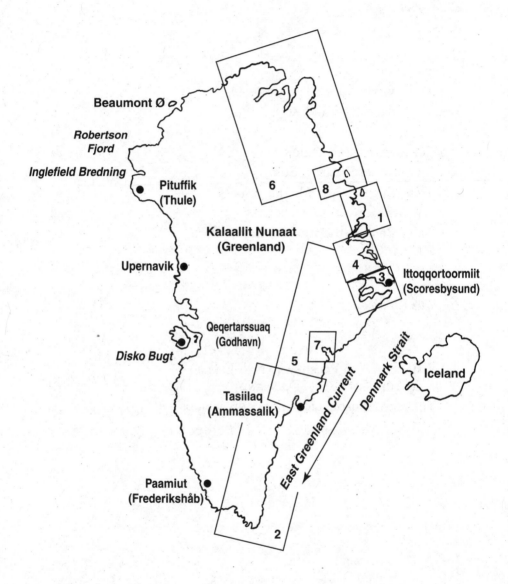

INDEX MAP

Foreword

I think of this as an *informal* history, simply a story, of East Greenland. It was while enjoying the book *Arctic Riviera*, a collection of magnificent photographs of Northeast Greenland by the Swiss photographer Ernst Hofer, that it occurred to me that the story of East Greenland ought to be compiled. *Arctic Riviera* is now fifty years old, but it is the most recent book of which I am aware that says anything about the nature of East Greenland. There are very few other, much older, books concerning the region, and there are no histories of that land. This is remarkable. Books about the polar regions are numerous, and many of the well-known stories are told and retold in new publications. There is a history of Northwest Greenland, but East Greenland, a much larger area, has been neglected, overlooked, ignored. A publisher told me that no one is interested in East Greenland. That may be true, but if so it may be because its story has never been told.

A reviewer of the manuscript was disappointed by my effort. He or she found it deficient in critical analysis and synthesis – a comprehensive summing up – of the diverse and rich scientific results (tens of thousands of pages, in fact) of the numerous explorations. Such a purpose would call for a particularly qualified person. My qualifications are modest. My only trip to the east coast of Greenland was one brief visit to Station Nord in 1953 when I hitchhiked, without authorization or any excuse at all, on a resupply flight by the U.S. Air Force. Such a journey does not qualify one to speak with authority concerning such a vast land, especially a journey to Nord, particularly flat and uninteresting, not at all like the rest of East Greenland. My qualification for this effort is no more than the recognition that its story ought to be told. My purpose is simply to put in one place the remarkable stories of remarkable people who carried out the task of revealing a vast region, not for conquest or exploitation but because of their love of the land. My purpose also is to try to convey something of the nature of that land that attracted and held those people for so many years in its exploration.

East Greenland is appealing for several reasons. It is truly a land of splendour, as many of its explorers testify here. Its history is rather simple and can be readily grasped and encompassed, a fact that is encouraging and reassuring to those of us who are not historians; we are not over-whelmed or bewildered by a complexity of events and motives. And it is a benign history full of comprehensible and constructive purpose. There are relatively few tragedies in the European exploration. Even when war came to East Greenland, we know of only two fatalities due to hostile action, and both of those were unintended. Perhaps the most attractive qualities of the story of East Greenland are those of indigenous people who for thousands of years made their homes in one of the most difficult lands on earth, and of the explorers who have revealed it for us. Their narratives are full of enthusiasm for the lands they found and explored, and so many returned for so many years because they were held spellbound by this harsh but entrancing region.

 Preface

First, since the largest island in the world became an autonomous province of Denmark in 1979 and attained a large measure of Home Rule it is officially Kalaallit Nunaat – that is to say, The Land of the People. But that part of Kalaallit Nunaat of interest to us here is still known as East Greenland.

The east coast of the great island is divided into two administrative districts – North Greenland and East Greenland. In this book, however, the term East Greenland encompasses all of the east coast from Kap Farvel, Greenland's southernmost point, to Kap Morris Jesup, the northernmost land in the world. Distances are presented in kilometres and in statute miles.

Indigenous peoples are referred to by three terms – Eskimos, Inuit, and Greenlanders. Eskimos means those people prior to and of the Thule Culture. Inuit (singular form, Inuk; plural form, Inuit) refers to people descendent from the Thule Culture. Greenlanders refers to those people of mixed Inuit and European ancestry.

Danish and indigenous place names are used except in the cases of initial name-giving or where English equivalents are used in original direct quotations. Danish and English geographical equivalents are:

bjerg	mountain	gletscher	glacier	ø, øer	island,
brae	glacier	halvø	peninsula		islands
bredning	gulf	hav	sea	skær	rock
bugt	bay	havn	harbor	sø	lake
dal	valley	kap	cape	sund	sound
elv	river	klippe	cliff		
fjeld	mountain	kyst	coast		

Scoresby Sund refers to the fjord. Scoresbysund (now Ittoqqortoormiit) refers to the village in Scoresby Sund.

Acknowledgments

I wish to thank all of the following: Kirsten Caning, Aka Lynge and Hauge Andersen of the Danish Polar Center and Sissel Hansen of the Norwegian Polar Institute for providing information on factual details of this work; and Mark Edwards of the Whitby Museum for providing the image of William Scoresby, Jr. Kirsten Klüver at the Danish Polar Center was infinitely patient in finding images for this work. William Barr of the Arctic Institute of North America encouraged completion of the story and offered substantial information that facilitated my task. Genevieve LeMoine, Curator of the Peary-MacMillan Arctic Museum at Bowdoin College, identified essential references and gave good advice on the anthropology of East Greenland. Several anonymous reviewers suggested a number of additions and improvements. Douglas Bart, my neighbour and friend, generously provided essential computer support at a critical and perilous time and thereby saved the project from extinction. Robert Lane of Friendship, Maine, read an early draft and suggested modifications. James Rollins of Boothbay, Maine, prepared the maps. Peter Enman was a thorough manuscript editor. I thank them all most sincerely.

Credits

The University of Calgary Press gratefully acknowledges permissions from the following to use quoted material:

- The families of Augustine Courtauld, John Rymill, and Sir James Wordie
- KVUG Sekretariatet c/o Danish Polar Center for numerous quotations from *Meddelelser om Grønland*.
- The American Geographical Society for quotations from the publications of Louise A. Boyd.
- Texas A & M University Press for quotations from Wallace Hansen, *Greenland's Icy Fury* (1994).

Introduction: The Nature of the Land

> "Far north, hidden behind grim barriers of pack ice, are lands that hold one spellbound. Gigantic imaginary gates, with hinges set in the horizon, seem to guard these lands. Slowly the gates swing open, and one enters another world where men are insignificant amid the awesome immensity of lonely mountains, fjords, and glaciers."

So wrote Louise Boyd (1935:1), for whom the gates of the Arctic swung open seven times. Four times the gates led her spellbound into East Greenland, and she would have returned again if World War II had not descended upon the world – even upon remotest East Greenland.

Greenland is four times the size of France. Its east coast stretches over 2,880 km (1,790 mi), from Kap Farvel in the south, at latitude 59°45' N – farther south than Bergen, Norway, to Kap Morris Jesup at latitude 83°39' N, about 550 km (342 mi) from the North Pole. The total length of the east coast, measuring all its sinuosities, has been estimated at 16,360 km (10,143 mi) and the area at about 100,000 square km – about the size of Portugal or Greece and twice the size of Denmark – some 38,400 square mi of mountainous Arctic territory, scored by deep fjords and mighty glaciers.

The east coast is difficult to reach overland from the west coast because one must cross the Greenland ice sheet several hundred kilometres wide. From the east one must cross the East Greenland Current, a powerful stream of ocean water that carries with it innumerable icebergs and immense quantities of thick sea ice, some from the Arctic Ocean itself, and packs them along the Greenland shore. The ice belt in the current may be as much as 480 km (300 mi) wide. The ice of the current can be very dangerous for ships caught in it or trying to reach the coast. Many ships and lives have been lost in that ice pack. One can approach East Greenland from the south, from Kap Farvel or Prins Christian Sund, but then one must work one's way against both the strong current flowing from the north and the ice floes carried against the coast. The approach to East Greenland from the north is by way of the northernmost land in the world. The only people who have ever approached East Greenland from the north were Paleo-Eskimos and Inuit who on at least four migrations made those journeys thousands and hundreds of years ago. Truly there are formidable gates guarding the entry to East Greenland.

Once one passes from the east through the ice-belt gates guarding the coast, one comes upon an unforgettable land. East Greenland is a land of great and strikingly beautiful mountains and with the largest fjord systems in the world. It is rich in glaciers discharging icebergs into the sea. Its waters are everywhere the bearers of icebergs of great beauty and great menace.

This Arctic land experiences astonishing varieties of weather. The East Greenland Current and its ice pack have a great effect on the weather of the coast. If the ice belt is narrow and scattered, then moist and stormy weather patterns from the North Atlantic Ocean can move toward the coast and bring their depressing weather with them. The outermost coastal fringe in summer can be cold, bleak, and soaked by torrential rains. The densest fogs imaginable are not uncommon along the outer coast. If the ice belt is wide and dense, however, the weather along the coast and in the fjords will be clear and calm. There may be quiet sunlit days with unsurpassed atmospheric clarity and phantasmagorical refractions that are unequalled anywhere. Bears, walruses, and seals are numerous along the outer coast. Deep within the fjords, the midnight sun of summer may shine for days and weeks on end, the temperatures may rise to very comfortable levels, plants grow in abundance, and muskoxen, hares, and foxes roam the meadows. Birds can be found in countless numbers. And so can mosquitoes. Snowfall may be very deep – 15 m (50 ft) fell one winter at Skjoldungen on the southeast coast. Snowfall is much greater in the south than in the north, and even in winter torrential rains can fall.

East Greenland is not a uniform ribbon of unchanging glacial and stony wastes. Most simplistically, it consists of two coasts, one from the southernmost point trending north-northeast 1,600 km (1,000 mi) to Scoresby Sund, where it intersects with the second coast which runs almost due north 1,250 km (780 mi) to 81°36' N, at which point it trends northwest to Kap Morris Jesup. The two coasts are quite different in physical characteristics that greatly affect the circumstances of human and other life. The southern coast is so mountainous and broken by glaciers and fjords that travel for any distance on land is almost impossible. Foxes seem to be the only land mammals, and they are not numerous. Muskoxen and hares are nearly absent along this coast. There are very few plains extensive enough to support an abundance of those grazing animals, and passage from one grazing area to another would be very difficult because the terrain is so fractured by glaciers and steep high mountains. Sledge travel on sea ice on that coast is uncertain and dangerous because the frequent storms of winter break up the ice and send the ice floes drifting to sea. The people of Ammassalik had a poor reputation for sledging simply because they had few opportunities on the uncertain winter ice to perfect the technique. Only by kayak and umiak could the original peoples travel along the coast south of Ammassalik; indeed, archaeologists have speculated that not until they had developed seaworthy kayaks able to survive in the exposed waters of Greenland's southwest coast could they migrate beyond Kap Farvel and settle along that eastern land.

There is a remarkable change at Scoresby Sund, where the trend of the coast shifts to the north. Within Scoresby Sund and as far north as the land extends there may be found wide plains, rich meadows of grasses, numerous muskoxen, and, formerly, reindeer. Muskoxen are found at Scoresby Sund and Jameson Land, on the interior shores of Kejser Franz Joseph Fjord, on Ymer Ø, on Hold With Hope, on Wollaston Forland, on Germania Land, in the interior of Danmark Fjord, on Vildtland, and around Jørgen Brønlund Fjord, and even on the lowlands along the eastern and northern shores of northernmost Peary Land. Mountains and glaciers are numerous from Scoresby Sund northward, but grazing plains share the land equally and lend a very different character to this northern land from that found on the southern coast.

The southern coast is indented by innumerable fjords, most of them quite small. The northern coast is broken by immense fjords that extend 290 km (180 mi) inland from the outer coast. The inner shores of these fjords, far from the winds, fogs, and frigid waters of the Greenland Sea, make possible a summer climate and benign growing conditions that are astonishing for such far northern habitats.

The terrain of the southern and northern coasts to a large extent determined the nature of the European explorations. Land and sea-ice travel in the south is very difficult. All investigations were dependent first upon small boats that were able to make their passages, with great difficulty and danger, through the pack ice. Later, aircraft could more easily be used to explore the complex southern coasts. In the north long journeys by dog sledges were possible that explored and mapped much of the land.

The climate differs between the two coasts. South of Scoresby Sund in the first half of winter there may be frequent periods of rain and thaw and high humidity and thick fogs arising from the nearby open water. The northern coast could be stormy but much drier in early winter. The Danish zoologist Alwin Pedersen believed that this difference in climate explains the near absence of muskoxen south of Scoresby Sund. Muskoxen are well equipped to withstand the extreme cold of the North, but the moisture of the South would freeze and form ice within their thick coat. Other Arctic mammals could lick their fur dry or break icicles with their teeth. Muskoxen cannot do that, nor can they shake ice free from their fur. An accumulation of ice impedes their ability to move and would make them easier prey for their enemies.

Humans have discovered and explored this land more than seven different times over thousands of years. The earliest people came here on at least three occasions from the south, from the southwest coast of Greenland by way of Kap Farvel, and four times from the north on several migrations that were each separated by hundreds of years. The remains of those ancient peoples and the evidence of their migrations have been found throughout much, but not all, of the length of this immense coast.

Knud Rasmussen, Greenland's most famous son, who knew and understood the Inuit and Greenlanders better than anyone else, wrote (1932:169) that for the original inhabitants it was never the country's barrenness, the glaciers, the winter ice or the tremendous breakers of the ocean that clung to the mind and made them afraid. All those who have lived up there, and built a house in some sheltered cove, have never allowed their spirit to be broken by its severity; rather were they enthralled by its grand beauty – and by the idyll, the camp idyll, which seemed to become more intimate because the surroundings were so prodigious and wild.

Any one who has had merely the slightest contact with Greenland knows the legend of the old hunter from Aluk, the old man whose heart broke, overwhelmed with joy of recognition, when, after many years of absence in richer and more luxuriant parts of the West Coast, he came back to his old dwelling-place and one morning saw the sun rising out of the sea; so sublime was the love that bound him to the coast of East Greenland.

Only relatively recently have Europeans discovered, explored, and mapped the land. The Danes have made most of the explorations, but Norwegians, Swedes, Germans, British, French, Dutch, and Americans have contributed. After the earliest years of European exploration before 1880, there has been a remarkable continuity of discoverers, particularly Danes, returning year after year to East Greenland, with one generation passing the baton of responsibility on to the next. There has been remarkable commitment of individuals to the investigations of this land.

Helge Ingstad, a Norwegian who spent years in the Arctic and in East Greenland, tried to express the feelings of Europeans for this seemingly hostile land:

> the land, framed between ice-capped mountains and a blue fjord; icebergs, in rank and file, cruising slowly out toward the fjord mouth; heads of seal and walrus silently peering about above the surface of the water; schools of narwhal plunging gaily along their way; sea birds in million droves, haunting the bright air above the fjord – and on land, the broad plain, with grasses and bog cotton nodding in a sunlit breeze, while the

fragrance of willow and crowberry, of flowers both red and yellow, adds spice to the air; musk-oxen grazing slowly along the coast, as peacefully as kine on a *sæter*[1] knoll; terns sitting about on tussocks and whipping their tails.… Ah yes, here was the place at last where one could settle down, live and die and leave the world to take care of itself (Ingstad 1937:229–30).

East Greenland has benefited greatly from possibly unique personal commitments to science and exploration. There is something compelling about this remarkable land that holds one spellbound. Dedicated men and women have returned year after year for thirty, fifty, even sixty years to the harsh realities and sublime attractions of this land of splendour. We shall meet them in this narrative.

---

1 In Norway a *sæter* is an outlying farm where cattle are kept for summer grazing.

THE DISCOVERY FROM THE WEST

The people who first saw and chose to live in Greenland came from Ellesmere Island and the central Canadian Arctic and before that, more than 5,000 years ago, from Alaska and from the northeastern parts of Asia. They are called Paleo-Eskimos, and they arrived in Greenland over 4,400 years ago. Their journeys were made during or toward the end of the Climatic Optimum (8,000–5,000 BP), a period of relative warming, that encouraged or facilitated their wanderings ever northward and eastward, following their hunting prey into empty lands (Schledermann 1996). Their inventory of tools was smaller than that of the later Neo-Eskimos, the ancestors of present-day Greenlanders. The Paleo-Eskimos had not developed the material culture that is typical of the Neo-Eskimo lifestyle, which is more fully adapted to the demands and resources of the Arctic. Even so, the earliest people hunted ringed and bearded seals, muskoxen, char-salmon, birds, Arctic hare, polar bears, walrus, and possibly narwhal.

The Paleo-Eskimos came to Greenland in several migrations over at least 3,000 years. Their very earliest remains in Greenland are found in Peary Land, the northernmost land in the world. Anthropologists called them the Independence I people because the remains of their shelters and tools were first found in the vicinity of Independence Fjord. Their closest cultural affinities are with the Cape Denbigh Flint Complex originally found in Alaska. Count Eigil Knuth, who first identified the Independence I Culture, described the nature of their shelters – they cannot be called houses: "Many of the tent rings possessed a remarkably solid and house-like construction masonry and a central corridor of similar stone

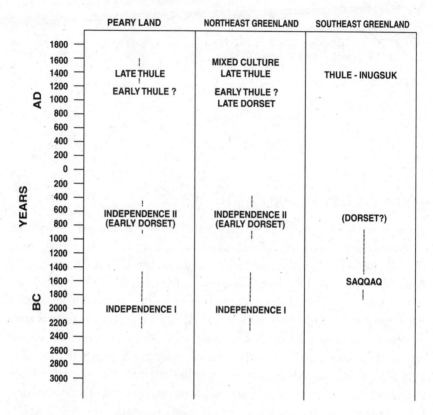

	PEARY LAND	NORTHEAST GREENLAND	SOUTHEAST GREENLAND

(The figure shows a time-line chart with a vertical years axis from 3000 BC at the bottom to 1800 AD at the top, divided into three regional columns.)

- PEARY LAND: LATE THULE / EARLY THULE ? ; INDEPENDENCE II (EARLY DORSET) ; INDEPENDENCE I
- NORTHEAST GREENLAND: MIXED CULTURE LATE THULE / EARLY THULE ? LATE DORSET ; INDEPENDENCE II (EARLY DORSET) ; INDEPENDENCE I
- SOUTHEAST GREENLAND: THULE - INUGSUK ; (DORSET?) ; SAQQAQ

Time-lines for Paleo- and Neo-Eskimo cultures in East Greenland

slabs placed edgewise, yet all so low that they presupposed a skin tent as a roof. In the centre of the middle of the corridors there were seen hearths with thick layers of charcoal and burnt bones" (Knuth 1967:13). Most of the bones were from muskoxen, and Knuth referred to this region of Peary Land as "The Musk Ox Way." The bones of hares, foxes, and char-salmon are also found in the ruins. It was a strange life those people lived in Peary Land. The sun is below the horizon for four and a half months of the year, and it is quite dark for two and a half months. There could have been little fuel – willow, heather, or muskox bones – for either heat or light. Knuth wrote that in the dark and the intense cold and the violent winds of Peary Land winters, families must have passed a lethargic indoor existence. "The people of the Musk-ox way must have lived through the dark period in a kind of torpor" (Knuth 1967:50). In the light period they roamed far across that great empty land, sunlit for months on end, searching for muskoxen, hares, and foxes. Knuth estimated there were about 200 people in the region of Jørgen Brønlund Fjord and Midsommer Sø, the location of most of the archaeological sites in Peary Land. It was a small group of people for such an immense land – indeed, there could not be a much larger population largely dependent upon muskoxen grazing on minimal Arctic meadows. From Peary Land the earliest people, as shown by archaeologists, migrated down the east coast of Greenland as far as Scoresby Sund, 1,350 km (838 mi) from Peary Land, hunting seals and walrus on the ice and in open waters along the outer coast. They apparently died out about 3,300 years ago after about 1,000 years in the region.

The second group of Paleo-Eskimos reached the northwest coast of Greenland about 4,000 years ago. They have been called the Saqqaq people, and they too had their origins in the Cape Denbigh Flint Complex of Alaska. Archaeologists now consider that the Independence I and Saqqaq peoples to be of essentially the same culture (Elling 1996). The Saqqaq people seem to have migrated down the west coast of Greenland, around Kap Farvel, and up the east coast to Ammassalik by about 1900 BC and to Scoresby Sund, where their remains have been found, and perhaps farther north than Shannon Ø. The Saqqaq people lived in Southeast Greenland for at least 1,100 years until about 800 BC, and then disappeared. But before that happened a new group of people passed around the north of Greenland into Peary Land and later moved southward along the east coast. These people are considered the earliest phase of the Dorset Culture that arose less than 3,000 years ago in the eastern Canadian Arctic. Peter Schledermann (1996) believes there are strong indications that early Dorset people amalgamated with Saqqaq people, producing the hybrid culture that Eigil Knuth, from their remains in Peary Land, called the Independence II people. They are now known as early Dorset people, and they lived in Northeast Greenland about 2,600 years ago. The Saqqaq and Dorset cultures are distinguished primarily by small but consistent differences in their tools. The Dorset people are known for delicate, detailed, faultless carvings in ivory of humans and animals. Traces of them have been found at Skjoldungen and Ammassalik in southeastern Greenland, but early Dorset remains on the east coast are found mainly in Peary

Land and Northeast Greenland. Two large sites of these people have been studied, one on the northern edge of Holm Land and the other on Ile de France (Andreasen 1998). The Holm Land site, now called the Eigil Knuth Site, contains about 100 structures, and the site on Ile de France contains about 400. The shelter remains of both the Saqqaq (Independence I) and early Dorset (Independence II) peoples are marked mainly by central rectangular hearths, formed by narrow vertical stones, which provided some heat and some light. No lamps or cooking pots have been found with those sites. Their cooking evidently was accomplished by hot stones in skin bags. No skeletal remains of either Independence I or II people have been found in East Greenland.

There was then apparently a period of about 1,000 years in which no Paleo-Eskimos lived in northern Greenland. A later phase of the Dorset people, later than the Saqqaq or early Dorset Cultures, arrived in Greenland about 800 AD. The late Dorset people also were a Paleo-Eskimo people and have been called "consummate hunters" (Odess, Loring and Fitzhugh 2000); seal bones and those of other marine mammals are found with some of their ruins. Unlike their Paleo-Eskimo predecessors and the Neo-Eskimos who succeeded them, there is no evidence that the late Dorset people used the bow and arrow or had dogs. Some Dorset people passed around northern Greenland and down the east coast as far as Young Sund just north of Clavering Ø and even on to Scoresby Sund. It is possible that late Dorset people survived long enough to encounter the next group of people to migrate into East Greenland (Schledermann 1996).

About the time that the Norse started their westward voyagings from Scandinavia into the North Atlantic, another group of people began an eastward migration from Alaska. The Norse arrived in Greenland about 1,000 years ago. The new arrivals from Alaska reached North Greenland about 800 years ago, near the end of a relatively warmer period – the Neo-Atlantic warming – that lasted from 800 to about 1200 AD. They are known as Neo-Eskimos. They were better adapted than their predecessors to the Arctic, living largely upon sea mammals, including the large bow-head whale, and with a culture that reflects that technological evolution. They were part of the Arctic Whale Hunting Culture that originated in Alaska somewhat more than 2,000 years ago and gradually spread eastward across the Canadian Arctic. They had developed skin boats – the umiak for hunting whales and other sea mammals – thus gaining full access to the most productive resources, those of the Arctic seas. Land animals were now a side issue with them, and they found their fuel not from Arctic willow or driftwood or the bones of muskoxen, as had the Paleo-Eskimos, but from the blubber of whales and seals. Their winter houses were solid, substantial, semi-subterranean structures well protected from the cold. The houses were built with timber in Alaska or with stones and whalebones and turf in Greenland. They also apparently had learned the technique of building snow houses – igloos – from the Dorset people whom they had encountered in their migrations. Neo-Eskimos had invented stone lamps for light, heat, and cooking, and they had cooking pots of clay or stone. The Neo-Eskimos had a larger inventory of tools than the Paleo-Eskimos, much of it adopted for the efficient hunting of sea mammals. In Greenland this culture is called the Thule Culture, because it was first described in the early 1920s as a result of Knud Rasmussen's Fifth Thule Expedition. These people are the ancestors of today's Greenlanders. Archaeological discoveries in Northeast Greenland show that the early Thule people passed around the north coast of Greenland and down the east coast, reaching Scoresby Sund about 1300 AD (Gulløv 2000). A more recent group of Thule people arrived in Northwest Greenland and also passed north about Greenland.

A remarkable archaeological discovery in 1949 in Peary Land was that of a nearly complete wooden framework of an umiak, a whale-hunting boat, about 10 m (35 ft) long. It was in a excellent state of preservation and has been reassembled in the National Museum of Denmark. The umiak has been dated by the carbon-14 method as 476 years old ± 100 years. The boat had been repaired with a small piece of oak, and it contained a few iron nails which means that its owners must have had contact with the Norse colonists of West Greenland. It is the only vessel known to have ever passed north around Greenland. Near the remains of the umiak were numerous tools of the whale hunting culture – whaling harpoon heads, blubber pounders, a whalebone spade, a box made in part of whale baleen, an umiak paddle. Bones of the Greenland, or bowhead, whale were found here. Bones of narwhal, bearded seal, and ringed seal as well as bones of muskoxen, reindeer, and foxes were also found at this site. The Thule people, including those in East Greenland, hunted large whales probably until European whaling in the eighteenth and nineteenth centuries greatly reduced the number of bowheads in the far northern waters; as many as seven European countries hunted whales in those waters (Robert-Lamblin 1986).

Shortly after they arrived in West Greenland, the Thule people came in contact with the Norse who had colonized southwestern Greenland late in the tenth century. The Norse contact led to a modification of the Thule Culture such that it is sometimes known as the Inugsuk Culture, named for an island in the Upernavik district where the Norse may have had trading contacts with the Thule people.

The Inugsuk people, like the Saqqaq before them, also passed around the southernmost part of Greenland and then north again, probably in the fifteenth century, and their remains are found along the east coast. There is an archaeological site called *Dødemandsbugten* (Dead Man's Bay) on Clavering Ø on the northeast coast of Greenland where the Thule people migrating from the north and the Inugsuk people from the south met and formed what the Swiss archaeologist Hans-Georg Bandi (1964:171) called "a peculiar hybrid culture." This mixed culture has been dated from both the sixteenth century and from the eighteenth century. Beginning in the seventeenth century there ensued a long period of population decline. The people of Kangerdlugssuaq on the northern part of the southeastern coast became extinct, but why is not clear; that region is rich in game. The last of those living in Northeast Greenland, only twelve people, were encountered briefly in 1823. They had disappeared by 1870. About 630 people were found on the southeasternmost coast in 1830, but only 120–130 remained in 1884. Beyond them to the north in the region around Ammassalik a previously unknown group of Inuit numbering 413 souls was found in 1885. By 1894 they were reduced to 293. Some of the east coast inhabitants had migrated to the west coast, and many had died from disease, or murder and blood feuds. In 1881–82 seventy people – more than 15 per cent of the population around Ammassalik – had died of starvation. The establishment of the Danish mission at Ammassalik in 1894 came just in time to preserve the population from extinction. Fifty years later the population numbered about 1,400.

EARLY EUROPEAN APPROACHES AND THE GREAT DISASTER OF 1777

East Greenland is said to be visible, on a clear day, from the highest land on the west coast of Iceland. The distance between the two lands is 300 km (185 mi), and the distance from a 914-m (3,000-ft) mountain in Iceland to the highest mountain in Greenland, over 3,700 m (12,200 ft) high, is about 370 km (230 mi), which is just within visible range in clear weather and with atmospheric refraction. The earliest settlers of Iceland, whether Irish or Norse in the ninth or tenth centuries, may very well have seen the land to the west.

The earliest European believed to have sighted the east coast of Greenland was Gunnbjørn Ulf-Krakason, an Icelander, between the years AD 900 and 930. He is thought to have been blown off his course as he sailed to or around Iceland. Gunnbjørn reported land to the west when he finally made his harbour in Iceland, and the sagas thereafter mentioned Gunnbjørn's Skerries, islands now thought to be in the Ammassalik area. It was this report of Gunnbjørn that led Erik the Red to voyage westward looking for a new home when in 985 or 986 he was exiled from Iceland for murder. Erik and his followers established homesteads and farms on Greenland's west coast.

During the 500-year Norse colonization of West Greenland there are vague reports of mariners wrecked on the east coast as they voyaged from Norway or Iceland to the Greenland colonies. In the *Floamanna Saga*, which contains some fantastic tales, there is an account of a shipwreck with a thread of truth to it. The saga relates that Thorgils Orrabeinsfostre lost his ship at a northerly point of the east coast in October 998, or perhaps in 1000 or 1001. Only in the autumn would that coast be sufficiently free of ice to permit such a ship to get through the ice belt and reach the shore. Thorgils had his wife and household of thralls with him, accompanied by Jostein of Kalfholft with his wife and son and thralls, altogether about twenty-six souls. They struggled with great hardships for three summers and winters to survive and finally to make their way south. In the first winter they built a hut near the site of the shipwreck. Seal hunting sustained them, but many were afflicted with scurvy and some died. Thorgils' wife bore a son during their first winter. Ice packed on the shore in the following summer and prevented escape by their small boat; for the second winter they were imprisoned at the hut. In the second spring Thorgils with three others climbed the mountain heights to view the state of the ice. On their return Thorgils found his wife murdered, but the infant son was still alive. The thralls, the boat, and the stores were gone. Thorgils and the remaining companions built a boat of skins stretched over a driftwood frame, and in that fragile craft they struggled south with great difficulty. In this period they may have come upon a few Eskimos; archaeology has confirmed that Eskimos were on the coast in the eleventh century and such an encounter was possible.

Thorgils' party spent a third winter on the coast. The next summer they came upon one of those who had stolen their boat and deserted them. They killed him. Near the southern end of the east coast they came upon the solitary homestead of Rolf, who had been outlawed from the Norse settlements. Thorgils' party spent their fourth winter with Rolf. The next spring they borrowed Rolf's ship with a promise to do what they could, because of Rolf's hospitality, to get his outlawry rescinded. Thorgils reached the southernmost Norse settlement on the west coast with a small remnant of his party. Among the colonies on the west coast he found the thralls who had deserted him. With swift, rough, Viking justice, Thorgils seized their property and sold them again as thralls.

The Norse undoubtedly made hunting trips to the southernmost coast of East Greenland; remains of a Norse hunting camp have been found in Lindenow Fjord. Helge Ingstad (1966) suggests that such trips were frequent, and there are hints from sagas and artefacts found on the coast that the hunters might have reached nearly as far north as Scoresby Sund. About the year 1200, Norse hunters on the east coast found the wreck of the Norwegian vessel *Stangarfoli*. They also found the skeletons of six men and the undecomposed body of the Icelandic priest Ingemund Thorgeirsson. The hunters found wax tablets with his body on which Ingemund had carved runes to tell the story of his death by starvation. Ingemund had been the archbishop's first choice for Bishop of Greenland; even though he had declined the honour, he found his final rest there while attempting to visit that remote diocese.

The last recorded visit by Europeans to the Norse colonies was in 1408. Efforts to re-establish contact with the lost colonists began in the late sixteenth century, with the belief that the so-called East Settlement of the Norse was located on the east coast of Greenland.[1] In 1579 two ships under Jacob Allday, an Englishman, were sent by the Danish king. They sighted the east coast near Kap Dan, not far from Ammassalik, and at one point they were within a few kilometres of the coast; but they could not break through the ice. Voyages in 1581, 1605, 1606, and 1607 attempted to reach the east coast without success. Henry Hudson, seeking not lost Norse colonies but a northern passage to the Orient, came upon the east coast on June 13, 1607, when after eighteen days at sea and after a night of "great fogge with much wind," he saw the sun and got a glimpse of an unknown land. Hudson wrote (Purchase 1906:295–98; Wordie 1927:236):

> This was a very high Land, most part covered with Snow. The neather part was uncovered. At the top it looked reddish, and underneath a blackish Clay, with much ice lying about it. The part which we saw when wee cast about, trended East and West: And the Norther part which we saw, trended North-east and by North, and North-east: and the length which wee saw was nine leagues; we saw much Fowle. Also we saw a Whale close by the shoare. We called the Head-land which we saw, Youngs Cape and neere it standeth a very high Mount like a round Castle, which wee called the Mount of Gods Mercie.

Then fog shut in again and for the next seven days there was fog and rain and snow and gales, and Hudson manoeuvred his ship to keep clear of the land. On June 19 Hudson hoped to learn whether the land they had seen "were a part of an Iland or part of Groneland," but again "the fogge increased very thicke with much wind." The weather later cleared when he had "a prettie gale." On June 22 it was clear and calm with the land in view, and he was able to determine his position at latitude 72°38' N and about 12 leagues (60 km, 37 mi) from the land. Hudson wrote:

---

1 The sources for these attempts to reach East Greenland are Nansen 1890 Vol. 1:274–308, Bobé 1928, and Gad 1971, Vol. 1.

It was a mayne high Land, nothing at all covered with snow: and the North part of that mayne high Land was very high Mountaynes, but we could see no snow on them.... The many fogs and calmes with contrary winds, and much Ice neere the shoare, held us from farther Discovery of it.... The chiefe cause that moved us thereunto, was our desire to see that part of Groneland, which (for ought that we know) was to any Christian unknowne.... And considering wee found Land contrarie to that which our Cards make mention of; we accounted our labour so much the more worth. And for ought that wee could see, it is like to bee a good land and worth seeing.... And considering wee knew no name given to this Land wee thought good to name it, *Hold with Hope*, lying in 73. degrees of latitude.

Thus was discovered the northeast coast of Greenland by Europeans, and that particular land is known today as Hudson named it – Hold with Hope. Hudson did not land there and never returned.

Then in 1652, 1653, and 1654 a wealthy Dane, Henrik Møller, sent expeditions under a Dutchman, David Danell. Danell was able in the first year to sail close to the east coast at 64° N and followed it south to Kap Farvel. He was unable to land, again blocked by ice. It was the same story in 1653 and 1654. Dutch whalers, Gael Hamkes in 1654 and Broer Ruys in 1655, reached the coast near Hudson's Hold with Hope, but as far as we know they did not land. Their names now appear on the map of a nearby bay and a cape. In 1670 the whaler Lambert saw land at the high latitude of 78°30' N. The Danish king sent Otto Axelsen in 1670 and 1671. There is no record of the first voyage and Axelsen did not return from the second. Very likely his ship was crushed in the ice.

For three months in 1724 Captain Hans Faester cruised along the coast from 66°30' N to 60°28' N. He got within 8 km (5 mi) of the coast but could not land. A similar unsuccessful attempt in 1786 inspired Christian Egede to make six attempts upon the coast in that year and in the following year, each unsuccessful.

Several unsuccessful attempts to reach the east coast from the west coast were made in the early eighteenth century, including a scheme to cross the inland ice sheet with horses. Peder Olsen Walløe, who lived as a trader in Greenland, made a successful attempt in 1752. He passed by Kap Farvel in an umiak – an indigenous boat – and managed to travel about 60 km (37 mi) up the east coast, where he was obliged to turn back. His farthest point was named Kap Walløe by W.A. Graah in 1829. Peder Walløe was the first European known with certainty to have landed in modern times on the east coast.

The ice of the East Greenland Current fully justified its evil reputation in 1777. It was a very bad season for navigation on that coast. Between June 24 and 28 twenty-seven or twenty-eight whaling ships from Britain, Hamburg, Holland, Sweden, Denmark, and Bremen were caught in the pack-ice off Shannon and Clavering Øer. Some were later able to work free of the ice. Twelve ships could not escape and drifted south. Six of those vessels were crushed on August 19 and 20 565 km (350 mi) south of their point of entrapment. The rest drifted farther south, about 80 km (50 mi) off the shore. The last of them was crushed on October 11 about 48 km (30 mi) from the land and 2,000 km (1,240 mi) from the start of its drift. As the ships were destroyed and sank one by one, their crews took refuge in the remaining ships; 286 men were huddled on the last remaining ship. When it too was lost the crews camped as best they could on the ice floes. Attempts to reach the land across the ice failed. Some whalers died of cold, some by drowning, some of exhaustion; most died of starvation. Near the end of their drift they were living on ten spoonfuls of porridge a day. Ultimately, the surviving whalers – about 155 – reached several small settlements on the west coast. Three hundred and twenty men had perished.

The French naval lieutenant Jules de Blosseville sighted the east coast between 68° and 69° N in 1833. He returned to Iceland for repairs to his ship and to make a report of his discovery and then sailed back to East Greenland, where he and thirty-eight crewmen disappeared. Three search expeditions found no trace of them. That coast is now known as the Blosseville Kyst.

Attempts to lay transatlantic cables in 1859 and 1860 brought several vessels close to the southernmost East Greenland coast. Landings were not made because of storms and ice.

Attempts were made in 1863 and 1865 to found trading stations on the east coast. Again the ice stopped approaches. A Danish naval captain,

A. Mourier, cruised the coast in a survey vessel, *Ingolf*, in 1879, from 69°
N southward. The survey measured ocean depths, investigated the submarine ridge between Iceland and Greenland, and measured sea-water
temperatures on both sides of the ridge. Captain Mourier was unable to
reach the east coast and concluded that it was altogether impossible to
reach the east coast from the sea.

The Swedish Baron Adolf Nordenskiöld in mid-June 1883 steamed
on his ship *Sofia* within sight of Kap Dan. He too was unable to break
through the ice and therefore sailed south. Three days later, on June 15, he
was off Kap Farvel, still held from the shore by ice. Nordenskiöld steamed
on to the west coast, but in September he returned to the east coast. On
September 4 he anchored in and named Kong Oscar Havn, the site of the
present settlement of Tasiilaq (Ammasslik). Nordenskiöld's party spent
two days on shore making scientific collections. Even though they had
landed in what we now know was the populated part of the coast, they
found no people. They did find numerous and recent signs of people, and
when the inhabitants returned to the site they discovered what they held
to be something "exceeding strange and supernatural," wrote Fridtjof
Nansen (1890:292) – a beer bottle from the Carlsberg Brewery in Copenhagen. Nordenskjöld then made an unsuccessful attempt to reach the
coast farther north.

The earliest landings on the east coast, other than Nordenskjöld's
single brief visit, were all made much farther north.

SCORESBY, THE FIRST POLAR SCIENTIST, 1822

At the beginning of the nineteenth century the East Greenland seas north
and west of Iceland were well known to be dangerous waters to be avoided
because of the heavy ice that trapped and destroyed ships, and the ice
was a formidable barrier to the land that was known to lie beyond. A
few mariners, beginning with Gunnbjørn in the tenth century, had seen
the mountains that towered above the western horizon, but as far as we
know no Europeans since Thorgils Orrabeinstfostre nine hundred years
before had actually reached the northeast coast of Greenland and landed
on its shores. The charts for that part of the world were hardly more than
guesswork, greatly in error in most respects; they "were a snare rather than

a safeguard to the navigator," as William Scoresby, Junior, wrote (1823: xvii).

The great pioneer and explorer of that forbidding coast was William Scoresby, Junior, a whaling captain, one of the most remarkable men of his time, and one of the foremost of all polar explorers. Scoresby came from Whitby, England, from whence had earlier come the legendary Captain James Cook. Scoresby's father, William, Senior, was a whaling captain. The son had gone to sea at age ten when he stowed away on his father's ship for a cruise to the Arctic whale fishery. The younger Scoresby followed that trade each year thereafter until he commanded his own whaling ship, acquiring intimate knowledge of the Arctic seas and Arctic ice; he knew more of the ways of the Arctic than anyone else of his time. In the winters, when his ships had returned, Scoresby attended Edinburgh University, which laid the foundation for his scientific studies of the North. Scoresby published two books based on his whaling cruises and his scientific observations of Arctic phenomena. He recorded, analyzed, and speculated upon explanations for everything that came to his attention: the speed and direction of ocean currents, the temperatures at the surface and at depth of Arctic waters, tides, the causes of fog, the structure of snow crystals, the nature of aurorae and of solar coronae, atmospheric refraction, the nature of sea ice, the anatomy of narwhals, the geology of the lands he was the first to visit, archaeological remains on the Greenland shores, the plants and animals, and the Earth's magnetic variations for corrections of ships' compasses for accurate navigation. His books are full of such observations, and they are all interesting. He was in fact the first Arctic scientist.

Captain Scoresby sailed from Liverpool in the spring of 1822 in his ship *Baffin*, recently constructed specifically for the Arctic whaling trade. He first cruised off the west coast of Svalbard. Finding few whales, he sailed to the west and south, which brought him into the ice of the East Greenland Current, where previous experience suggested whales were to be found. His relative proximity to the barely known land of Greenland to the west excited his hopes of finding a way to reach the coast. In particular, he hoped to discover traces of the Icelandic or Norse colonists of Greenland last heard of four hundred years earlier. Scoresby, like most scholars of his time, believed that Østerbygd, or the Eastern Settlement of the Norse sagas, was to be found on the east coast of Greenland.

William Scoresby, Jr.
Courtesy of the Whitby Museum

The skill and danger of navigating within the ice off East Greenland were a large part of the whalers' trade, as they were of any vessel trying to reach that coast. The ice and weather of the East Greenland Current are as much a part of the story of East Greenland as the land itself, because everyone trying to reach or depart from the land had to deal with the current and ice belt in all their moods. Scoresby wrote (1823:46–47):

> The nautical operations of this day were of the most difficult kind which the whale-fishers have to encounter, and in which numbers of ships are annually damaged. Most of the masses of drift ice, among which we had to force a passage, were at least twenty times the weight of the ship, and as hard as some kinds of marble; a violent shock against some of them might have been fatal. But the difficulties and intricacies of such situations, affording exercise for the highest possible exertion of nautical skill, are capable of yielding, to the person who has the management of a ship, under such circumstances, a degree of enjoyment, which it would be difficult for navigators, accustomed to mere common-place operations, duly to appreciate. The ordinary management of a ship, under a strong gale, and with great velocity, exhibits evolutions of considerable elegance; but these cannot be comparable with the navigation in the intricacies of floating-ice, where the evolutions are frequent, and perpetually trying, – where manouevers are to be accomplished, that extend to the very limits of possibility, – and where a degree of hazard attaches to some of the operations, which would render a mistake of the helm, or a miscalculation of the powers of a ship, irremediable and destructive.

In spite of those "irremediable and destructive" possibilities, it was within the mass of ice that whales were to be found; there the whale hunters must go. Scoresby on June 3 found an extraordinary number of whales in pods of half a dozen or more, "sporting occasionally, and enlivening, by their frequent appearance, this otherwise barren region of solemn stillness and desolation" (Scoresby 1823:72). One whale boat came upon seven or eight whales of the largest size lying at the surface, huddled together remarkably

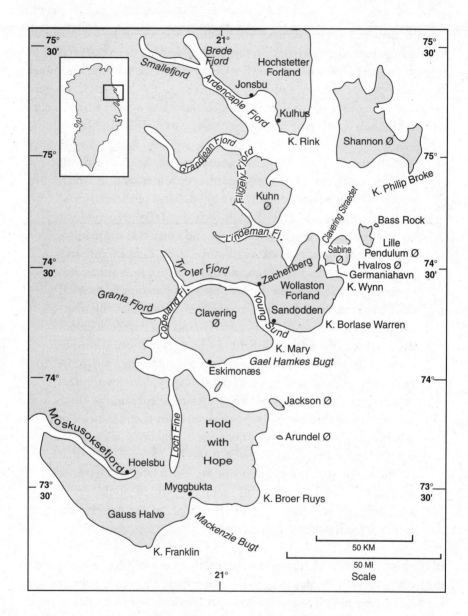

HOLD WITH HOPE TO SHANNON Ø

close. The weather was very still and calm, and ⸎
the slight noise of the boat and the whole pod made .
thrown up by their tails flew in showers over the boat in
sea for a hundred yards around was filled with eddies and wı.

Scoresby looked upon the coast of Northeast Greenland afteɪ
night on June 7–8; as far as we know it was the first recorded sightıₙ
this coast in 150 years. The wind subsided and the sky became perfectₗy
clear. Eighty km (50 mi) away, the land extended from N by E to NW.
Another voyager to Greenland described that extraordinary experience
when, after passing through the ice, the gloom of clouds and fog suddenly
lifted and thus revealed the mountainous coast that "being richly tainted
by a glorious western sun formed an unusually splendid sight. Greenland
unveiled to our anxious gaze that memorable evening, all the magnificence of her natural beauty. Was it to welcome us that she thus cast off her
dingy outer mantle, and shone forth with radiant smiles? – such winning
smiles!" (M'Clintock 1860:16).

Captain Scoresby wrote of the land (1823:82): "I looked on it with
intense interest, and flattered myself with the hope of being able to land
upon some of its picturesque crags, where no European foot had never
trod, before the season for the fishery should come to a close."

Captain Scoresby was at 74°06' N and concluded that the nearer
land in sight was Hold with Hope first seen by Henry Hudson in 1607;
beyond was the headland of Gael Hamkes Bugt, discovered by a Dutch
whaler in 1654. Early in June, however, there was little chance of getting
closer to this land; the ice was still too close and thick. Scoresby would
have to wait.

On June 18 *Baffin* was at 73°01' N and Scoresby began to discover
new land in the vicinity of Mackenzie Bugt, which he named. By mid-July
fog became common. For fifteen out of twenty days dense fog – Scoresby
(1823:159) called it "this bewildering obscurity" – prevailed, a common
event in the ice. In the previous year only three out of forty-one days had
been free of fog, and when the fog disappeared, the land was transformed
by refraction into curious appearances. "The whole exhibition is frequently
a grand and interesting phantasmagoria," wrote Scoresby (1823:167).

Scoresby used his astronomically determined positions of *Baffin* as
he drifted in the ice as a base line from which he took angles to the

newly discovered headlands and mountains. He was able to check the rate, or accuracy, of his chronometer because the moon was at a convenient distance from the sun for determining longitude – an uncommon skill among whaling captains or indeed any mariners of the time. The weather now was "uncommonly favourable" and enabled him to determine distances with "the greatest precision." He was thus able to chart the coast from Gael Hamkes Bugt to Bontekoe Ø with considerable accuracy. At other times, though the atmosphere was very clear, his survey was frustrated by a common Arctic phenomenon. He wrote (1823:143–45):

> ...the whole coast was found to be so disfigured by refraction, that I could not recognize a single monument or headland.... The land, and a number of ships that came within sight, as well as the ice, and indeed all distant objects were strangely distorted. Inverted images of two ships, occasionally double, were seen in the air, which, I imagine, were at least ten miles beyond the limit of direct vision; for we approached them about this distance without being able to see them.... These interesting exhibitions were at length closed by the commencement of a dense fog, which was productive of a most disagreeable transition of feeling: – from the exhilarating enjoyment of a pure atmosphere, and warm sunshine, with extensive and interesting prospects, we were in a moment enveloped by a depressing and impenetrable gloom.

Scoresby next came in upon the land along the Liverpool Kyst at 71°02' N. He wrote (1823:176–78):

> The land at this time in sight was the most extraordinary of any that I have ever seen before.... The land ... is mountainous, dark, and sterile in the extreme. Nothing can be conceived more rugged than it is; yet nothing that I have ever seen equals it in bold grandeur, and interesting character. There is nothing in it that is tame, smooth, or insignificant. The mountains consist of an innumerable series of elevated peaks, cones, or pyramids, with the most rugged assemblage of

sharp rocks jutting from the sides. They take their rise from the very beach, and ascend by steep and precipitous cliffs…. Most of the summits … are surmounted by ranges of vertical pinnacles, so uniform and parallel, as to resemble ranks of soldiers … .although they are probably of the height of near 500 feet [152 m] above the connected summit of the mountain, they stand singly and detached from each other.

Scoresby was at last able to land on the coast on July 24. He went ashore at 70°30' N, where the coast had become less mountainous, on a rocky point that he named Kap Lister, of which he gave a detailed description of the geology and plants. There he found marks of Inuit habitations, tent rings, tools, and old meat caches. By the discovery of light ash in fireplaces, not yet dispersed by wind, he concluded that the place had been inhabited earlier in that summer. The inhabitants had perhaps been frightened away by the strange sight of ships along their coast.

The next day, July 25, *Baffin* sailed westward into a "spacious" inlet. (See map, page 74) Scoresby's father, in his whale ship *Fame*, had entered the inlet the day before. The two vessels met in the newly discovered Hurry Fjord, a branch of the main inlet stretching northward 45–65 km (28–40 mi), where *Fame* had seen two whales. Scoresby the younger named the large body of water for his father as the first then known to have entered it.[2] The Scoresbys, father and son, spent two days cruising in Scoresby Sund, and Scoresby the younger landed at several points. He found that in the interior of Hurry Fjord "the heat among the rocks was most oppressive; so much so, that my excursion was greatly contracted, and my research limited, by the painful languor which the uncommonly high temperature produced…. I think the temperature could not be below 70° [21° C]: to my feelings, it was equal to the greatest heat of summer in England" (Scoresby 1823:204). The Scoresbys found that 80 km (50 mi) in from the sea the sound is divided into two branches by high land

---

2   According to a treatise in the Transactions of the Scandinavian Literary Society of 1814, it is likely that Scoresby Sund was discovered in 1761 by the Danish whaler Volquard Boon, who entered the sound but apparently did not go ashore. The southern shore of the entrance of Scoresby Sund is now known as Volquard Boons Kyst.

which they called Milne Land. They surmised that the branches extended considerable distances beyond the limits of their visibility. In fact, the branches extend 160 km (100 mi) beyond their visibility, and there are nine fjords branching from them into the interior. The Scoresbys had discovered the largest fjord system in the world, but almost seventy years would pass before Scoresby Sund was explored in its entirety.

Leaving Scoresby Sund, William Scoresby, Junior, sailed south along the coast and met such an extraordinary chain of icebergs off Kap Brewster that he was obliged to sail nearly 50 km (30 mi) offshore to get past it. At one point 140 icebergs were counted from the masthead. He was able to roughly map the coast as far south as 69°12' N, 70 km (43 mi) southwest of Scoresby Sund. Because whales were nearly absent along this coast, he again sailed northward; he loved exploration, but whaling was his business. Icebergs were now, as he sailed north, even more numerous off Kap Brewster; he counted 500 at one time from the masthead. By August 10 *Baffin*, in company with *Fame* and a third whaler, was close in to Traill Ø, named "in compliment to a highly esteemed friend ... of Liverpool." The southeast end of it, Scoresby wrote (1823:247), "is a stupendous cliff, rising from the very sea, without a yard of beach ... to a height of about 1,300 feet [400 m]. This cliff is of singular beauty. The prevailing colour, which is slate blue, or bluish-grey, is intersected and variegated by zig-zag strata of bright yellow and red."

Scoreby called it Vandyke Cliffs. The *Sailing Directions for East Greenland and Iceland*, published 120 years later by the Hydrographic Office of the U.S. Navy (Hydrographic Office 1943:175), states that the cliffs are in fact more than 700 m (2,300 ft) high and uses Scoresby's very words to describe them. Just north of Vandyke Klipper is Kap Moorsom. There Scoresby was able to go ashore again. He wrote (1823:247):

> The summit of the ridge on Cape Moorsom, consists of a series of sharp and elevated pinnacles. Some of these are so particularly slender, so full of rents, and so devoid of support, excepting from the narrow base on which they stand, that it seems surprising how they retain their position. It appeared indeed probable, from the great mass of rocks at the foot of

the ridge, apparently the ruins of the pinnacled summits, that every heavy gale of wind brings some of them down.

Scoresby's account (1823:249–50) of climbing Kap Moorsom is worth quoting at length:

> After one unsuccessful attempt to ascend, I entered upon a slope included between two precipitous rocks, and with much labour accomplished 500 feet [154 m], above which, the cliff rising vertically, prevented further progress in that direction; but, after skirting the brow of another precipice below me, where the inclination was at least 50°, and the surface entirely composed of loose sharp stones, I reached the bottom of a chasm between two prodigious pinnacles, and again proceeded upward. This attempt, which I was induced to undertake for the purpose of collecting specimens of the rocks and plants, eventually assumed such a hazardous aspect, that I would gladly have relinquished it, could I have conveniently returned. The rocks of the pinnacles bounding the chasm, distant about twenty feet from each other, were vertical on both sides. One of these rocks, which was greatly decomposed and broken, so as to afford by no means a firm hand hold, I was obliged to grasp with my left hand, and to thrust my right hand among the loose stones, while every step was accomplished; and it frequently required considerable deliberation before a second step could be attempted. A slip of the foot here might have been fatal, as the bottom of the chasm opened on a precipice of 400 or 500 feet, over which, whenever I moved, a large shower of the loose stones about me, were immediately precipitated. At the top, I expected to find at least some portion of flat surface, that I hoped would repay me by its productions, for the hazardous exploit into which my anxiety for specimens of minerals, plants, and animals, had unexpectedly betrayed me. But, to my surprise, the top proved to be a ridge (with the sea on both sides) narrower and sharper than the top of the highest pitched roof. Here I sat for a few minutes, seated on the ridge, with

a leg over each side, pointed to the water, under two terrific vertical pinnacles, between two and three hundred feet [60–90 m] in elevation. These actually vibrated with the force of the wind, and appeared altogether so shattered and unstable, that it was astonishing how they remained erect. I was far from being at ease in such a threatening situation, and therefore made a hasty retreat, by sliding down the side opposite to that by which I had ascended, a good deal rejoiced to find that this, being less steep, and not so dangerously interrupted by precipices, afforded a much safer descent than the other.

Scoresby brought back specimens of "curious and interesting rocks" (1823:251), mostly of slate-clay and some of bituminous shale. Farther along the coast, near what he called Cape Mewburn, he found signs of Inuit habitation. His father, meanwhile, had found remains of at least fifty summer habitations and great numbers of animal bones scattered about.

The tides just off Vandyke Klipper were so "fierce" as to greatly hinder the boats searching for whales in Davy Sund and to place the ships in jeopardy among the ice floes. A long and tedious gale from August 10 to 13 added to their troubles, and heavy and incessant rain fell with little intermission for 130 hours. "The quantity of rain that fell far exceeded any thing of the kind I ever before witnessed. Our boats were likely to be torn from the tackles by the weight of water that collected in them before it was observed; and, after that, they were emptied repeatedly" (1823:267).

Another hard gale followed on August 23 with heavy rain changing to thick snow by evening. *Baffin* was among drifting ice floes and icebergs. A berg thrust the ship completely up on a broad underwater tongue of a floe 1.6 km (1 mi) in circumference and 12 m (40 ft) thick. The vessel stayed there two hours, in danger of being crushed throughout. They were saved by new ice pressure which took the ship by the bow and forced her astern and off the tongue. It was late in the season and it was clear that the time had come to leave the coast.

For more than three months Scoresby had pursued whales among the ice of the East Greenland Current. In spite of fogs, gales, atmospheric refractions, heavy rains and snow, and his primary responsibility of catching whales, he had for the first time charted 650 km (400 mi) of coast, from 75° to 69° N, hardly known before his voyage. The distance of coast charted, following all its convolutions, was closer to 1,300 km (800 mi). Scoresby had taken advantage of every opportunity to determine his latitude and longitude and the compass variation; he had determined the position of fifty stations and taken nearly 500 angles upon which his chart was based. He wrote (1823:324):

> As a part of the eastern coast of Greenland was discovered by Henry Hudson, in 1607, (from latitude 72° to 73 1/2°) and as some insulated points have been seen by some of the whalers within the last few years, it is difficult, and indeed impossible, to ascertain what proportion of the researches of this voyage is original discovery. The position and form, however, given to this coast in our best charts, are so different from the reality, that the greater part, if not the whole extent of these investigation, may perhaps be considered as a *new country*.

Scoresby found many signs of habitation along the coast, but he found no people and no signs of the lost Norse colony that he had hoped to discover. With lingering hope he discussed his findings at length in his journal (1823:337): "... on the whole ... I conceive, that the remains we met with were not entirely Esquimaux. They indicated practices among the inhabitants that were in favour of the supposition of the admixture with some other nation, – doubtless the ancient colonies planted by the Icelanders. Hence, there is some reason to believe, that these colonies were not entirely depopulated, – that they are not yet extinct." He was greatly disappointed that his whaling duties and obligations did not permit him to search for Norse colonies south of 69°30' N, where he could observe no hindrance to his penetration along the coast. Nevertheless, this voyage of 1822, so rich in results, must have been of great satisfaction to William Scoresby. He made twenty voyages to the whaling grounds of the East Greenland Sea, from 1803 to 1823. This penultimate voyage, however, was the only one on which he had been able to land on the shores of East Greenland and partially satisfy his great interest in the land that lay beyond the ice of the East Greenland Current and which until then was known to Europeans only from the report of Henry Hudson from 1607. Scoresby indeed was the great pioneer of the exploration of East Greenland.

Baffin returned to Liverpool on September 18, 1822, having accomplished a satisfactory voyage in the northern whale fishery. William Scoresby made one more voyage to the Arctic. He then left his active sea career in his early thirties and entered the Church. He contributed many papers to the Royal Society, to which he had been elected a Fellow, and to the British Association. All his papers, log books, magnetic instruments, and botanical and geological specimens were left to the Whitby Museum.

Scoresby's reports of ice conditions from his earlier voyages had led to the renewal of British voyages in search of a northwest passage – a long-hoped-for route of commerce – across the top of North America to Asia. Because Scoresby, with good reason and more Arctic experience than anyone, was no believer in an open polar sea – a belief of the Secretary of the Admiralty – this exceptionally energetic and most experienced Arctic navigator and scientist was passed over as a leader of the new endeavour – to Scoresby's great disappointment. Scoresby was apparently passed over, also, because he was merely a whaling captain rather than an officer of the Royal Navy. His two published journals from his voyages to East Greenland are his claims to pre-eminence in polar science and Arctic navigation, and to immortality. He died in 1857, aged sixty-eight.

CLAVERING AND THE LOST INUIT FAMILY, 1823

The British Board of Longitude commissioned Captain Edward Sabine of the Royal Artillery to conduct pendulum observations of the force of gravity at various points around the Atlantic Ocean for the purpose of determining the correct shape of the Earth, a matter of practical importance for world-wide navigation. In 1821 Sabine, then on the coast of Africa, met Captain Douglas Clavering, who had just been appointed commander of the ship *Pheasant*. At Sabine's request, Clavering and *Pheasant* were ordered to carry Sabine to eight locations on both shores of the Atlantic for Sabine's observations. Upon their return to England, the Board of Longitude decided that Sabine's observations should be extended to northernmost latitudes. The vessel *Griper*, which had been engaged in a search for the Northwest Passage in 1819–20, was assigned for the voyage. *Griper* was reputed to be a slow and unhandy sailer, but she had been greatly strengthened for the 1819–20 voyage and was capable of surviving heavy blows from ice. Captain Clavering and Captain Sabine got along very well together, and Clavering had greatly aided Sabine's earlier scientific observations. Captain Clavering was appointed to command *Griper* for Sabine's new voyage.

The program specified pendulum observations at Hammerfest in northern Norway followed by observations on Spitsbergen. From there Clavering was to proceed to East Greenland, then only imperfectly known from Scoresby's reports of the previous year, for additional pendulum observations. *Griper* sailed from the Thames on May 11, 1823, and "without any material occurrence," wrote Clavering (1830:6), arrived at Hammerfest on June 2. The ship departed Hammerfest three weeks later, and by July 22 Sabine had completed the observations on Spitsbergen, from whence they sailed for Greenland.

Clavering entered the ice of the East Greenland Current at 75°10' N on August 2 and "soon found ourselves hampered amongst immense fields of ice" (Clavering 1830:16). By the 4th the weather was clear and they discovered land about 80 km (50 mi) distant. The crew dragged the heavy vessel through the ice until they gained clear water along the shore on August 8. Clavering went ashore. "Never was a more desolate spot seen; in many places not a vestige of vegetation … no reindeer, no birds, or whales…. Spitsbergen was, on the whole, a paradise to this place" (Clavering 1830:17). He named the point Kap Borlase Warren, which is on the mainland of Wollaston Forland. There he found remains of indigenous huts.

The ship coasted toward the northeast and on the 10th they discovered and named the Pendulum Øer, where they found an anchorage and a favourable location at which Captain Sabine could make his observations. With a fair wind Clavering was able to sail as far as 75°12' N until stopped by thick, fast ice. He discovered and landed on the shore of what he named Shannon Ø. Clavering named the island for the man-of-war on which he had served when it captured the United States frigate *Chesapeake* in the War of 1812; and he named the cape on which he landed for the *Shannon*'s "gallant commander," Philip Broke. Far to the west he could see Ardencaple Fjord, which he named for the residence of a friend and relative. Clavering had reached what he thought was the northeast point of Greenland. That point is in fact 740 km (460 mi) farther north.

A gale of wind sped *Griper* back to the Pendulum Øer. She went aground briefly. The crew got off her without trouble, and the vessel was securely anchored while Captain Sabine's party was landed for the pendulum observations.

Leaving Sabine to carry on his work, a matter of days, Captain Clavering and nineteen of his officers and crew departed in two rowing boats on August 16 for explorations to the westward. Working their way through ice, they camped at Kap Borlase Warren, where they found recent traces of people, particularly mounds of blubber covered by stones to keep scavengers from the store. The next day one of the boats was damaged by ice. While repairing it on shore, more traces of people were found "so that we began to look anxiously for them" (Clavering 1830:20). The following day they found them.

Clavering and his party first found a small sealskin tent pitched close to the water, but with no inhabitants. The owners, on seeing the sailors, had retreated a short distance and stood watching their visitors, who in time spotted them among protective rock outcrops. Clavering laid down a looking-glass and a pair of mittens nearby and retired to watch. The people immediately came down to examine the gifts. They then allowed the sailors to approach and shake hands, "trembling violently the whole time," wrote Clavering (1830:21), "in spite of our best endeavours to inspire them with confidence."

The visitors and the Inuit returned to the tent, 1.5 m (5 ft) high and with a framework of whalebone and driftwood. Nearby was a sealskin kayak with harpoons and spears of wood tipped with bone. Some were tipped with what appeared to be meteoric iron. The next day men, women, and children visited Clavering's tent, bringing large pieces of seal and walrus blubber as gifts. Clavering gave them biscuits and salt meat, which they immediately spat out. The people were dressed in sealskin with the hair inwards and were much astonished at everything they saw at the sailors' camp. To their great surprise, Clavering had the face of one of the children washed, "for they were so stained with dirt and oil, it was impossible, without this proceeding, to know what was their real colour, which now exhibited a tawny coppery appearance" (Clavering 1830:22).

Clavering left the people on the afternoon of the 19th and continued westward into what he now believed was the bay discovered by the Dutch whaler Gael Hamkes in 1654. "At this point it opened into an extensive basin, the circumference of which could not be less than fifty miles [80 km]" (Clavering 1830:22). The bay was perfectly free of ice. Following the shore for 32 km (20 mi), first to the north and then northeast, they realized they had been skirting an island; it was later named Clavering Ø. Clavering climbed a 1,370-m (4,500-ft) mountain at the inner end of the bay, "hoping to have an extensive view of the different openings and arms of the sea that surrounded us on all sides" (Clavering 1830:23). He called the mountain Jordanhill after the residence of a friend. From the height he saw an opening, an inlet, to the south, across the bay, for which they set off the next day, and on August 22 they reached the head of the inlet 29 km (18 mi) from the bay, "the face of the country presenting a less barren and heath-like appearance." Clavering named it Loch Fine.

They had enjoyed a constant calm, except for one night, and "most beautiful and serene weather" (Clavering 1830:23). For lack of wind Clavering's party had rowed all the way of their exploration. With a south wind in Loch Fine they sailed back to the Inuit camp on the evening of August 22, and they spent the next two days with the people. "We were well received by them, but our attempts at making ourselves understood were very unsuccessful." Clavering wrote (1830:24):

> Their amazement at seeing one of the seamen shoot a seal was quite unbounded. They heard for the first time the report of a musket, and turning round in the direction in which the animal was killed, and floating on the water, one of them was desired to go in his canoe and fetch it. Before landing it he turned it round and round, till he observed where the ball had penetrated, and, putting his finger into the hole, set up a most extraordinary shout of astonishment, dancing and capering in the most absurd manner. He was afterwards desired to skin it, which he did expeditiously and well.

... A pistol was afterwards put into their hands, and one of them fired into the water: the recoil startled him so much, that he immediately slunk away into his tent. The following morning we found they had all left us, leaving their tents and everything behind, which I have no doubt was occasioned by their alarm at the firing.

And that was the last ever seen of indigenous people north of Ammassalik on the east coast of Greenland.

On Clavering's return toward the ship the boats penetrated 24 km (15 mi) into Young Sund on the north side of Clavering Ø. There they saw a large bear – the first they had seen – which they pursued. "The animal, however, as soon as he saw us, set off at a gallop much exceeding our ideas of his speed, having imagined these animals to be slow and unwieldy" (Clavering 1830:25).

They reached the ship on August 29; they had been gone thirteen days. Sabine's pendulum observations were completed the next day, and on August 31 *Griper* got under way. With calms and light winds they proceeded slowly to the southwest along the coast, occasionally working through loose drifting ice. On September 4 "the reappearance of the stars warned us how rapidly the days shortened at this season." They landed at two or three points to make latitude observations, and they shot two bears and captured a third which they carried as far as Norway (but there it was accidentally strangled by a line when it got loose in a boat).

On September 12 the fine weather they had enjoyed since they arrived on the coast of Greenland was broken by a strong NNE gale very thick with sleet. Rather than drive before the wind through thick ice and with bad visibility, they secured the vessel with two hawsers and two chain cables to a large ice floe. Before morning the hawsers and cables had broken. "Our situation was now a most anxious one, the gale continued with unabated violence, and the ship drove to the southward amongst loose ice and heavy floes, which, from the darkness of the night, we could neither see nor avoid. We received many shocks, but, from the admirable manner in which our little vessel was strengthened, without any serious injury" (Clavering 1830:28).

Off Kap Parry, discovered by Scoresby the previous year and 225 km (140 mi) south of the Pendulum Øer, they broke through the edge of the ice, arrived at open water, and left the coast of Greenland on September 13. For the next week they suffered severe gales and reached the coast of Norway on September 23. On October 6 they anchored in Trondheim, where Captain Sabine commenced a new set of observations. They got away from Trondheim on November 13, but gales kept them on the Norwegian coast until December 3. Persistent gales that pressed them toward the shore followed them until off the entrance to the Baltic. This eight-month voyage came to an end when they reached the Thames on December 19.

Edward Sabine went on to a distinguished scientific career, attained the rank of general, was knighted in 1869, and served as president of the Royal Society for ten years. Douglas Clavering sailed from Sierra Leone aboard *Redwing* in 1827 and was never heard from again. Part of the wreckage of *Redwing* was found on the African coast. Clavering was twenty-eight years old when he commanded *Griper* on her voyage to Greenland. He was characterized (by James Smith in Clavering 1830:1) as "not less distinguished for his upright and honourable feelings, than for the most amiable and affectionate disposition."

GRAAH AND THE MOST DIFFICULT EXPLORATION, 1828–30

The Icelandic sagas had spoken of two Norse settlements in Greenland, the Western Settlement and the Eastern Settlement. In the early nineteenth century it was believed by some, such as William Scoresby, that the Eastern Settlement had been located on the east coast. Scoresby had searched for indications of the ancient Norse settlements on the east coast in 1822, and he thought he might have found some indications of them. At least he did not rule out the possibility. The Danish government commissioned Lieutenant Wilhelm August Graah of the Royal Danish Navy to investigate the question, "to explore the East coast of Greenland, from Cape Farewell to lat. 69° North" (Graah 1837:vii). He was instructed "As early as possible in 1829, [to] set out on your Expedition, whose limit is to be the southernmost extremity of the land seen by Captain Scoresby in

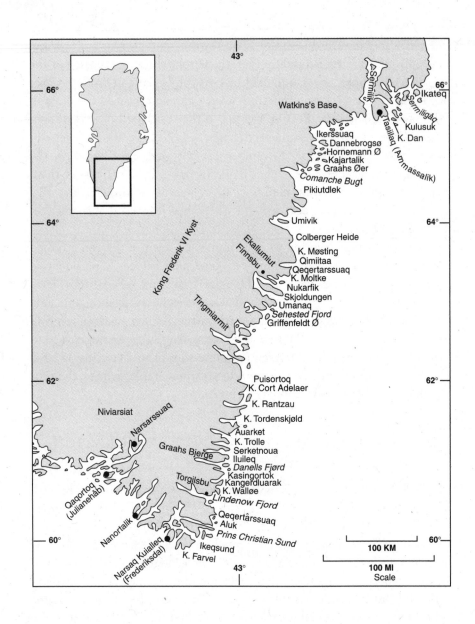

KAP FARVEL TO TASIILAQ

1822 ... the aim and the end of the Expedition is to seek for traces of the old Icelandic colonists supposed to have inhabited these coasts" (Graah 1837:x). In seeking for the old Norse, he would also provide knowledge of the coast, connecting the known land of southernmost eastern Greenland, seen until then only by Peder Walløe in 1752, together with Scoresby's survey from 69° N as far north as 75° N.

Lieutenant Graah was no stranger to Greenland. He had visited the country, surveying the west coast between 68°05' and 73° N, that is, from Godhavn (now Qeqertarssuak) to Upernavik, in 1823 and 1824. For the east coast expedition Graah was accompanied by the naturalist Jens Laurentius Moestue Vahl and by the superintendent of the Greenland settlement of Frederikshåb (now since 1979 named Påmiut), Matthiessen, who could speak the dialect of the East Greenlanders. Graah was also assigned an unnamed sailor who would cook. Graah arrived with Vahl in Julianehåb (since 1979 named Qaqortoq), the principal settlement of southwest Greenland, in 1828 where he arranged for the construction of two umiaks, so-called women's boats, for the journey, and where he recruited an Inuit crew of five men and ten women. The women would row the umiaks and the men in kayaks would accompany the umiaks to hunt along the way.

Graah wrote that umiaks, the traditional boats made of driftwood frames and sealskin coverings, usually were 6.7–7.3 m (22–24 ft) long and 1.5–1.8 m wide. Those built for his expedition were 11.7 m (38.5 ft) in length and somewhat more than 2.1 m (7 ft) wide. He later found them too big for passage through the ice; nevertheless, he wrote (1837:30),

> No sort of boat is, probably, better adapted to the navigation of these icy seas than this umiak of the Greenlanders. It is not difficult to row; rooms a considerable cargo; may with ease be hauled ashore, or on the floes of ice, by three or four men; and though indeed more exposed than other boats to the risks of springing leaks, is capable, whenever this happens, of being easily repaired by the simple contrivance of thrusting a bit of blubber into the hole, until an opportunity arrive of sewing on a patch of skin over it. To guard against such accidents, accordingly, the Greenlanders, when navigating through new ice, or

brash ice, usually hang a skin out at the bows. As this, however, impedes the progress of their boats, I adopted, in lieu of it, a couple of ice-boards, so made as to fix, when required, into the water-way, and which, forming a sharp angle before the bows, were found to answer fully the purpose for which they were intended.... A boat with a cargo on board, rowed by four or five women, can, in calm weather and smooth water, accomplish a distance of thirty miles [48 km], or somewhat more, in a day … every fifth day, moreover, must be a day of rest, in order that the boat's skin, saturated by the sea, may dry.

For the remainder of the season of 1828 Graah surveyed and mapped in the vicinity of Julianehåb. Graah and Vahl spent the winter, during which "nothing occurred worthy of mention" (Graah 1837:51), at Nanortalik (which means "a place frequented by polar bears"), occupying their time with meteorological, auroral, and magnetic observations and arranging Vahl's botanical collections.

They left Nanortalik with the umiaks and kayaks on March 21, 1829, and by April 1 they had passed through Prins Christian Sund (which Lieutenant Graah so named), the gateway to the east coast. There they met heavy drift ice, "that most formidable enemy … which we had no hope of overcoming but by patience" (Graah 1837:63). They were forced to remain on Qeqertaq ("island") for twenty-five days in nearly total inactivity, shut in by ice and by storms from the northwest. At length they were able to proceed, always hindered by ice or stopped by gales. They were icebound again at Kap Walløe, only 60 km (37 mi) along their way, for three weeks. Beyond this point there was no historic record of any earlier European travel along the entire east coast as far as Scoresby's discoveries 1,450 km (900 mi) to the north. At Ikarisieitsiak ("a large sound or passage"), "a couple of gun-shots distant from Iluileq," they camped on a small island where they found a family of Inuit (East Greenlanders) who had their tent nearby at Ivimiut ("people of a grassy place"). Graah wrote (1837:69):

> This tent constitutes the Summer dwelling of the Green-lander, from May to October he makes use of no other; and one

must admit that it is excellently well adapted to the purposes of people who, during the whole Summer, are perpetually moving about, at one moment far in the recesses of the firths [fjords] looking for herrings, roots and berries, and at another among the islands along the coast in quest of seals, birds, and eggs. The ground on which the tent is to be pitched is usually marked out by a wall of about two feet in height, on which, as well as on the cross-beam of the doorframe, rest the rafters. Over these are then stretched two or three layers of hides, reaching down to the ground, where they are secured from being carried away by the wind by means of large, heavy stones. Instead of a door, a curtain is made use of, formed of the intestines of seals, in general handsomely ornamented, and so transparent as to admit a cheerful light into the tent. For the rest, the interior arrangements are precisely as in the ordinary Greenland houses, with the sole difference that a tent is seldom tenanted by more than two families together.

Another family was tented nearby and visited Graah's party. Throughout the journey Graah came upon Inuit in groups of various sizes, as well as camping places temporarily deserted; and he found ancient Inuit ruins, some with skeletons of people who had apparently died of starvation or disease.

Graah's party in its umiaks struggled on. The land became still more covered with snow than the country farther south, and above glaciers that covered the land in every direction he found a chain of mountains "no less remarkable for their beauty of contour, than for their height, which, I think, must be upwards of 3,000 feet [915 m], while the rest of the country, hereabouts, falls considerably short of half that elevation" (Graah 1837:71). They were subsequently named the Graah Fjelde. At their landing place, Graah found the rocks to be highly magnetic.

They were icebound for seventeen days at Serketnoua ("a sunny promontory"), and snow and storms continued almost every day. It was now mid-June, and still the ice pack remained thick along the coast. It would remain so throughout the summer. Just beyond Kap Herulf Trolle they were told of a large mass of iron, a mystery to the local people. Graah investigated and found it to be a small ship's cannon, 1.7 m (5.5 ft) long, which he surmised to be from a whaler wrecked upon the coast at least forty years earlier. Graah cleaned it out and fired it, "to the great delight of the Greenlanders" (Graah 1837:74). These folk were entertained by a cannon shot even though the Inuit found by Clavering had disappeared upon the discharge of small arms. Near their camp site Graah found a natural vault or grotto, about 45 m long, 30 m wide, and 30 to 36 m high (148 x 98 x 108 ft) into which the sea surged. Within "was a singular harmonic echo, which caught up and repeated innumerable times, every sound, even the lowest, ... and with a change of tone at every repetition.... While we were there, sea-birds were flying about it, and within it, in flocks of thousands, taking pleasure, apparently, in listening to their own shrill cries, so melodiously re-echoed from the rocks" (Graah 1837:74).

By June 18 they had rowed past Kap Tordenskjøld, 137 km (85 mi) north of Prins Christian Sund and over 670 m (2200 ft) high and one of the best sea marks on the coast; and on June 20 they camped just south of Kap Cort Adelaer. To the north lay Puisortoq ("where the ice rises to the surface"), the glacier that protrudes into the sea and rises perpendicularly 185 m (600 ft) at its face. It was notorious locally and reputedly dangerous to pass because of the frequency it discharged ice into the sea; the ice could shoot out like missiles. Puisortoq, Graah was told, was "frequently impassable for years together" (Graah 1837:77). At this point Graah sent back one of the umiaks with Vahl, Matthiesen, and the sailor. His intent was to reduce his party to improve its chances of having enough food to get through the coming winter. He considered the possibility that, given the reputation of Puisortoq, they might be able to pass by it to the north but be unable to return to the south.

Graah then proceeded with his Inuit companions. Puisortoq calved ice twenty times during the three hours it took them to pass it, but they had no accident. Just beyond they found three families encamped, as they had at fairly regular intervals north of Prins Christian Sund.

The ice held them for three days at Griffenfeldt Ø. Graah and a companion used the time for a laborious five-hour climb of a 915-m (3,000-ft) mountain whose "ascent is exceedingly difficult, it sides being everywhere steep ... its highest peak consists of a vast accumulation of loose stones, that roll down from under one's feet at every step" (Graah 1837:85). From the summit they thought they could see westward across the Greenland ice cap to the Niviarsiat ("the young girls"), 1,525-m (5,000-ft) high mountains in the Julianahåb District of the west coast and 260 km (162 mi) from their peak.

Graah found seventy or eighty East Greenlanders camped at Qeetartivaq ("the large island"), an island north of Kap Moltke and surrounded by a multitude of icebergs. From them Graah bought as much dried seal's flesh and blubber as the Inuit could spare. Just beyond was Qimiitaa ("the inner part of a boot or *kamik*") where about 100 Inuit had tents. "Qimiitaa was one of the prettiest spots I yet had seen upon this coast. Its valleys were, indeed, still, in a great degree, filled up with snow [on July 10] ... but wherever this was not the case, the soil was covered with a vigorous growth of grass, and a number of sweet-smelling flowers adorned the rocks" (Graah 1837:89). Few of the people there had ever seen a European. Of them Graah asked about any signs of the ancient Norse, as he had of all Eastlanders he had encountered. He inquired about ruins, of hot springs said to be common in the eastern settlement of the Norse, of nails and bits of iron? Had they seen runes or grave stones? Had they seen mice, thought to be descendants of mice of the Norse colonies? He asked in vain. These people had no knowledge of such things.

Graah's crew was reluctant to go north of this point because they were told of five boats that had perished in the ice just north of Qimiitaa in the previous year. Graah enlisted new crew and went on, always struggling with ice. *Sailing Directions for East Greenland and Iceland* (Hydrographic Office 1943:97) stated:

> This is one of the most difficult stretches of the southern east coast, navigation being especially hazardous just south of Bernstorff Fjord. A rapid current sets out of this fjord, which produces more ice than any other in southeastern Greenland. Usually a large bank of icebergs lies off the mouth of the fjord; inside of this bank are such violent whirlpools, filled with icebergs and calf ice, that navigation is often impossible. The waters northward, between Bernstorff Fjord and Umivik are always in an inexplicable state of unrest, even in calm weather.

North of Kap Møsting, Graah encountered ice floes – some 1.6 km (1 mi) in length – larger than any met farther south and upwards of 9 m (30 ft) in thickness. "Here the coast is bold and precipitous," says *Sailing Directions for East Greenland and Iceland* (Hydrographic Office 1943:98), "covered with glaciers that protrude into the sea at every cleft or ravine." Graah and his crew had to row for thirty-four hours across Umivik ("where the boat is kept when hunting") Bugt before finding a landing place, and there they found an island with 130 people full of curiosity about the strangers.

By July 24, Graah, in a heavy rain, had reached Hornemann Ø at 65°10' N. He waited three days hoping to proceed. "A vast number of icebergs had grounded under the shore, and the spaces between them were blocked up by drift and solid field-ice." By this time he had "not the most distant hope of finding any vestiges of the old colony under a more northerly latitude than that we now were in" (Graah 1837:99–100). After a terrible storm on July 30 he saw far off to the northeast a few islands, probably those islands near Kap Dan east of Ammassalik, which he thought could be Gunnbjørn's Skerries. The Icelandic sagas, noted Graah, state that the skerries "lay mid-way between Iceland and Greenland, that is to say … midway between Iceland and the Bygd in Greenland, which, in fact, they do exactly, if, by the Bygd, we are to understand the present district of Juliana's-hope" (Graah 1837:100).

Lieutenant Graah now, on August 21, travelled a few more kilometres to Dannebrogs Ø, where he hoisted the Danish flag, constructed a cairn, deposited a record and a silver medal presented to him by the king, and took possession of the country in the king's name. He called it Kong Frederik VIs Kyst. He found the island to be in 65°15'36" N; this was in fact his farthest north. These several islands at Graah's furthest now appear on maps as Graahs Øer.

Lieutenant Graah had come nearly 645 km (400 mi) in a straight-line distance from Prins Christian Sund, but he was only halfway to the intended goal of 69° N as given in his orders from the king. Ice prevented progress for three weeks, and the country about Dannebrogs Ø was utterly destitute of all means of subsistence. "Finally, my people, if not absolutely in a state of mutiny, were exceedingly averse from going further, and, indeed, would not have held out even thus far, but for the bribes I daily offered them of spirits, coffee, etc., my stock of which was now almost exhausted" (Graah 1837:102). Lieutenant Graah had made a remarkable journey against unending difficulties – storms, ice, and the reluctance of his companions to proceed – but he could go no farther.

They retreated south through thick ice to a place called Nukarfik on an island south of Kap Moltke where Graah intended to spend the winter. Nukarfik means "a place where one is not active." Leaving part of his party there to build a winter house, Graah went farther south to buy food for the winter. He went on to Ekallumiut (referring to "people who live near trout") on the inner end of a large island he named Skjoldungen, far from the influence of the ice pack of the outer coast. It was "the handsomest tract of land I had yet seen along this coast," with a rich growth of willows, berries, and grasses, and with a stream abounding in Arctic char. "Various flowers, among which the sweet-smelling lychnis, everywhere adorned the fields" (Graah 1837:105–6). In this "delightful place" he found between 200 and 250 East Greenlanders gathered to harvest the berries and char before they dispersed to their winter lodgings. This was the largest number of Inuit he had met. He estimated that fairly recently there had been about 600 people along that coast, from Kap Farvel to Dannebrogs Ø, of which about 120 had emigrated to Frederiksdal (now Narsaq Kujalleq) and Nanortalik on the west coast.

By October 29, Graah moved from his tent into an Inuit winter house his crew had found on Nukarfik. The house was about 3.6 m (12 ft) on a side. He divided it into three sections and shared it with his boat crew. They were south of the Arctic Circle and the sun was above the horizon for at least a few hours each day; they were spared a prolonged period of darkness. Graah spent his time by working on the map of the coast he had explored and by learning the Greenland language. He was ill a good part of the winter and food was very scarce. They often ate rotten seal flesh and even some skins. The Inuit in the vicinity shared some food with Graah, in part from the hope that he would assist them to move to Nanortalik on the west coast. Through the winter he had ample opportunity to study their ways of life and character. He wrote (1837:118–9):

> In the interior of their dwellings they are filthy in the ex-
> treme; and not less so in their persons, their hands and faces
> being constantly begrimed with blubber. Their food is cooked in

the most disgusting manner ... [and there is] an odour through their huts which I lack words to describe. [Even so, wrote Graah] ... they are modest, friendly, obliging, and forbearing.... And I had frequent opportunities ... to be convinced of the genuine civility and hospitality of these Eastlanders.

Further, wrote Graah (1837:122–3),

> In regard to morals, the Eastlanders deserve much commendation ... [and] though they had constant opportunities of robbing me ... during the nineteen months I spent upon King Frederick's Coast, I never lost so much as a needle – a circumstance the more surprising, because they all well knew what sort of articles I had with me, and because there were all things precisely that which must have seemed most valuable in their eyes.... They are, in a word, a gentle, civil, well-intentioned, and well-behaved set of people, among whom one's life and property are perfectly secure, as long as one treats them with civility, and does them no wrong or injury.... Their worst faults are – ingratitude, a total want of sympathy for the distressed and destitute (those excepted who are related to themselves), and cruelty to dumb animals, which, whether useful or useless to them, they torment and persecute without mercy. To this list of faults, I may add, insincerity and dissimulation.

Early in April, in spite of illness, very scarce supplies, and the reluctance of his companions – "they were heartily tired of the expedition" (1837:132), Graah renewed his attempt to travel farther north. On the first day they reached Kap Moltke, and there a northeast gale began that lasted for fourteen days. They travelled along a coast with many glaciers, some of them calving icebergs as they went, "throwing up the sea in huge foaming billows" (Graah 1837:132). They landed at Kap Møsting, only 21 km (13 mi) from Kap Moltke, where they were held into July. Lieutenant Graah made eighteen attempts to get farther north, all frustrated by the state of the ice; "The state of the ice ... was such, that it was absolutely impossible to make one's way over it, a single mile's length North of Kap Møsting, on foot, or in a sledge, or in a boat" (Graah 1837:134). When at last they did manage to travel a few more kilometres to the north, they were again icebound for fifteen days on a small, low-lying skerry close to the glacier of Colberger Heide. It was a perilous place; a few years earlier a party of Inuit camping on that rock had been swept away when the glacier calved. During Graah's confinement, he wrote, the glacier calved some hundred times a day, causing seas to sweep over the rock. Nevertheless, his party escaped any serious injury. By the end of July they were eating old seal skins. Graah had to retreat. It was a very difficult struggle. For five days they had to eat only whale's blubber disgorged by sharks. They had to carry their umiak over ice floes. "During this most painful and laborious journey, I had frequent opportunities of admiring the patience, resignation, and perseverance of the Greenlanders" (Graah 1837:140). They reached open water on August 2 and then caught a small seal which they ate raw, "hide, hair, and all" (Graah 1837:140). They rested a bit and then went slowly on down the coast, the threat of imminent starvation lifted, but with winter rapidly coming on. Graah had to quell small mutinies on the part of his tired and hungry companions. Heavy rains added to their troubles. Graah himself was seriously ill in August, mainly from the "miserable fare I had been necessitated to put up with, being some year-old, sun-dried, and half-rotten seal's flesh, and, next to that the extreme fatigue I had lately undergone. Perhaps, too, my late squabbles with my Greenland followers may have, in some degree, contributed to produce the same result ... I ... was almost in a state of insensibility" (Graah 1837:147). At the end of August they again passed the dangerous glacier Puisortoq. Then they came upon a great plain upon which black crakeberries and whortleberries or bilberries were found in great abundance. Graah wrote that without those berries he would have perished on "this inhospitable coast" (1837:147).

New ice was now, by September 8, forming among the floes. A northeast gale with snow came the next day. "We were lucky enough ... to reach Serketnoua before the gale was at its height. Here we now remained eight days, exposed to all the miseries of cold, and famine, and sickness" (Graah 1837:149). Another hard gale came from the northwest on September 30 from which there was little shelter for their umiak near their camping place. The boat was swept away. "Speechless with horror, my Greenlanders stood gazing at it, as it drifted away" (1837:149). Fortunately, the wind shifted and drove it back – surely an amazing piece of good luck – and it was recovered and repaired. "I myself, however, in endeavouring to save it, sustained an injury in the right hand, which unfitted me for duty, or nearly so, for the rest of the voyage" (1837:149). Once again, south of Kap Walløe, the boat and their supplies were damaged. Graah lost some of the charts he had made. They reached Prins Christian Sund late in the day of October 8. The supplies that he had arranged for when he left Julianehåb the previous year and which Graah expected to find at this point had not been sent, apparently from negligence. Graah sent two kayakers to Frederiksdal for assistance and provisions. The missionary, Mr. Klein-schmidt, responded quickly with bread and wine, and Graah, in a state of utter exhaustion, received a letter informing him that the king was satisfied with the manner in which he had executed his commission. Graah reached Nanortalik, his starting place, on October 19, 1830. He spent the winter at Julianehåb and arrived back in Copenhagen on September 13, 1831.

Lieutenant Graah's journey was the first deliberate and successful attempt to explore and map the east coast of Greenland. He had investigated 550 km (341 mi) of unknown coast and collected much information about the country and its inhabitants. His journal contains many descriptions of the coast that were used without alteration 110 years later in *Sailing Directions for East Greenland and Iceland*. The extent of the east coast that he explored for the first time with such difficulty and diligence was never exceeded and only equalled by Amdrup in 1900 and by Mylius-Erichsen in 1907. The king had good reason to be satisfied with Lieutenant Graah's work, but apparently had little realization of the cost to his faithful servant.

KOLDEWEY AND THE FIRST SLEDGE EXPEDITION, 1869–70

The German geographer August Petermann initiated a summer expedition, the First German Arctic Expedition, in 1868. It was commanded by Captain Karl Koldewey and worked in the waters around Svalbard. This brief voyage had the effect of stimulating greater interest in Germany in Arctic exploration, and that in fact was its primary purpose. In

1869 Petermann and Koldewey launched the Second German Arctic Expedition. Its purpose was to reach the highest possible northern latitude. Petermann was a believer, as Captain William Scoresby, Jr., was not, in an open sea at the North Pole surrounded by the barrier of ice that all northern voyagers had encountered. Petermann hoped that Koldewey might break through that barrier and reach the North Pole. Petermann wanted the expedition to push north between Novaya Zemlya and Svalbard. Captain Koldewey, like Scoresby, had no great belief in the likelihood of an open polar sea and successfully argued that he should proceed to East Greenland. If ice there prevented his ship from getting far north by sea, he could hope to make new discoveries by following the coast northward, beyond Clavering's discoveries, with the ship or by sledges. In any case, East Greenland had been seldom visited and there was ample opportunity for discovery and exploration.

A new vessel, *Germania*, 27.5 m (90 ft) long, was specially built and reinforced for the expedition and equipped with sails and a steam engine. A second vessel, *Hansa*, was purchased and reinforced. Under the command of Captain Friedrich Hegemann, she was to carry extra coal for *Germania* and be the consort for the expedition. *Hansa*, however, had no engine. Koldewey's orders were on no account to spend more than one year in East Greenland.

Germania encountered the ice edge on July 15 in thick fog, and for most of the next two weeks the ship was in fog working its way through the ice, but on the 28th, Captain Koldewey wrote (1874:271):

> it was a fine still midnight, too wonderfully solemn and grand to be easily forgotten. The fog had almost entirely disappeared, and lay to the east, like a bank over the water. The sea was perfectly calm, so that the ice was clearly reflected, and where the water was visible it had taken different colours; under the clouds it lay dark, and from blackish brown to yellowish; and where the atmosphere was clear it glistened a transparent green. Even to the brush of an experienced artist, it would be no light task to render the different colours and lights truly; this soft red of the sun upon the ice; on the shady side of the blocks, the softest blue and violet ...

Early on the 29th Koldewey saw the land of East Greenland at Kap Broer Ruys, but it was not until August 4 that they broke into open water along the coast. They anchored the following day at the Pendulum Øer, discovered by Captain Clavering, where they were greeted with a fall of snow that covered the ship, and there they repeated Captain Edward Sabine's pendulum observations. When the observations were finished, after several days, they sailed north along the east coast of Shannon Ø, closely observing the set of the tides and currents, which prevailed to the south, until stopped on August 14 by ice at 75°30' N. Then they retreated to the south side of Shannon Ø, out of the ice stream. There they killed their first muskox. These were the first of these impressive animals to be seen by Europeans in East Greenland, for Scoresby, Clavering, and Graah had seen none. Until the end of August Koldewey's explorers investigated and mapped Shannon Ø. There they found bears, muskoxen, a walrus, basaltic columns, and ancient Inuit ruins. They noted that muskoxen seemed to be found mostly north of about 75°30' N and that reindeer were numerous only south of that parallel. In the meantime Koldewey continued to observe the sea ice, always hoping for a chance to take *Germania* farther north. The chances seemed small, therefore the ship steamed south to investigate Lille Pendulum Ø. By the end of August it was clear that there was no hope of getting farther north; they retreated to the small, secure harbour – Germaniahavn – on Sabine Ø (the larger of the two Pendulum Øer) where they had first anchored. There they would winter. The next day, September 2, saw the first of the violent storms with heavy snowfall from the NNW that would recur throughout the winter.

On September 10 the ship steamed a short distance westward where they landed for the first time on the mainland shore of Greenland. A short excursion took them up Dronning Augustadalen. Lieutenant Julius Payer, the surveyor and geologist of the expedition, wrote (Koldewey 1874:306): "a tiring, monotonous road led us up and down the mountains and slopes covered with scanty vegetation, through rough water-rifts, and, lastly, over a small steep glacier on to the Dolerite-crest of the Sattelberg" more than 1,130 m (3,700 ft) high. Payer (Koldewey 1874:306) continued:

A violent north wind made the moderate cold of 14° Fahr. [–10° C] particularly painful to the travellers during their stay on the summit, especially while carrying on their work.

The view westward was unimpeded, and afforded a most interesting view of the interior of the Greenland Fjord, the exploration of which, by means of extensive sledge-journeys … seemed desirable. The opposite view, too, of a broad, smooth, icy sea losing itself in the distance, and the wild, imposing, rocky land to the west and north was, in a purely landscape point of view, most beautiful.

Meanwhile, a boat excursion southward along the shore was stopped short of Kap Borlase Warren by heavy ice. The ship returned to Germaniahavn.

On September 14 they began a sledge journey to the northwest of Sabine Ø to investigate what they named Fligely Fjord. Along the way they shot a bear and, Payer wrote (Koldewey 1874:318), "Reindeer came from all sides of the strand in a state of wonder." From the 1,235-m (4,050-ft) top of a mountain they found that the fjord turned north and joined with Ardencaple Fjord discovered by Clavering. The confluence of the two fjords surrounded what they named Kuhn Ø. The mountain climbers returned to their camp after dark. Payer wrote (Koldewey 1874:320):

> It was a glorious night; a perfect calm and a cloudless sky. A whitish northern light, which we saw to the south of us, together with the lights of the stars, shed a feeble glimmer over the icy landscape around us, and the ice-crowned tops of the surrounding mountains were distinctly to be seen. Nowhere does Nature show herself with greater power and expression than in the Arctic regions; and on such a September night as this it was truly majestic.

While on their return toward the ship the sledge and one of the seamen broke through the ice. All were recovered, but of course everything was soaked. Payer (Koldewey 1874:321) described "[t]he saturated and frozen tent we could with difficulty raise at all; the folds were like lead. We suffered not a little from the cold that night." They encountered muskoxen and reindeer very close the next day which they did not hunt, and Lieutenant Payer found an enormous layer of coal on Kuhn Ø. They reached the ship on September 21 after a journey of 215 km (133 mi).

While the sledging party was away, the men on the ship had killed reindeer and the largest bear they saw in Greenland, and three violent storms had struck the ship. Apparently the storms followed the coast and spared the inner fjords where the sledge party had travelled. By mid-September the ship was firmly frozen in for the winter and covered with a canvas shelter. It would be the first European ship to winter safely on the coast of East Greenland, and its crew were the first Europeans to winter north of Graah's Nukarfik, over 970 km (600 mi) to the south; they were the first Europeans on the east coast (after Thorgils Orrabeinsfostre) to winter north of the Arctic Circle. The autumn was largely occupied with the scientific observations in meteorology, magnetism, and some dredging of the ocean bottom. The weather was sufficiently good to encourage botanical studies of plants showing in wind-swept, snow-free areas.

Unlike the storms of September, "The whole of October and some part of November," wrote Doctor Adolphus Pansch, the surgeon, biologist and archaeologist, "we enjoyed the finest autumn weather ... ' Fine, clear weather with calm,' – such was the ever-repeated entry in the ship's log, and we had, indeed, 'over East Greenland an ever-smiling heaven'" (Koldewey 1874:339).

They took advantage of the fine weather. A sledge party left on October 27 to travel south toward Clavering Ø to examine geology and glaciology along the coast and to learn whether the Inuit visited by Captain Clavering in 1823 still lived there. The way around Kap Borlase Warren was difficult because of broken sea ice piled against the cape. On the 30th they had reached the northeast side of Clavering Ø and found a thick growth of birches, willows, and grasses, all several centimetres high. Payer wrote (Koldewey 1874:362): "This spot was the richest in vegetation of any I had seen in Greenland; and we might count on the presence of reindeer, which was all the more welcome, as the continuation of our journey depended upon the success of our hunters." An abundance of driftwood along the shore told them that it was unlikely there were any people in the vicinity; Inuit would have carefully gathered the invaluable wood into a safe place. That day they discovered and entered Tyroler Fjord northwest of Clavering

Ø. There, Payer wrote (Koldewey 1874:364), they found "a beautiful semi-circle of glaciers…. Scarcely anywhere can the traces of glacier formation be so strikingly followed out as on this spot." They had hoped that perhaps Tyroler Fjord might lead them back to and join with Fligely Fjord and thus open an easy route back to the ship. Such was not the case, and they had to return the way they had come. Close to home they had to cross thin, newly frozen, sea ice. Payer wrote (Koldewey 1874:368–69):

> As with difficulty we were following the road, we were startled by a walrus breaking through the ice close to us. We fled as quickly as we could, for any attempt to defend ourselves would have been madness. But the walrus swam as quickly under the ice after us, breaking through it near us, evidently intending to stay in our company. We dispersed as much as possible, springing over the ice-crust, through which the alpenstock constantly broke, followed by the rustling and flapping caused by the monster. Had any one fallen in, it would have been impossible to have pulled him out again. Fortunately, near Cape Wynn, a screen of old ice relieved us of our pursuer.

They were back on the ship on November 4 after a journey of 320 km (200 mi). Payer summarized (Koldewey 1874:370) the results of the journey: "The passage conjectured by Clavering to exist to the north of the island of the same name, the discovery of some Fjords, the enlargement of our geographical knowledge of the neighbourhood, and, lastly, the highly interesting study of the Greenland glaciers, were the fruits of this difficult journey."

Stormy weather returned shortly thereafter with heavy snowfalls and violent winds striking the ship frequently and lasting for days at a time. Doctor Pansch wrote (Koldewey 1874:372) that on November 7, for example, "From time to time there were perfect hurricane gusts, causing the ice-bound ship to quiver throughout: such weather we had never experienced. If we ventured beyond the closely-shut hatchways on to the deck, we were nearly deafened by the blustering, roaring, and crashing with which the wind broke upon the ship and howled around it." These recurring storms were separated by periods of fine and calm and cold days in which work on the ship and at the observatory on land was possible. The sun had long since disappeared, but the darkness was relieved by the afterglow to the south, by the moon that shone without setting from the 19th to the 25th of November, and by northern lights. Doctor Pansch recorded that "[w]eeks passed without any unusual interruption. Everything went its usual way, the increasing darkness of the days turning our thoughts to Christmas and the new year." On December 16 began the worst and most lasting storm they experienced. Karl Börgen, the astronomer, on his way from the observatory, Pansch wrote (Koldewey 1874:383), "was once taken up and bodily thrown at least ten paces forward, and not without great exertion did he reach the guiding rope, and then on his way to the ship he was lifted up several times and thrown aside." The storm lasted into December 20. It raged more than 103 hours and blew with an average speed of 90 km (56 mi) per hour. They celebrated Christmas with calm weather and a tree made of Andromeda shoots found under the snow.

With the new year, 1870, planning for the main journey of exploration to the north began. What the ship had been unable to do because of the ice fields, they hoped to do by a sledge journey – reach a high latitude. While preparations for the journey were underway in the dark days of January, bears visited the ship. The ship's engineer was followed home by a bear who was delayed in his pursuit by the engineer shedding clothing to divert the bear and attract his curiosity. The engineer's cries attracted help from the ship which scared the bear off with gunfire.

The sun returned for the first time on February 3. Doctor Pansch wrote (Koldewey 1874:400–401): "To our great joy the horizon here was quite clear; only a few clouds stood in the heavens. These added to the beauty of the scene, for they were of the brightest red and yellow.... Moved to the depths of our hearts, we thought to look upon the sun, but the long-unseen light was blinding, the eyes could not bear it, and we were compelled to have protecting-glasses before we could tell whether the sun's disc was above the horizon.... It was a joyous and a glorious sight."

On March 6, the day before the intended start of the long northern journey, there was a near-fatal accident. Karl Börgen, when about fifty steps from the ship, was seized by a bear and dragged away. His cries for help were heard by Captain Koldewey, who roused the crew. Börgen wrote (Koldewey 1874:408–9): "The grip was so sudden and rapid, that I am unable to say how it was done; whether the bear rose and struck me down with his fore-paws, or whether he ran me down.… The next thing I felt was the tearing of my scalp which was only protected by a skull-cap.… The cry for help which I uttered frightened the animal for a moment; but he turned again and bit me several times on the head." The bear dragged Börgen by the head. A shot from the aroused crew caused him to drop Börgen. The bear then seized the victim by the hand, fortunately protected by a thick fur glove, and dragged him for 300 paces. The bear was crossing rough shore ice and heading for smooth sea ice beyond. If he had reached it, the victim would have been lost because the bear could have easily outrun the pursuers. The rescuers caught up with and drove off the bear before he got to the smooth ice.

Börgen's injuries were mainly in the head. The bear had torn his scalp in several places, some tears were 10–15 cm (4–6 in) long, and there were about twenty injuries elsewhere on his body, in part from striking rough, sharp edges of broken shore ice as he was dragged along. His clothes and hair were saturated with blood. Payer wrote (Koldewey 1874:408) that Börgen had been "carried more than 100 paces with his skull almost laid bare, at a temperature of −13° Fahr. [−25° C]; his scalp healed so perfectly that not a single portion was missing." Börgen wrote (Koldewey 1874:410) that "neither during the act of receiving the wounds nor during the process of healing, which progressed favourably, did I experience the smallest pain."

The northern party began its journey the day after the accident. They dragged a sledge heavy-laden with supplies for fifty to sixty days, and they were accompanied by a supporting team of four men and a smaller sledge. They hoped to reach 80° N, – over 550 km (340 mi) away – and they started auspiciously; "The weather is lovely," Payer wrote, but they ran into difficulties almost immediately. "The first day our advance was rendered so difficult by the hard, rough, sharp-edged snow-drifts, that we could only get the sledges along half laden, thus having to go over the road three times" (Payer in Koldewey 1874:426). Then unmistakable signs of a heavy storm came upon them. They decided to return to the ship and await a more favourable opportunity. It was just as well. They would have made no progress in the storm, which prevailed for several days. Only on March 24 did conditions improve enough to warrant a new beginning.

Julius Payer wrote (Koldewey 1874:412): "Sledge journeys, particularly in spring-time, are attended by great expenditure of strength and troubles of all kinds." Six sailors – Herzberg, Mieders, Thomas Klentzer, Wagner, the carpenter, and Peter Ellinger – and Captain Koldewey and Lieutenant Payer dragged the big sledge. Four men dragged the support sledge. Their supplies included coffee, chocolate, boiled beef, ham, butter, suet, salt, dry black bread, pemmican extract of beef, beans, lentils, peas, barley, flour mixed with melted butter, and twenty bottles of brandy. The medicine chest provided for only frostbite, snow-blindness, and dysentery. Each man was allowed 2.25 kg (5 lb) of personal baggage. Arctic sledge travellers had not then learned that it is essential to reduce weights to the minimum.

The support sledge had to return on the second day when one man's foot was frostbitten. From then on the northern party struggled across the frozen sea against blizzards that kept them in their tent for days at a time, in much lower temperatures than those at the ship, and through deep snow. The north wind blew in their faces and chilled their bodies struggling with the sledge.

Payer wrote (Koldewey 1874:417) that they frequently witnessed parhelia, or mock suns, caused by the refraction of the sun's light by the ice-crystals floating in the upper strata of air. These mock suns sometimes form a double circle around the sun, with a coloured bow beyond, and horizontal stripes of light emanating from the sun itself. The inner part of this bow is always red, the outer shading off into pale green and a very light sky-blue. The first circle is bright yellow within; the second of a yellowish grey. This phenomenon only takes place in a yellow, vaporish atmosphere, with horizontal strata, and a somewhat cloudy sky.

New lands arose above the northern horizon, and the hardships and slow pace of their progress did not diminish their enthusiasm for the new lands revealed to them. Lieutenant Payer wrote (Koldewey 1874:429) that "The rosy sloping masses of Koldewey Island in the northeast, looked in the splendour of setting sun like fairy-land." They made geological observations as they went along, encountered muskoxen from time to time, climbed mountains to survey the route ahead and to map the country, and found Inuit tent-ring ruins at Kap Carl Ritter. Bears were common there, and occasionally they came up to the sledgers or the tent. The travellers had to keep no special bear watch because the cold kept at least one of them awake during the night. As they travelled north, icebergs frozen in the sea ice increased in size and number and the snow had drifted in great mounds among the bergs. So little was then known of the geography of Greenland that Payer speculated (Koldewey 1874:432) that icebergs formed from East Greenland glaciers might "be carried to the west coast by a connexion of the different fjords and currents, or that by interior channels they arrive in Scoresby's or Davis' Strait."

Payer described (Koldewey 1874:434) the changing scenery. A new mountain chain to the west "was of wonderful beauty. Glacier cascades, more than a mile broad, fell from a snow plateau 4,800 feet high [1,220 m].... Icebergs of monstrous height, which on that very account we mistook for islands, were iced up in the interior of the bays."

They reached the end of their northern journey on April 11 just north of Kap Bismarck. Storm kept them in their tent until April 15, when four of them (Koldewey, Payer, Thomas Klentzer, Peter Ellinger) walked to 77°1' N, 278 km (172 mi) north of their winter quarters, but 334 km (207 mi) short of their hoped-for goal of 80° N. They could go no farther. Payer wrote (Koldewey 1874:436): "our object gained fell far short of our bold flights of fancy." As far as they could see from a 300-m (1,000-ft) mountain, the sea was solidly covered with ice; there was no suggestion of an open polar sea beyond an ice barrier. "The conjecture, once broached, of an open Arctic Sea," Payer concluded, "we could, from our standpoint, only reject as idle." They flew the North-German and Austrian flags on the mountain top and erected a cairn in which they deposited a record of their endeavours, a cairn, Payer wrote (Koldewey 1874:437), "which will doubtless remain unmoved, though perhaps never again seen to the end of time."

Little did they guess that, far from remaining unseen until the end of time, that land would again be visited in less than forty years. Sledging parties would then far surpass the northern record of Koldewey's expedition. It was an expedition rich in scientific talent and blessed by enthusiastic and dedicated support teams made from the ship's crew. The expedition accomplished much. The crude technologies of their time, however, greatly limited what they were able to do.

Two muskoxen and a bear provided meat for the travellers that lasted until their return to the ship. Beyond Kap Helgoland was a large snowy waste. Payer described (Koldewey 1874:439) the struggle to advance. "We waded through it during Easter time, as step by step we sank up to the thighs through the crusted surface, and in spite of the greatest exertions could only make a short day's journey. Panting and almost bent double we tugged at the traces; with struggles the sledge followed, sinking deep into the snow-dust, almost as much swimming as gliding." They reached the ship on April 27. They had covered 556 km (345 mi) in a month.

On May 8 Lieutenant Payer with four men started out again to explore Fligely and Ardencaple Fjords. Temperatures were then much more moderate than a month earlier, but deep snow made sledging very difficult. On May 10 they gained less than a kilometre in a march of four hours, sinking deep in the snow at every step. Conditions got worse as they entered the fjords. Payer wrote (Koldewey 1874:453): "The continued jerking of the sledge had given us all a violent headache, the throbbing of which was most painful." They had to relay their loads. At one point they saw three bears partially destroy food in a cache. A sailor returned from a muskox hunt empty-handed, with a broken gun and torn clothing; he had been thrown down and trampled by a muskox. With rising spring temperatures, thick fog added to their troubles. They found it impossible to enter far into the fjords covered with deep snow. They confined their examination of Ardencaple Fjord to a view from a mountain – a three-and-a-half hour climb – at its southeastern corner. Their view followed the fjord inland 80 km (50 mi) where it curved to the west and disappeared from view, and so they mapped it. They gave particular attention to the geology of Kuhn Ø, where in the autumn they had discovered coal. They reached the ship on May 29, trudging and hauling their sledge the last few days through snow made dense, wet, and sticky by the thaw. Rain fell on the next few days after their return.

While the northern party was away, and later as Payer attempted to enter the fjords, Ralph Copeland and Börgen were carrying on triangulating and mapping surveys of the area from the Pendulum Øer north to Hochstetter Forland, erecting tall survey beacons on all prominent elevations visible from other points of the area. The job took from early April until mid-June. As they traversed Lille Pendulum Ø they came across remarkable formations of basaltic columns 1.8–2.7 m (6–9 ft) thick and *hundreds* of feet high. Muskoxen were frequently encountered, and as the season progressed the surveyors laboured through soft, deep snow that gradually melted and flooded the sea ice. They were compensated by the scenery: "The prospect from Ruthner to westward," Borgen and Copeland wrote (Koldewey 1874:500), "is wonderfully beautiful. The wildly rent mountains, with broad ravines and narrow gorges, and the wonderful contrast of the granite sandstone and basaltic rocks against the blinding white snow, made a never-to-be-forgotten impression." By the end of May the melting snow made it impossible to continue farther north. On their retreat south, "so much water had collected on the ice that the mountains were reflected in it; we might therefore make up our minds to wade from thirteen to fourteen hours through water at 32°" (Koldewey 1874:502). When on land they had to cross streams full of meltwater, once up to their waists. Bears, often females with cubs, were common on the way back to the ship where they arrived on June 17.

One of the expedition's priorities was to try to locate the Inuit seen by Clavering in 1823, forty-seven years earlier. The excursion to the north side of Clavering Ø in the previous autumn had not been conclusive as to their fate. By mid-July there was enough open water to permit a boat trip to the south side of the island where the Inuit had last been seen. The boat was stopped by ice a few kilometres from the site, and they walked the rest of the way to the settlement site described by Captain Clavering. Along the way the botanist Doctor Pansch examined the vegetation now in full bloom or even beginning its autumn stages. He wrote (Koldewey 1874:521):

> We were ... delighted by ... the slender rich-leaved *Epilobium latifolium* (L.), [fireweed] with large lovely red flowers; also the yellow-head of the *Arnica alpina* (Murr.); ... a bellflower (*Campanula uniflora*, L.) was unfolding its first dark blue bells; thus all the elements of a lovely bouquet were present.

And further (Koldewey 1874:522–23):

> Growing among the loose pebbles and in the rocky crevices
> was the beautiful *Polemonium humile* (Willd.). Such blossoming
> splendour we had not yet seen in Greenland, and for the moment
> forgot that we were in the far North; we had already known the
> plant in Germaniaberg and Klein Pendulum, but there it was
> nothing to this luxuriance! The vigorous pinnate leaves were
> more than half a foot long, the blossom the bulk of a good-sized
> apple, and on this the flowers were crowded of the clearest and
> most lovely blue, and at some considerable distance we could
> smell the aromatic perfume of its leaves.

Reindeer were common and unafraid along the way. Graves, tent rings,
and houses marked the site of Clavering's visit with the Inuit, but they
found no traces of living peoples. Examination of two houses gave them to
believe that on this spot there could be no question of the slow dying-out
of a once numerous population. Indeed, they had found numerous tent
rings, ancient houses, and other artefacts of human occupations wherever
they had travelled on the shores of Shannon, Lille Pendulum, Sabine, and
Clavering Øer, and Wollaston Forland.

Germania was freed from the ice on July 22. Captain Koldewey again
steamed north, slowly threading his way through channels within the ice
fields on the east side of Shannon Ø By the 28th it was clear that they
would get very little farther north than had been possible the previous
year. Captain Koldewey recorded (1874:537) "nothing but thick ice and a
white ice-sky to the north. It was evident that until the beginning of the
autumn storms nothing could set the enormous mass in motion." Their orders were to go north as far as possible, but with such a doubtful prospect
in view Koldewey, with the concurrence of his officers and scientists, decided that their time would be better spent farther south, where Scoresby
had indicated there might be large unexplored fjords or bays. On July 30
they steamed south again.

They landed on Jackson Ø for further scientific observations and to
increase their scientific collections. The ship steamed westward along the
coast, encountered a barrier of ice, and anchored. A boat crew threaded its

way further west between the ice and the shore. They landed in Mackenzie Bugt and shot five reindeer, "the herd being so confiding," Koldewey wrote (1874:545) "that they allowed themselves to be surrounded before they thought of moving. We therefore rejoiced in some fresh meat, which lately had been scarce." On August 8 the boat reached Kap Franklin, where they were on the verge of the great discovery of the expedition, a discovery that with good reason would amaze them.

> Börgen and the Captain mounted a rocky height ... from whence their astonished eyes beheld a landscape, which was indescribable in its extraordinary grandeur. The interior of Greenland lay there like a splendid picture, displaying the Alpine world in its highest style. At our feet lay the mouth of a great Fjord, or rather arm of the sea, perfectly free from drifting ice, but covered with numerous icebergs of from 95 to 190 feet [29–59 m] high, and stretching westward in the far, far distance, then seeming to divide into several arms, rising even higher and higher into the regions of eternal snow and ice.
>
> This was a moment that richly rewarded us for all our troubles and difficulties (Koldewey 1874:547–48).

Thus they discovered Kejser Franz Joseph Fjord, one of the great fjord systems of the world.

While they lingered, the ice barrier drifted east and cleared the way for *Germania*. The weather remained fine and clear and they steamed into the fjord. "What strange feelings arose within us as we advanced into these lonely waters, as yet uncleft by the keel of any vessel." Julius Payer wrote (Koldewey 1874:552):

> We had entered a basin, the shores of which were formed by rocks, which for glorious form and colour I had never seen equalled. Here were congregated all the peculiarities of the Alpine world: huge walls, deep erosion-fissures, wild peaks, mighty crevassed glaciers, raging torrents, and waterfalls; which in Europe, as a rule, come but singly. All these pictures of wild beauty were taken in at a glance.... A colossal cubic

rock ... stretched itself far into the Fjord, rising out of the blue water to a height of at least 5600 feet [1,700 m].... The terraces and towers on its edges resembled a ruined castle; we therefore called it the Devil's Castle.

Never in the Alps had I seen anything even approaching this in grandeur.

They anchored on August 11 far in the fjord, and Lieutenant Payer and Doctor Copeland with the sailor Peter Ellinger climbed a mountain, later named Payer Fjeld, to get a general view of the entire neighborhood. They reached 2,090 m (6,850 ft) and from that height, Payer wrote (Koldewey 1874:561), they saw "a monstrous pyramid of ice to the west, rising 4,850 ft [1,480 m] above a high mountain ridge. This glorious peak could bear none other name than that of Petermann, the honoured originator of the first German Arctic Expedition: its real height must have approached 11,000 feet [3,354 m]." And they could trace their great fjord 65 km (40 mi) farther towards the west southwest. In the meantime, Doctor Pansch examined the rich and varied vegetation that flourished in the twenty-four-hour sunlight and the warmth radiating from the sun-heated high dark cliffs. "We found it much in the same freshness and vigour as on the higher Alps in Switzerland ... all the mountain slopes were green; though there were large spots of low, woody bushes, namely, willow, birch, and bilberry" (Pansch in Koldewey 1874:556–57).

Now it was mid-August and they were running out of time. Their orders forbade them to spend a second winter in Greenland, and they still had to pass through the pack ice off the outer coast. Their steam engine began to break down. The engineer made such repairs as he could and they made their way to the mouth of the fjord, where they found the pack ice quite dense. On August 16, Captain Koldewey wrote (1874:565), their "poor, patched boiler was heated once more, but as soon as steam was up more pipes began to leak." In the absence of wind to drive them with their sails through the ice, however, one more trial under steam had to be made. With a failing engine, with little or no wind, and in dense fog common to the outer coast in summer, they weighed anchor homeward bound. On the 21st the engine expired forever and they were dependent upon sails alone. On the 24th a usable breeze helped them along banging through the floes, and by the end of the day they were clear of the pack ice. They entered the Weser and arrived at Bremerhaven on September 11, 1870. They had all returned safely with a rich harvest of results and a wonderful story of adventure and discovery to tell.

And what had become of *Hansa*, *Germania's* sailing consort? The story was included in Captain Koldewey's narrative of the expedition. In addition, the ship's log of *Hansa* kept by Captain Hegemann was recently translated and published; we have a detailed account of *Hansa's* fate. The ships were separated in the ice as they approached Greenland on July 20, 1869, and never met again. *Hansa*, which had no steam power but only sail, spent August struggling to get through the ice. At times her crew could see their goal, the land north of Kap Broer Ruys. They got off the ship and onto the ice and pushed and pulled their vessel, but calms and the thick drifting ice frustrated their efforts and hopes. At other times storms drove the pack even closer together. Captain Hegemann retreated and managed to break free from the pack early in August and sailed north to try again to penetrate the ice at 75° N. Again the ice closed around and held *Hansa*. At one point they could see the land only 15.5 km (10 mi) from what would be *Germania's* winter harbour. From the 14th "the captain's log-book unfolds a succession of reverses, troubles and dangers" (Koldewey 1874:86). They had blizzard conditions on August 22, and five days later heavy ice pressure came upon the ship "with terrible force, so that she is constantly cracking and rose up about 1.5 feet" (Hegemann 1993:278). Later the sailors tried an unsuccessful boat excursion across the ice to land. The ship was under sail for the last time, but still confined in the ice, on September 2. With steam power they could have reached the open water that they saw along the coast. After that last futile effort to break through, the ship could only drift with the southerly current. The crew secured the ship to a large, heavy, thick ice floe which later would become their refuge. Bears visited them; some they shot, others escaped. Two foxes appeared, showing that there was continuous ice from the land. On September 7 the log notes (Hegemann 1993:281) that "Our hope of reaching the coast is vanishing steadily, and hence we now probably will soon have to try to get out again." By the end of September they knew that they would not escape the ice that winter. They built a house of coal blocks from their cargo and of snow and ice blocks on their ice floe in the event that the ship might be crushed and lost.

Three sailors attempted to reach the land, about 16 km (10 mi) distant, on October 17, but open water and drifting snow forced them back. And then ice pressure on the ship began to be serious. She began to leak and they moved all usable materials to their coal- and snow-block house on the floe. The ice pressure continued and the pumps could not control the water rising in the ship. The masts fell, and on October 22, in calm and clear weather, the ship sank 9.7 km (6 mi) from Liverpool Land.

The sailors settled as best they could into their coal- and ice-block house for the winter. The routine of maintaining their camp amid the drifting snow kept them busy, and their health remained good, sustained by fresh meat from the occasional bear. They killed a walrus that provided meat and fuel from its three-inch [8 cm] layer of fat. The monotony was relieved by auroral displays of "dazzling coloured rays," by the ever-changing sculptures in the shifting ice around them, and by the changing aspect of the coast as they drifted along. At times they were within 6.5 km (4 mi) of the shore and could identify points described by Scoresby and later, when they were farther south, by Graah. On November 23 in fine, calm weather they could see both Greenland to the northwest and Iceland to the southeast. The ship's log frequently recorded days of fine and even very fine weather and at intervals violent blizzards from the northeast. The log notes: "The remarkable feature of this Christmas Day is that it rained all day; even a thorough down pour towards evening" (Hegemann 1993:299).

Their floe remained intact and undamaged into January, keeping its original diameter of 4 km (2.5 mi) and thickness of about 12 m (40 ft). Then the ice became active. The log (Hegemann 1993:301):

> 11 January. This was a terrifying day for us. At 4 a.m. a severe NE gale with thick blowing snow. Much open water with heavy waves. Our floe started to break up all around. From 4 a.m. onwards we stood all day near the boats in this terrible weather, afraid that they might break away at any moment.... It is only due to a miracle of Providence that we are still in

possession of the boats and the hut. The floe is now only a pan 150 paces wide, but we hope it is very strong ...

Captain Hegemann's narrative (Koldewey 1874:130–31) noted that "The days from the 11th to the 15th of January were destined to bring us new horrors. On the 11th, heavy storm from the north-east with driving snow.... Our field again began to break on all sides." They were aroused by noise before any motion was visible. The crisis came during a storm when blinding snow made visibility almost impossible. Their floe was battered and greatly reduced in size. The sea was close to their house and they found the coast hardly two miles away, but the chaos of broken ice between their floe and the coast made it impossible to reach the land. The northeast storm on January 11 split the floe between their house and their pile of firewood. The floe was reduced to a diameter of 46 m (150 ft), and then at midnight they barely escaped destruction as they drifted close by an iceberg. For five nights following a second storm they slept in their two boats, anticipating that their house might be destroyed while they slept within. With better weather they built another house, but half as big. "Throughout all the discomfort, want, hardship, danger of all kinds, the frame of mind among the men was good, undaunted, and exalted. The cook kept a right seamanlike humour, even in the most critical moments. As long as he had tobacco he made no trouble of anything" (Koldewey 1874:134–35). Much of the turmoil of the ice in January was undoubtedly the result of spring tides and of pressure arising from the Greenland current and sea ice passing in the narrowest constriction between Iceland and Greenland. The weather continued to alternate between "extremely bad weather" (January 31) and "very fine weather" (February 1) – and even on the same day (February 12). Most of February passed quietly. Icebergs increased around them, but their floe suffered no further reduction in size. March brought abundant snow. Again they risked destruction by striking a grounded iceberg. "As we came nearer the mass, we suddenly saw directly above us numerous points and jagged spikes; one projecting angle indeed we could grasp.... But – wonderful! our floe was unshaken; it did not even graze it" (Koldewey 1874:141). Captain Hegemann (1993:308) noted: "The 20 minutes during which we sped past the berg were terrifying. It was especially the SW tip, which was badly crevassed and threatened to collapse at any moment, which inspired concern in us…. The iceberg was 2000 feet long and about 800 feet wide and a fairly regular height of 90 feet." They drifted safely by.

Rain came early in May. By May 6 they were at 61º4' N; they had drifted nearly 1,600 km (1,000 mi) since they were beset. "Grand was the appearance of 'Puisortoq' glacier, a mighty ice field extending thirty nautical miles [55 km] along the coast" (Koldewy 1874:144). On May 7 open water was visible along the coast; the time had come to take to their boats and leave their ice floe. They departed at 4 p.m. and had to spend the night camped on another floe. The following day they worked again through drifting ice, but such was the weather and the state of ice between them and the coast that it was slow going. Often they had to drag the heavy boats across ice floes. The log (Hegemann 1993:315) for May 8: "Hauling out and relaunching the boats is very heavy work and hence the men are all really exhausted." Bad weather, snow falls, and storm kept them confined to a floe for six days. Then after a brief hope of release, they were held for another five days. Such was their progress. May resembled January in the continued northern storms. It took them four *weeks* to cross those few kilometres to reach the shore. In fourteen days they were able to advance less than 4 km (2.5 mi) by dragging the boats. Only on June 4 did they succeed in reaching land for the first time since they left Bremen the previous June. They enjoyed delightful weather, now, as they made their way by oar and sail down the coast, hunting birds as they went. They found the entrance to Prins Christian Sund, the passage to West Greenland, after following a blind fjord, and on June 13 they reached Frederiksdal, a Moravian missionary station, where their fellow countrymen welcomed them to the southernmost European settlement in Greenland. Their safe return to Europe was now assured. It was just a matter of time until they reached Julianehåb, from whence they took a vessel to Copenhagen, where they arrived on September 1.

Danish Pre-eminence

HOLM AND GARDE AND THE KONESBAAD EXPEDITION, 1883–85

In the mid-nineteenth century a number of countries, such as Germany, had undertaken geographic and scientific explorations in Greenland, particularly in the northwest regions. With the exception of the important work of a few individuals, Denmark had not been able to participate in that work in any systematic or sustained way, in considerable part because of difficult economic conditions after a disastrous war in 1864 with Prussia and Austria in which Denmark lost Schleswig-Holstein.

Professor Frederik Johnstrup, Professor of Mineralogy at the University of Copenhagen, developed a plan for coordinated long-term research throughout Greenland. Parliament was receptive to the plan and provided funds annually for expeditions to West Greenland in 1872, 1874, 1876, and 1877. Johnstrup participated in that of 1874 and personally supervised those of 1876 and 1877. Late in 1877 he petitioned Parliament that the research program should be placed on a formal institutional basis to insure the long-term continuity of the work. On January 11, 1878, the Ministry of the Interior, impressed with Johnstrup's results, established the Commission for the Supervision of Geological Exploration in Greenland. In later years its name was modified to reflect its expansion to encompass a much wider range of scientific activities. The commission published the first volume of its research series, *Meddelelser om Grønland*, in 1879, and the series continues without interruption into the twenty-first century. Since 1879 all the major Danish explorations of East Greenland have been commissioned by or assisted by the commission, beginning with the umiak expedition of Gustaf Holm and Vilhelm Garde.

About 1850 rumours had reached the Danes in southwest Greenland of an unknown group of Inuit living in an area on the East Greenland coast north of that explored by W.A. Graah in 1829–30. Their living place was reported to be called Ammassalik because it was there that capelin (angmagssat), a small fish related to salmon that appeared inshore in the spring, were found in abundance. The rumours of unknown Inuit were persistent over the years and so in 1883 Lieutenants Gustav Holm and Vilhelm Garde together with scientists Hans Knutsen and Peter Eberlin were sent out to find them. Their purpose also was to re-examine and survey more carefully the coast that Lieutenant Graah had first explored over fifty years earlier. No European had visited that coast since Graah. Holm and his colleagues landed at Julianehåb and on July 18 established their base at the far southern village of Nanortalik, where umiaks, such as Lieutenant Graah had used and for the same reasons – they were believed to be the most suitable by far of any boat for such work in ice – were built for the expedition. In late July 1883 Holm's party set out for the east coast with four umiaks and ten kayaks and over thirty people. The kayakers would hunt along the way for the essential additions to the European supplies carried in the umiaks. Among them was Johan Petersen, a West Greenland interpreter who would serve with C.H. Ryder's expedition in 1891–92 and later would be station manager of the Danish posts to be established at Ammassalik in 1894 and at Scoresby Sund in 1924. Holm's expedition was known as the Konesbaad [women's boat] Expeditionen til Gronlands Østkyst 1883–1885.

Passing through Prins Christian Sund, Holm's party reached the east coast on July 31. There they met Navfalik, an "honest and clever" fellow who would give them much good advice and support for the duration of the expedition. They had already met and been delayed by difficult ice conditions, and Navfalik and other people were unanimous in their belief that Holm, at that late date, early August, could not hope to reach Ammassalik in that year. Holm could not spend two winters on the East Greenland coast, so he built a depot for their supplies at Kasingortok ("the much faded one" or "the one turning grey") near Danells Fjord, about 87 km (54 mi) north of Prins Christian Sund. Navfalik, who planned to spend the winter there, promised to look after it. Holm then sent back three umiaks and six kayakers. He intended to proceed with explorations in the area with one umiak and four kayakers until they would have to return to Nanortalik for the winter. From the mountain at Iluileq ("appears to be an island, but is connected") they found impenetrable ice to the north. Having no other choice, they slowly worked their way south again, examining the interiors of several fjords along the way. From the top of a nunatak in Kangerdluarak ("a small fjord") they had an "excellent view inland of the magnificent Alpine prospect" (Holm and Garde 1889:67). On the nunatak's top of 1,000 m (3,300 ft) they built a cairn. Exploring the interior of fjords was slow business; Holm reported that the rowers were lazy and reluctant to work their way through newly-forming ice in the fjords. "The steerer Gedion was the only one who did not grumble, and we kept on as long as possible, until much calf ice completely barred the way" (Holm and Garde 1889:68).

On September 1 the weather became very wintry with storm, rain, and snow. Heavy drift ice set into the fjords and kept the expedition shut in until September 7. They could not return to Nanortalik the way they had come, by way of Prins Christian Sund, because the rapid current in the sound driving dense ice floes made it too dangerous. They had to go further south, almost to Kap Farvel, to Ikeqsund. And there they had to work through rather thick skim ice and to struggle on in darkness among dense, thick, heavy (Stor) ice. They reached Nanortalik in the night of September 15–16.

The winter at Nanortalik was spent in observations on weather, tides, magnetic variations, soil temperatures, and ice movements. And the umiaks were overhauled and completely re-covered with new skins.

The expedition set out again on May 5, 1884, with four umiaks and seven kayakers and thirty-one people besides the four Europeans and two interpreters. The crew included Johannes Hansen, called Hanserak, the grandson of the Danish founder of Julianehåb. He could not speak Danish, but "he was a man with incredible persistence and unyielding courage … he was clever and resourceful and took on himself every kind of job … which he carried out fully and quickly" (Holm and Garde 1889:72). By his example he influenced the rest of the crew.

Because of the extent of ice, a month passed before they could pass through Prins Christian Sund and reach the east coast. Only on June 27 could they leave Kekertatsiak ("a rather good island") just a few kilometres north of Prins Christian Sund. They found that their depot at Kasingor-tok had been well looked after as promised by Navfalik. As they travelled toward Kap Cort Adelaer they were escorted for a time by nine umiaks, twenty kayakers, and about 119 people. From a camp site by Kap Rantzau, Holm climbed a 400-m (1,300-ft) mountain and saw a ship under sail and steam 7 or 8 km (4 or 5 mi) from land.

They reached Tingmiarmît (which refers to people who live in "bird land"), Navfalik's home and nearly 300 km (186 mi) from Prins Christian Sund, on July 28. Fifty years later this region would be described as an Arctic riviera by Knud Rasmussen's colleagues on his Sixth Thule Expedition. Holm laid down a supply depot here and again Navfalik promised to care for it. From here Garde, Eberlin, and Petersen were to return to Nanortalik with one umiak and two kayakers, examining fjords as they went. Garde's instructions were to return to the east coast with fresh supplies in the following year to meet Holm's party on its return from the Ammassalik area. This arrangement would give Holm greater freedom and flexibility of movement in his investigations of the Ammassalik area.

Gustaf Holm's party "had several rough struggles to break our way through [the ice] with axes and hooks and to press forward along the coast," and Holm noted that now "our Greenlanders' eagerness, cleverness, and endurance was praiseworthy" (Holm and Garde 1889:86). As they went north icebergs increased both in size and in number. On August 2 they reached the region of the Akorninarmiut (referring to "people living between headlands or bays"), where Graah had wintered, and there in fact on Nukarfik they found Graah's winter quarters of more than fifty years before. The local inhabitants told Holm that he could not possibly reach Ammassalik that year – perhaps because the local people wanted their company for the coming winter. Fortunately, they were joined by Ilinguaki, who was familiar with the Ammassalik region. "This extraordinarily clever and kind man became our escort to Ammassalik district; without his companionship, the expedition would have scarcely been successful" (Holm and Garde 1889:88). On August 25 they passed Lieutenant Graah's northernmost point, where they found Graah's large beacon or cairn untouched – "not a stone had fallen out of it" (1889:89) – though they could not find the silver medal that Graah had left. Holm left a report of his expedition in the cairn, and the next day they crossed the "huge" ice fjord Ikerssuaq ("the great sound"), filled with ice in all sizes from great icebergs to small calf ice.

They found three human bodies, apparently victims of starvation in the previous year, in a house at Inugsaliq ("a place with a beacon or cairn"). In fact, it appeared that the population of the southeast coast, exclusive of the Ammassalik district, had declined drastically since Graah's first exploration. He had estimated a population of about 630 people. Holm in comparison found the coast almost deserted: he counted only 120 people.[1] Some of the decline came from emigrations to the trading stations of the west coast, some came from starvation, and some of it was the result of deadly blood feuds which were not uncommon among the East Greenlanders. Holm's party reached Ammassalik on September 1.

In the meantime, Lieutenant Garde with Eberlin and Petersen on July 29 had started the return journey to Nanortalik as planned. Garde and Eberlin looked in vain for a rumoured inscribed stone before leaving the vicinity of Tingmiarmît, a rumour that had suggested the possibility of Norse ruins; there was still a lingering belief, in spite of Graah's report, that the Norse might have settled in East Greenland. None of the local people knew anything about such a stone.

On the journey south, Garde investigated the fjords from Tingmiarmît to Iluileq by Danells Fjord, which they had passed by on their way north. Because of limited time, the numerous fjords, and the presence of ice in so many of them, it was not possible to investigate all the fjords thoroughly The Greenlanders with him were very reluctant to enter far into the fjords for fear that newly formed ice of winter would trap them within and prevent their return to their homes on the west coast. By climbing mountains along the way Garde and Eberlin got a good idea of the general arrangement of the land inland from the coast and were able to continue their surveying measurements. Garde's party was slowed occasionally by ice along the coast, and low temperatures were causing new ice to form here and there, but they passed the great glacier front of Puisortoq without incident in clear and calm weather. Similarly, they passed with ease Kap

---

1 The anthropologist Helge Larsen revised the population estimates to 536 people in 1830 and 135 in 1883. (Larsen, H. n.d. (1970?)). The exploration of Greenland, pp. 139–54. In K. Hertling, E. Hesselbjerg, S. Klitgaard, E. Munck, O. Petersen, eds., *Greenland Past and Present*. Copenhagen: Edvard Henriksen.

Cort Adelaer, which had been difficult to pass on the way north because of rough water.

At Auarket ("a fjord with much colour") Garde saw the cannon that Graah had reported. His limited powder supply did not allow him to fire it, as had Graah, much to the disappointment of the Inuit. Garde and Eberlin reached with "great trouble" the site of the depot they had established in the autumn of 1883 at Kasingortok. And "long and laborious" was the remainder of the journey. Storm after storm and heavy seas along the open steep coast and an ominous mood among the Greenlanders who did not expect to reach their homes again made it a difficult journey. Only on September 27, quite late in the fall, did they finally reach Nanortalik. More than he expected and much to his pleasure, Garde's faithful Greenlanders immediately volunteered for the northward journey in the following year.

During the winter the covers of the umiaks were renewed with the best skins by the most able elder Greenlanders. With their other scientific observations through the winter, Garde and Eberlin "undertook observations and measurements of the extraordinarily frequent and very bright northern lights" (Holm and Garde 1889:110).

Lieutenant Garde again reached the east coast on May 23, 1885, only five days after his departure from Nanortalik, thanks to northwest winds that had cleared ice from the coast. The previous year the same journey had taken twenty-seven days. It was still winter on the east coast and the expedition was held for twenty days by ice masses at Qeqertârssuaq. Further progress was slow and much delayed by ice and winds and rowing against the strong current. They made 13 km (8 mi) in one day, but the last 2.5 km (1.6 mi) took 4.5 hours of effort. Garde found that extra coffee, schnapps, and a cigar all around (to male and female alike) would restore good humour among his crew. Like their other passages along this coast, this one was a struggle against ice forced against them and the land by winds and currents. The journey was also assisted by intervals of clear, even beautiful, and calm weather when they made good progress rowing their umiaks. Garde was anxious to use good weather to pass Puisortoq, but his Greenlanders were so pleased that they had passed Kap Cort Adelaer without trouble that they insisted on landing and feasting on a newly caught seal. While they waited, Puisortoq, with great and prolonged noise and turmoil, calved large quantities of ice, filling the sea before it with a mass of ice blocks and fragments. Garde was reprimanded for watching the glacier calve; the Inuit had turned their backs to the spectacle. Watching its discharges, Garde was told, could only bring misfortune.

Not until two days later did the ice clear enough to let them proceed. They arrived on July 8 at Tingmiarmît, where they were to wait for Holm. In 1884 it had taken them eighty-three days to reach Tingmiarmît; in 1885, fifty-two days. With the quick passage Garde had time to investigate the fjord behind Umanaq ("that which is shaped like a heart") about 48 km (30 mi) north of Tingmiarmît, and there on July 16 they met with Holm's party who had just arrived from Ammassalik.

When Lieutenant Holm arrived at Ammassalik on September 1, 1884, he chose a wintering site "that was excellent, at the outer end of an isthmus, behind which was a little fjord, Tasuisarsik ['a bay resembling a lake'], bordered by a high, steep picturesque mountain … if one went a little way into the hills one could see the whole inhabited part of Ammassalik Fjord. In old, overgrown house ruins … we would excavate and construct our winterhouses" (Holm and Garde 1889:92). There was plenty of driftwood for construction, and part of one of their umiaks, which was in mediocre condition and could no longer be used and was not to be repaired, was used for the houses.

Holm and his colleagues visited several of the inhabited places within the Ammassalik region. They estimated a total population of about 413 people and they found no less than forty places with old house ruins. In all the inhabited places they were "everywhere received with choice hospitality. Everywhere there was a great abundance of fat bags and seals, whose parts were dried, and parts frozen, stored for the winter stockpile" (Holm and Garde 1889:96). Holm traded for food for the winter. He moved into his winter house on October 3 when a raging snowstorm made life in a tent "the greatest unpleasantness."

Holm and Knutsen carried on their meteorological and tidal observations through the winter, and they studied their East Greenland neighbours, thirty-eight of whom lived in a house twenty minutes away. They had visitors through the winter from the distant parts of the Ammassalik district. The visitors thought little of walking for eight or ten hours over the mountains and through the deep snow of ice-covered fjords to visit the Danes. Holm could not take long winter sledge journeys because there were few dogs in the region. In recent years dogs had been killed and eaten because of the distress of hunger from poor hunting. But through the winter when bad weather kept the Ammassalik kayakers on shore, Holm's skilled hunter from West Greenland, Samuel, experienced in the turbulent winter seas of southwest Greenland, took his kayak to sea and brought home forty seals. On June 1 they visited the place where capelin fishing was taking place. Many people, perhaps the region's whole population, were gathered. Tents were set up, and in the evening there were drum dances and the young ones were playing games.

Holm built a large cairn by their winter house and left a record of their wintering. They left Ammassalik on June 9, 1885, but not until June 25 and only with much chopping and poling through the ice did they arrive at the great fjord Sermilik ("a place having glaciers"), only about 30 km (18 mi) away. Hurricane-like winds struck them there. Great efforts were needed to ensure that they and their tent, boat, and baggage were not all blown away. It was a warm, dry wind, the worst of it apparently very localized to their location on the west side of the fjord. Before leaving Sermilik, they rewarded Ilinguaki for his help with a rifle and two or three years' supply of ammunition and with a Danish flag with instructions on when to display it. The strong wind had driven ice away from the shore and so their travel to the south was relatively easy. On July 12 they learned from a kayaker that Lieutenant Garde had arrived and was waiting for them at Umanaq just north of Tingmiarmît. Here Holm and Garde rewarded and took leave of Navfalik and the East Greenlanders who had helped them for two years. Together Holm and Garde travelled south, and "in steady, beautiful weather and very scattered ice" they came on July 21 to Karra akungnak ("a rounded promontory"). It is a well-protected camp site in the bay just south of Kap Cort Adelaer where they were stopped for five days by stormy, rain-filled, northerly winds that drove ice in upon the land. Holm and Garde reached the west coast of Greenland on August 15 and finally arrived at Nanortalik on August 18. They boarded the ship *Constance* and left Greenland on August 29 and arrived in Copenhagen on October 3.

The expedition had accomplished its goals. It had found and become acquainted with the previously unknown people of Ammassalik and with "their life patterns, customs, speech, stories, beliefs, and so on" (Holm and Garde 1889:142), and it had brought home a rich ethnological collection of over 700 objects. Holm later published a three-volume report on the people with whom he had lived for nearly a year. He concluded (Holm 1914:147)

> that they are smart, clever, and understand how to turn to good account the things which fall into their possession. In their hunting expeditions they display endurance and audacity. They are lively, and are endowed with considerable powers of dissimulation. They are polite and accommodating in their behaviour to one another, but at the same time careful not to offend, reserved and suspicious. Deeper feelings, such as love, devotion, or real friendship are seldom met with among them.

The Danish ethnologist William Thalbitzer, after spending the period 1904–6 at Ammassalik, examined all the collections of Holm and Garde and of Gustav Amdrup made in 1899–1900. He concluded that the people were of a mixed culture made up of people who had come from the north and people who had come from the south, meeting and learning from each other how to live on the rich resources in the favourable location of the Ammassalik district. Thalbitzer noted that some of the ethnological objects were characteristically from the people of northwestern Greenland, such as dogs and dog sledges, winter seal hunting techniques and tools, and some were characteristically from southern Greenland, such as long houses, dip nets for capelin, cross bows, certain kinds of clothing for kayakers, and wooden boxes. Thalbitzer noted that many items were common to all of Greenland, and some were unique to the Ammassalik district. He concluded (Thalbitzer 1914:732) that "from this fusion has come Greenland's most exclusive, most complex and most artistic Eskimo community."

The expedition of Holm and Garde had revised and expanded upon Graah's map of the southeast coast, including new information on the fjords that Graah could not examine. Holm extended the map northward beyond Graah's farthest point. Holm and Knutsen recorded physical and geographical information from the Ammassalik district, including

GUSTAV HOLM
COURTESY ARCTIC INSTITUTE, DENMARK.

careful observations of sea ice which showed that access to the region from offshore was not as difficult as previously believed. For that reason in 1894 the Danes under Holm's leadership established a trading post and missionary station at Ammassalik, the first on the east coast, for the benefit of the Inuit and to reverse the decline of the population. When Holm had found those isolated people, they numbered about 416. When the station was established ten years later, the population was 293. Holm had found them just in time to prevent their extinction.

Three years after the return of Holm and Garde, Fridtjof Nansen began his pre-eminent Arctic explorations with the first crossing of the Greenland ice sheet. He and five companions with two rowing boats were set out on the pack ice from a Norwegian sealing vessel on July 17, 1888, just south of Ammassalik. They expected to cross the drifting ice and shortly reach the shore, but that was impossible. They drifted south until July 29, when at last they were able to reach open water along the land at about 61°35' N. They landed first on the island Qeqertârssuaq and then rowed north again, landing at various places and meeting people at several points along the way who welcomed them warmly. Nansen (1890:345–46) wrote that if one could handle the unique atmosphere within their tents and "is careful at first not to look too closely into their methods of preparing food, the general impression received is absolutely attractive. There is a frank and homely geniality in all their actions which is very winning, and can only make the stranger feel thoroughly comfortable in their society." The people offered the Norwegians food and gifts. Nansen (1890:351) wrote: "The hospitality, indeed, of this desolate coast is quite unbounded.... The nature of their surroundings and the wandering life which they lead have forced them to offer and accept universal hospitality, and the habit has gradually become a law among them."

Nansen commented upon the European goods he found among them, goods they had obtained by journeys to the Danish colonies beyond Kap Farvel (1890:367–69):

> These pilgrimages occur unfortunately too often, though their emporium lies at no trifling distance – a couple of years' journey, in fact, for those who live furthest up the coast.

One would almost expect that so long a journey would be followed by a long stay at the place of business. But this is not the case, and the Eskimo, in fact, spends little more time over his periodical shopping than a lady of the world over a similar but daily, visit. In half an hour, or an hour perhaps, he has often finished, and then disappears again on his long journey home. A shopping expedition of this kind will therefore often take four years at least, and consequently a man's opportunities are very limited .These are quite enough, however, to produce a mischievous effect. One is apt to suppose that it is the want of certain useful things, otherwise unattainable, that urges them to these; but this is scarcely so, for the real incentive is without doubt a craving for tobacco....Most of their purchases are things which are either altogether valueless or else actually injurious....

In addition to tobacco they buy other things which certainly have an injurious effect upon them, such as, for instance, tea....

In exchange for such things, which are of little value to us and still less real worth to them, they give fine large bearskins, fox-skins, and seal-skins which they ought to keep for their own clothes and the other numerous purposes for which they can be used....When the Eskimo have at length consumed their purchases and must needs return to the old manner of life, the net result is that they have lost a number of useful possessions and have acquired a feeling of want and longing for a number of unnecessary things.

Nansen's party landed on a small island off Mogens Heinesens Fjord which

seemed to us the loveliest spot we had ever seen on the face of the earth. All was green here; there was grass, heather, sorrel, and numbers of bright flowers. Up at the top we found the ruins of two old Eskimo houses, and here the vegetation was most luxuriant. It was a simple paradise, and wonderfully delightful we found it to lie here stretched on the greensward in the full blaze of the sun and roast ourselves to our heart's content, while we enjoyed the rare pleasure of a short rest. Then we gathered a few flowers in memory of this little Greenland Idyll, and taking to the boats again resumed our northward journey (1890:381–82).

Nansen, incidentally, believed that the traditional stout Norwegian rowing boat was superior to the umiaks used by Graah and Holm and Garde for travel on this coast. Farther on, Nansen wrote (1890:414–15),

> We came upon the most charming spot we had yet seen in Greenland, a little flat green meadow, and in front of it a big tarn of fresh water, with small fish swimming in it of a species which I could not determine On one side of the meadow were ruins of Eskimo houses, one of them very large, and the rest smaller. There were many skeletons in and outside the large house, including a particularly well-preserved Eskimo skull, which we carried off. These bones pointed to the conclusion that this settlement, too, had been depopulated by famine.

Nansen and his companions reached Colberger Heide, 64°04' N, where there was a practical route onto the ice sheet, on August 10. On the next day they began their ascent of the inland ice. They reached the west coast of Greenland in the latter part of September, a feat that had previously been thought to be impossible.

RYDER AND THE GREATEST FJORD IN THE WORLD, 1891–92

Scoresby Sund was not visited after the Scoresby's brief exploration in 1822 until 1891, when Lieutenant Carl Hartvig Ryder of the Royal Danish Navy set out for the region on the chartered sealing vessel *Hekla*. He was accompanied by Lieutenant Helge Vedel, the zoologist and geologist Edvard Bay, the botanist Nikolaj Hartz, by Henrik Deichmann, an ethnologist and physician, and by the West Greenland interpreter, Johan Petersen, who had been with Gustav Holm. The purpose of the expedition was to extend Holm's explorations of 1885 from 66° N near Ammassalik

Øjebliksfotografi.

CARL RYDER
COURTESY ARCTIC INSTITUTE, DENMARK.

northward to 73° N, near the entrance to Kejser Franz Joseph Fjord, discovered by Captain Koldewey in 1870. In the first year Ryder's expedition was to investigate the coast from the entrance to Scoresby Sund northward to Kejser Franz Joseph Fjord, partly with *Hekla* and partly with the aid of a steam launch. *Hekla* would depart in the fall, leaving a wintering party to explore the interior of Scoresby Sund. In the following summer, 1892, the unknown coast from Scoresby Sund to Ammassalik would be explored from the steam launch. *Hekla* would return to Ammassalik to pick up Ryder and his party in the autumn of 1892.

Hekla had great difficulty reaching the Greenland coast. The vessel met the outer edge of the pack ice on June 20, 355 km (220 mi) ESE of Kap Brewster, the southeastern corner of Scoresby Sund. Progress there proved impossible, so the ship went farther north, as far as the latitude of Shannon Ø, where the pack was somewhat more open, but the passage through the ice to the coast took thirty-three days. The ice off East Greenland that year extended as far as 485 km (300 mi) from the shore. Ryder and his scientists landed for a few hours at Kap Broer Ruys, where they shot three muskoxen for the Copenhagen museum. Ryder (1895:31) described the animals as "very peaceful, but … with its small scowling eye rather full of malice." They tried but found it impossible because of ice to enter Kejser Franz Joseph Fjord. Their passage south along the coast toward Scoresby Sund was very slow, greatly impeded by heavy, very difficult ice – "large unbroken floes of enormous extent" (Ryder 1895:27) – and by thick fog. On some days there was no progress at all through the ice and fog. They used the time in the ice for depth soundings, temperature measurements in the depths of the sea, and dredgings of animal life on the ocean bottom. "Day followed after day, and our patience was put to a severe trial" (Ryder 1895:35). When within 56 km (35 mi) of Kap Stewart in Scoresby Sund they were held within the pack for five days. They had planned to then follow the coast north, inside the belt of pack ice, but that proved impossible. The expedition finally entered Scoresby Sund at latitude 70° 20' on August 2. Within the sound they found beautiful, clear weather. The fog of the pack ice lay behind them, and "all were naturally on deck to enjoy that splendid panorama that gradually unfolded itself before us as we came into the fjord" (Ryder 1895:36). They landed at Kap Stewart, a pleasant spot in the warm sunshine and alive with birds and

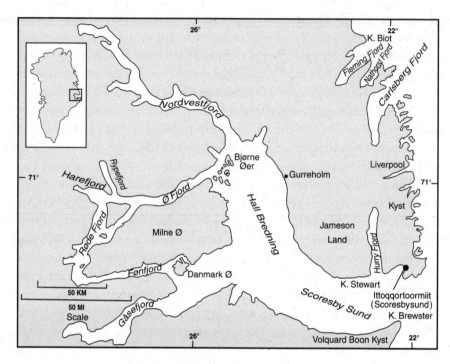

SCORESBY SUND

flowers and butterflies. Ryder wrote (1895:38) "as idyllic as the natural surroundings thus were, likewise were naive and trustfull the animals that lived in them. Reindeer ... appeared in a crowd.... They were so little shy that they came running to us in a herd at only 30 paces from me." Animal life was rich on Jameson Land. Reindeer were found "in wonderful numbers" (but they completely disappeared, for reasons not known, within a few years) and many muskoxen were grazing around Hurry Fjord. Indications of foxes, hares, bears, ermines, and lemmings were present on the plateau of Jameson Land. Similarly, vegetation was rich; 150 species of flowering plants were gathered in the region. Vegetation was even more abundant farther west toward the heads of the fjords far removed from the summer fogs of the outer coast. There they found dense thickets of willow, birch, and heather with myrtle growing to a metre in height, and among grasses and mosses were flowering plants forming thick carpets.

Such growth was favoured by the generally calm conditions that prevailed throughout the year, interrupted occasionally by strong and warm foehn winds that in spring and summer melt snow and ice and provide moisture for the vegetation.

Ryder penetrated deep into Scoresby Sund, where he quickly found that it divided into several branches reaching far inland. Near the entrance to the southwestern branch Ryder found an excellent site with a secure harbour for winter quarters on what he called Danmark Ø, just south of Scoresby's Milne Land. In fact, the harbour was the only secure anchorage for the ship they found in Scoresby Sund. Ryder decided to keep *Hekla* with his expedition for the winter. That would insure getting out more quickly in the spring to prosecute the planned explorations by steam launch along the outer coast. From their winter quarters, named Hekla Havn, a number of expeditions by the steam launch and rowboats probed into the branching fjords. The first journey, in August, took them into Gåsefjord, where they found that thick ice filled its interior. On their second journey they entered a fjord due west of Hekla Havn in calm weather, but in the evening it began to blow from the interior. "Icebergs now came sailing out of the fjord in a strong current, and with very frequent calving perhaps because of the warm temperature" (Ryder 1895:46). They named it Fønfjord. The farther west they went, they found that the basalt traprock that lay over the steep cliffs of the fjords became ever thinner until it disappeared, leaving only gneiss-granitic mountains that farther west became buried under ice. When they had reached what they thought to be the bottom of Fønfjord, they found that it turned abruptly and continued into the north. They climbed a hill to view the prospects and found themselves in a "knee-high thicket of willow, birch, blueberries, and crowberries, all interwoven with a richly blooming flora" (Ryder 1895:48). Farther north they came upon many reindeer that walked calmly past them. They did not complete their exploration of this region behind Milne Land in the fall, but saved that task for spring sledge journeys. On their return to the ship in Hekla Havn they passed several narwhals.

On September 3 they set out again with the steam launch along the east side of Milne Land; their goal was the interior of Hall Bredning, the other main branch of Scoresby Sund that stretched far into the north. On a sunny slope of one of the Bjørne Øer they came upon a fat old bear fast asleep in a blueberry heath. Apparently the bear had enjoyed the pleasures of a calm, sunny, summer day and gorged himself with a feast of blueberries. They shot the bear.

At the northernmost end of Hall Bredning they discovered Nordvestfjord. But by then, early September, winter threatened, a strong wind came from the fjord's interior, there were many very large icebergs, and new ice was forming. They could not reach the innermost end of the fjord, over 220 km (136 mi) from Hekla Havn, and they could not risk being frozen in so far from their ship, therefore they turned back. The strong wind turned into a storm raging with full force so that tops were blown off waves "and the whole fjord stood in a froth." They camped for shelter behind a small point of land. On September 10 they camped on the Bjørne Øer, where the weather gave them some relief.

> It was the first very beautiful evening we had had in a long time. It was completely calm and clear weather, but it began now to become dark at night. The mountains stood impressively up toward the clear star-filled sky. A pair of large fires of heather were lighted and while the fire blazed high and cast its flickering light over the nearby surroundings and smoke slowly rose skyward, pipes came out after the evening meal and conversation became comfortable accompanied by crackling heather (Ryder 1895:68).

Ryder returned to the ship on September 12. During the boat journeys between August 23 and September 25, 7,969 km (3,060 mi) were explored and mapped. They found that the interiors of the lands within the fjord system were everywhere from 1,524 to 1,830 m (5,000 to 6,000 ft) high and with glaciers numerous throughout the region.

The winter on Danmark Ø was marked by periods of clear, calm weather, and by periods, "day after day, week after week," of very heavy snow fall and blizzards. Ryder explained the changes in weather on the presence or absence of drift ice along the coast. The clear, calm, cold weather came when drift ice was thick and fast along the coast, shutting off a supply of moisture for the heavy snow falls. In clear weather, Ryder wrote (1895:81),

[w]hen the moon is up or when the northern lights perform with full light, the polar night is almost as beautiful as the summer day. The snow-covered mountains and the ice-covered fjord with its large icebergs formed a picture which everyone who has eyes for natural beauty must wish to see. Everything takes place in the subdued light so soft and harmonious as if one were in a strange world ... [there] comes only harmony in silver radiance and snow.... Icebergs become magnificent palaces more beautiful and bold in form than in reality.

As the sun left them late in the fall, he wrote (1895:81–82),

it stood only very low in the sky ... it spread itself along the top of the mountains south of us, while the colored sky in all possible nuances of green, blue, gold, and red. Especially after the sun had gone down was the illumination beautiful ... a glory of the most shining red ... farther to the east the sky was emerald green and farther north where the earth shadow raised itself higher and higher in the sky it was all dark blue. Toward the clear sky in the south the mountains were outlined with each little peak and point as sharp as if they were clipped out of metal, and in the north the mountain tops glowed ... in the most beautiful red, but the sun sank slowly, the shadows raised themselves and soon turned off the glow.

The winter passed with a round of scientific observations and preparation of maps and cataloguing collections made in the previous summer. The sun returned to Hekla Havn on January 30, when they began preparations for the spring journeys. In the first half of March bears were seen passing the station nearly every day. Ryder's first sledge party set out on March 27 to extend their explorations into the several fjords west of Milne Land. They enjoyed "beautiful, calm, sunshiny weather" for much of the way, but they had to pull their sledges and they found it hard travelling in deep and soft and increasingly wet snow. They found the west side of Milne Land to be "an enormous Alpen landscape with high jagged mountain ridges, peaked tops, and deep ravines" (Ryder 1895:89). An ice cap lay overall with six large glaciers approaching the sea. The party found a fjord running east on the north side of Milne Land, undoubtedly the fjord they had seen west of the Bjørne Øer in the autumn; thus Milne Land is in fact a very large island. And they trudged into the small Hare, Rype (grouse or ptarmigan), and Vest Fjords that ran off into the northwest and west, each with glaciers at their heads. A final journey in late May went into Gåsefjord, which they had tried to penetrate by steam launch in the previous fall. It was now full summer in the interior, at least fourteen days ahead of summer at Hekla Havn. On a plateau of 670 m (2,200 ft) they found exceptionally fertile vegetation. Their journeys reached the heads of all the branch fjords except Nordvestfjord; thus was revealed for the first time the full extent and wonderful complexity of the fjord region of Scoresby Sund. They found the edge of the inland ice sheet 283 km (175 mi) from the sea, and most of the interior fjords reached into the edge of the inland ice. From it are discharged immense icebergs into the fjords; some bergs were 90 m (300 ft) high and perhaps well over 300 m (1,000 ft) deep. Shallow parts of the fjords prevented such icebergs from escaping the fjords until they had melted substantially; the accumulation of big bergs are a serious obstacle to navigation of the inner fjords by both large and small boats.

Through all of June and July the weather at Hekla Havn was very calm with rain and fog, but when summer arrived, "flowers and plants burst forth in such abundance and with such speed, that one would believe them brought forth by magic" (Ryder 1895:110). Seals appeared on the ice, and brant geese and their goslings appeared in large flocks. But "ahead of the welcome guests, birds and flowers, however, also came other creatures which were not so welcome. They were mosquitoes, which for the rest of our stay here plagued us in a high degree" (Ryder 1895:110). Ryder's colleagues excavated old house ruins and graves when the snow disappeared, and they investigated the high basaltic mountain formations on the south side of Gåsefjord, across from their station. Ancient remains of animals plants, and humans were plentiful throughout the region. Ryder's people found many Jurassic and Tertiary plant and animal fossils on the western heights of Jameson Land, and they found fossils older than Jurassic at Kap Brewster. They found remains of fifty abandoned winter houses and graves and other human artefacts at seven locations, showing that a fairly numerous human population had relatively recently inhabited the region of Scoresby Sund. The expedition produced topographical and geological maps that for the first time showed the Scoresby Sund region in rich detail.

Not until August 8 could the *Hekla* leave the winter harbour, just a year after her arrival. Lieutenant Ryder wrote (1895:112):

> The weather was the most beautiful – dead calm with a baking sun ... sunshine glittered from the glaciers and icebergs; all the mountains stood sunlit against the sky; they had begun to put on their winter dress, because fallen snow now lay from the tops down to 1,000 feet [305 m] above the water. The small sea kings [Little Auks or Dovekies] swam in large flocks about the ship or flapped frightened away along the water surface, uncertain whether they should seek refuge by flying or by diving.

Large ice floes and many icebergs and fog hindered the ship's passage out of Scoresby Sund. At times they were stopped completely. Lieutenant Ryder put supplies ashore in a depot at Kap Stewart as a fall-back reserve for the hoped-for small-boat journey along the coast to Ammassalik, and he left a record of their work during the last year in a cairn there. On August 13 *Hekla* left Scoresby Sund and began to voyage southwest along the outer coast looking for a starting point for the steam launch journey. Ice floes and icebergs were thick and close-packed, and thick snow limited visibility so that the ship made little progress. On August 19 they abandoned the effort and turned toward Iceland to replenish their coal supplies. They left Iceland on August 29 to sail back to the Greenland coast to try again. When close to the Greenland shore, Ryder wrote (1895:122):

> ... there followed a period with persistent violent storms with snow and rain. Several times we were near the ice edge, but every time we had to keep away because of storm and violent seas ... the storm reached its height on the night between September 3–4, when it blew like a hurricane, while at the same time there was a very irregular sea, which seemed to come from several directions.

They arrived at Ammassalik, from whence Ryder hoped to travel north along the coast in small boats inside the ice belt. In fact it was very late in the fall, with new ice forming, and he could only travel in the vicinity of Ammassalik, visiting a number of the Inuit settlements. They stayed for two weeks and made a large ethnological collection. The expedition left Greenland on September 24 and arrived in Copenhagen on October 12. Three years later a trading and missionary station was established at Ammassalik.

NATHORST AND A "BEAUTIFUL AND SPLENDID" DISCOVERY, 1899

Salomon Andrée and two companions disappeared in the Arctic Ocean in 1897 while trying to travel from Spitsbergen to the North Pole in a hot air balloon.[2] His fellow Swede, Doctor Alfred G. Nathorst, a very experienced geographer, geologist, and Arctic authority, led a party to East Greenland in 1899 for three purposes: (1) to search for Andrée on the chance that his balloon might have drifted that way; (2) to lay supply depots for Otto Sverdrup who was then in the vicinity of Northwest Greenland and was believed to be travelling north around Greenland to the east coast; and (3) to continue his own Arctic explorations and scientific investigations. Nathorst's ship, *Antarctic*, met the edge of pack ice on June 24 and followed it north and northeast until June 27, when at 73°12' N the ship began to work northwestward through the ice toward the Greenland coast. Nathorst reached open water along the coast on July 2 after "some very hard work in the last part of the way, the ice being very dense" (Nathorst 1899:535). They had arrived at the coast a little south of Shannon Ø, last visited by Captain Karl Koldewey in 1870. After laying a cache for Otto Sverdrup and leaving messages for him at various places, *Antarctic* passed south within the open landwater along the coast touching at several points. Because Kejser Franz Joseph Fjord was still blocked with ice, Nathorst went farther south on July 22 to Scoresby Sund, where

---

2 Only in 1930 were Andrée's remains discovered on Kvitøya off the northeast coast of Svalbard. After their balloon landed on the ice, far short of the North Pole, they had made their way on foot across the ice back to land, only to succumb, apparently, to carbon monoxide poisoning in their tent, or perhaps to poisoning from eating polar bear liver.

the ship anchored at Kap Stewart on July 29. They examined Lieutenant Ryder's house and depot and then anchored in and mapped Hurry Fjord and waited there until August 7 for the ice to break up farther north. They returned to Kejser Franz Joseph Fjord, now ice-free, on August 9. Not since its discovery in 1870 by Koldewey had anyone entered the fjord. Nathorst arrived at its innermost reaches on August 10, the first party to do so, and they spent the rest of August exploring and mapping that extraordinary fjord system. On August 14 Nathorst discovered a branch trending south from Kejser Franz Joseph Fjord which led into Antarctic Sund, named for his ship, and then into a "hitherto unknown magnificent great fjord, which was named Kong Oscar Fjord.... The surroundings of Kong Oscar Fjord are beautiful and splendid" (Nathorst 1899:536).

When Nathorst understood the magnitude and complexity of the fjord system he had found, he had a difficult decision to make. The limited navigation season would not permit both mapping surveys of the two fjords and scientific investigations. Mapping would lay the foundation of future scientific work, and it was uncertain that such a favourable opportunity for surveys would "ever again occur." He therefore decided that the vessel would support the work of the surveyors, and the scientists would land on the shore only when it was necessary to anchor for astronomical observations. A number of promising locations for particularly desirable scientific work had to be passed by. Without the mapping work, the results of biological, ethnographic, geological, and hydrographic work would have been considerably greater. But subsequent explorers would have the benefit of accurate maps and should be in a stronger position than otherwise. The researches Nathorst had to leave incomplete were still to be undertaken.

The southeastern end of Kong Oscar Fjord enters Davy Sund, discovered by Scoresby in 1822, but Davy Sund was blocked by ice so Nathorst returned up the fjord. "It was most interesting indeed to go about 800 nautical miles [1,480 km] in these waters, where no ship had plunged its keel before us" (Nathorst 1899:536). They found that two branches stretch to the west from Kong Oscar Fjord, the southern one, Segelsällskapet (Royal Yacht Club) Fjord, itself divides into two branches and the northern branch, Kempes Fjord, into three branches. They found two straits, Sofia and Vega Sunds, that led eastward from Kong

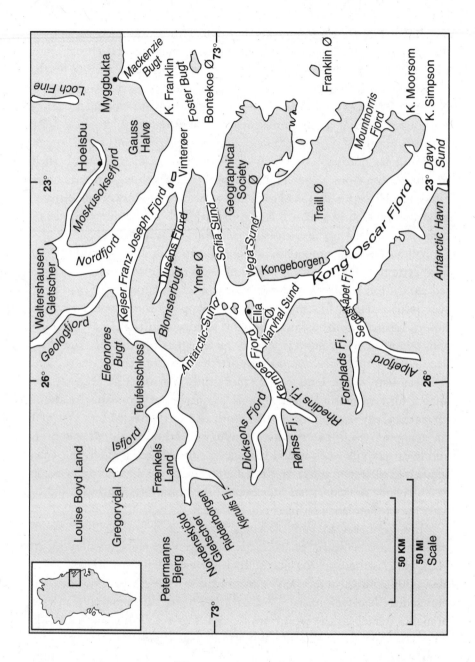

THE GREAT FJORD REGION

Oscar Fjord to the open sea, separating the large Ymer and Geographical Society Øer (which islands Nathorst named) and Traill Ø from each other. Returning through Antarctic Sund to Kejser Franz Joseph Fjord on August 24, they entered Nordfjord and discovered Moskusoksefjord stretching far off to the east. Their brief summer voyage thus completed the discovery of the second largest fjord system in the world.

Otto Nordenskjöld, a geologist with Nathorst, wrote: [3]

> The scenery there is the most magnificent of its kind that I know of. The rock walls plunge abruptly down to the narrow blue fjord, on whose surface float icebergs which, compared to works of man, our ship for example, are immense but appear quite insignificant when compared with this gigantic nature. Here the mountains are plateau-like in character, there they rise, especially where the strata are steeply inclined, to wild-looking peaks and ridges. Yet what makes the picture especially noteworthy is the glorious coloring, lacking elsewhere in the Arctic world, where white and blue in varying shades do indeed produce the most wonderful light effects but nevertheless prevail to the extent of monotony. Here the basement rock proper consists of highly colored, dark, violet, green, yellow, white, and especially glaring red strata. No vegetation cover conceals the aspect of the mountain slopes, which are crowned by a shining blue-white band of ice – a mighty mass which looks so thin only in consequence of its great height. Only in certain desert lands can the bare skeleton of the earth be seen in such colors as here. There, however, one misses the life and the contrast which sea and ice lend to this picture of the Greenland fjords.

Throughout the voyage within the fjords the weather had been unusually fine, with sunshine and often calm days. The benign weather permitted the completion of a map, on a scale of 1:200,000, of the whole of Kejser Franz Joseph Fjord and the newly discovered Kong Oscar Fjord with all

---

3 Quoted by Mecking in Nordenskjöld and Mecking 1928:276.

their numerous branches. James Wordie (1927:226) later wrote: "The result of this expedition was to make the interior fjords extremely well known."

Even with priority given to mapping rather than scientific investigations, Nathorst's scientists discovered Silurian and Devonian geological systems previously unknown on this coast. They mapped archaeological sites and made collections of artefacts and parts of skeletons. The botanical collections were very complete, including species new to Greenland and to East Greenland. They secured twenty-eight muskoxen, seventeen polar bears, and nine reindeer, the skins, interior parts, and skeletons of which were preserved for study in Sweden. They found that the polar wolf had made an invasion around North Greenland, two of them having been seen in Scoresby Sund, and Nathorst was the last explorer to find living reindeer on the east coast of Greenland. The zoologist Alwin Pedersen (1966:24) later wrote:

> Since then [1900] they have disappeared, leaving no trace except for a few antlers and occasional skeletons of animals which had probably died a natural death. There is no doubt that they must have migrated elsewhere, probably to West Greenland. The route they must have taken is not known, but it is quite possible that they may have crossed part of the inland ice. Perhaps we shall never know whether they reached their destination or perished on the way.

Nathorst's expedition left the coast on August 30 and was clear of the ice on September 1.

PEARY AND THE SEEDS OF DISASTER, 1892, 1900

Robert E. Peary was a civil engineer employed by the United States Navy who made a career of trying to reach the North Pole. He had made a short journey to acquire Arctic experience on the Greenland ice sheet in 1886, and in 1891 he obtained a year's leave of absence to make explorations in northern Greenland. The northernmost and northeastern coasts of Greenland were then completely unknown, and Peary wanted to determine the northern limits of Greenland. It was then thought that Greenland might extend as far north as the pole itself. On the last day of April 1892 he set off from McCormick Bugt in Northwest Greenland to cross the ice sheet. With Eivind Astrup, a Norwegian skiing champion, and thirteen dogs and two sledges, Peary reached land on the eastern edge of the ice sheet on July 1. They walked 43 km (27 mi) in two days across barren, frost-shattered rocks until they came to the edge of an almost vertical cliff they thought to be 914 m (2,800 ft) above a bay below. Peary called it Navy Cliff, and from it they gazed out across new land. The weather was clear in brilliant sunshine and "the view that spread away before us was magnificent beyond description" (Peary 1898:343). On their right, descending to the sea, was a great river of ice that Peary called Academy Glacier. Beyond the glacier, some 24 km (15 mi) from where they stood, cliffs ended in a bold cape, which Peary named Glacier Cape, and there dark clouds seemed to indicate to Peary that the shoreline trended away to the east or southeast. He "christened the great bay spreading its white expanse before us Independence Bay in honour of the date, July 4th" (Peary 1898:349), and on the map included in his book just beyond the bay Peary wrote in the "East Greenland Sea." He estimated that the most distant land they could just make out, far to the northeast, was 97 km (60 mi) away.

Peary summarized his discoveries with the conclusions that: (1) he had reached the northern shore of Greenland and had seen an archipelago beyond (called Peary Land), separated from mainland Greenland by a channel – he called it Peary Channel; (2) the frozen sea at the foot of Navy Klippe was a bay even though in the cairn on the cliff he left a note in which he called it a fjord; and (3) that from Independence Bay the coast of Greenland trended away east and southeast.

Unfortunately, Peary was mistaken in each of these conclusions. The land he saw north of Navy Klippe was not an archipelago, but an integral part of Greenland; the bay at his feet is in fact a relatively narrow fjord about 185 km (115 mi) long, and from Navy Klippe the coast of Greenland trends, along the south shore of Independence Fjord, northeast for 83 km (52 mi) and then east for about 130 km (81 mi). The easternmost point of Greenland is slightly south of east and almost 370 km (230 mi) from Navy Klippe. These mistakes had serious consequences for three later exploring parties. They led one of them to disaster and a second to the very edge of catastrophe.

Peary returned over the inland ice to his base early in August. He made a second trip to Navy Klippe in 1895, but because he was very short of food, the trip became a desperate race against starvation and nothing was accomplished.

Robert Peary returned once more to the northeast coast of Greenland. He was on an unsuccessful four-year (1898–1902) struggle to reach the North Pole. In 1900 he decided to try for the pole by departing from the northernmost point of Greenland, then unknown. With two companions, Matthew Henson and Ahngmalakto, and with three sledges and sixteen dogs, he sledged past the then farthest known point of northern Greenland, Kap Washington, and on May 13 he reached the northernmost point of land in Greenland and in the world, which he named Cape Morris Jesup. By so doing he proved the insularity of Greenland and that the only way to reach the North Pole was over the sea ice of the Arctic Ocean. He very soon found that it was a hopeless business to try to travel from that point over the fractured, jumbled sea ice, and after two or three days[4] on the ice he returned to the land at Kap Morris Jesup on May 17. Here he found fifteen muskoxen, but left them in peace. Peary started east into unknown land, passing into Northeast Greenland, and for three marches he "made great distances over good going, in blinding sunshine and in the face of a wind from the east which burned our faces like a sirocco" (Peary 1907:327–28). He reached Kap Bridgman, 83 km (52 mi) from Kap Morris Jesup, on the first march; there the land turns away to the southeast. Peary reached 83° N after two more marches, passing Frederick E. Hyde Fjord along the way. Beyond the fjord he recognized a "magnificent mountain," Mt. Wistar, which he asserted he recognized from his 1895 trip. This seems doubtful, since in 1892 he estimated the furthest land visible from Navy Klippe at 97 km (60 mi); Mt. Wistar is 225 km (140 mi) from Navy Klippe. He was then stopped by fog at a point he called Clarence Wycoff Island. There he remained two nights waiting for the fog to lift, but it did not. He erected a cairn, deposited a record, and began his return on May 22. Peary arrived back at Kap Morris Jesup, after killing ten muskoxen nearby, on May 26, travelling in fog most of the way.

---

4 It is impossible to learn from Peary's report how far north he went or how long he stayed on the ice, but it was not far nor long.

And this is as much as Peary had to say about this 167 km (104 mi) of new land in East Greenland that he was the first to describe.

AMDRUP AND THE MOST DANGEROUS COAST, 1898, 1900

By 1898 a considerable part of the coast of East Greenland had been roughly surveyed. Captain Koldewey had reached as far north as Germania Land at about 77° N. Gustav Holm had expanded upon Lieutenant Graah's explorations of the southeast coast from Prins Christian Sund to Ammassalik, and Lieutenant C.H. Ryder had explored the innermost reaches of Scoresby Sund. And Nathorst in 1899 would map the great Kejser Franz Joseph and Kong Oscar Fjords. But there remained a great unknown gap along the coast from Holm's farthest north near Ammassalik at 66° to Kap Brewster near Scoresby Sund at 70° N, over 800 km (500 mi) in a straight line of coast very difficult to reach. Several vessels had attempted to reach that coast, but heavy ice conditions had stopped them all because it is there that the East Greenland Current is forced into the funnel created by Iceland lying 300 km (186 mi) to the southeast. The funnel concentrates the drifting ice and accelerates the current, causing dangerous conditions for any vessel. The French explorer Blosseville was lost without a trace in 1833 when he sailed into that pack.

The exploration of the east coast from Ammassalik to Scoresby Sund now became a priority for the Danes. There was concern in Denmark that because of foreign interests in this locality another country might take the initiative of exploration, with adverse implications for Danish claims to sovereignty.

The Carlsberg Fund provided funds and Lieutenant Georg Carl Amdrup of the Royal Danish Navy was appointed exploration leader. He was to spend the winter of 1898–99 in Ammassalik, where a mission and trading post had been established in 1894, to become familiar with conditions in East Greenland. In the following year he would go by ship to Scoresby Sund and then travel south by small boat close inshore along the coast back to Ammassalik, thus filling the unexplored gap. The expedition was called The Carlsberg Fund Expedition to the East Coast of Greenland. Amdrup was accompanied to Ammassalik in 1898 by the

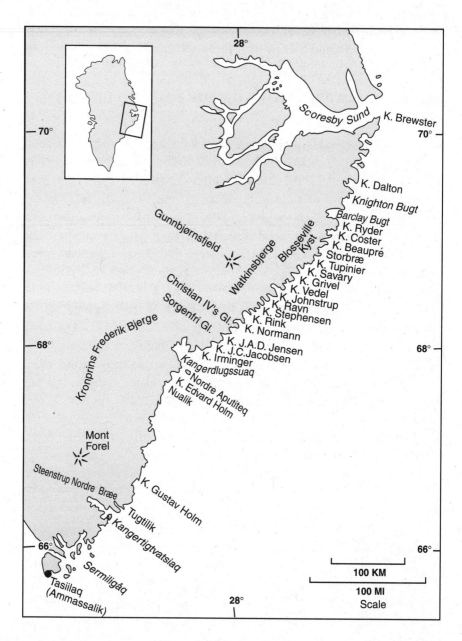

28°

Scoresby Sund

K. Brewster
70°

70°

K. Dalton

Knighton Bugt

Barclay Bugt
K. Ryder
K. Coster
K. Beaupré
Storbræ
K. Tupinier
K. Savary
K. Grivel
K. Vedel
K. Johnstrup
K. Ravn
K. Stephensen
K. Rink
K. Normann
K. J.A.D. Jensen
K. J.C.Jacobsen
K. Irminger
Kangerdlugssuaq
Nordre Aputiteq
K. Edvard Holm
Nualik

Gunnbjørnsfjeld

Watkinsbjerge

Blosseville Kyst

Christian IV's Gl.

Sorgenfri Gl.

Kronprins Frederik Bjerge

68°

68°

Mont
Forel

Steenstrup Nordre Bræe

K. Gustav Holm

Tugtilik

Kangertigtvatsiaq

66°

66°

Sermiligâq

Tasiilaq
(Ammassalik)

28°

100 KM

100 MI
Scale

TASIILAQ TO SCORESBY SUND

botanist Christian Kruuse, a physician Knud Poulsen, a naval petty officer N.A. Jacobsen, and a mechanic Søren Nielsen. Their main job was to lay down supply depots northward from Ammassalik to support the long boat journey planned for 1900. They hoped particularly to lay a depot at a fjord called Kangerdlugssuaq (which means "the great fjord"), known only from Inuit reports, about halfway between Ammassalik and Scoresby Sund. In the autumn of 1898 Amdrup carried out a depot-laying boat journey to Depot Ø about 80 km (50 mi) north of the settlement, and in the winter the party carried on magnetic and astronomic observations and studies of Inuit life. They undertook two reconnoitring sledge journeys northward in the spring of 1899.

On June 21 Amdrup and his four companions began the long depot-laying boat journey northward toward Kangerdlugssuaq. It became a continuous struggle against dense ice and the south-flowing current. Frequently they had to unload to haul the boat out of the water and across the ice. They had to wait eleven days on an island for the ice to loosen enough to allow them to proceed. But the enforced delay gave them ample time to repair the damage to the boat caused by ice pressures. Along one stretch it took them eighteen days to cover only 22 km (13.5 mi). This is a coast of many fjords with glaciers discharging icebergs into them, and it is a coast of steep cliffs and headlands rising 600–900 m (2–3,000 ft) vertically from the sea. It was difficult in many places to find a landing and camping site, but where they did find such sites they often found Inuit ruins, many of them clearly only of a temporary nature. Remains of earlier inhabitants were especially numerous – house ruins, tent rings, and graves – in Kangertigtvatsiaq ("a smaller large fjord"), a district with as many signs of former inhabitants as the Ammassalik district. One wonders what Amdrup's party thought of such settlements on that difficult coast.

It was dangerous work rowing among rapidly moving masses of glacial and thick polar ocean ice. Pieces of ice were constantly breaking off icebergs under water and surging to the surface. The travellers had just concluded that there was relatively little chance of harm "when the boat suddenly got a violent jolt under the keel. The stern rose half way out of the water, and a massive, hard, blue-ice block pitched up straight astern of us, while the waters foamed behind" (Amdrup 1902:81).

Georg Amdrup
Courtesy Arctic Institute, Denmark.

There were compensations for their toil and danger and the thick fog that often enshrouded them. On July 14 there was "radiant sunshine. Before us lay the most splendidly imposing ice panorama one could imagine. In a long, crevassed, and indented tongue the great Steenstrup nordre Bræ protruded out into the water and sent out to sea countless masses of icebergs, most of them very large" (Amdrup 1902:80).

At Kap Christiansen they camped by a vertical cliff wall at which there were a number of isolated needle-like granite pillars that rose to a height of 30 m (100 ft). Just across from their camp site at Nualik ("the place which has a smell") there was a 300-m (1000-ft) high cliff over which flowed glacial ice and from which broke great blocks that "with a deafening spectacle crashed down the steep mountain wall. This spectacle repeated itself every hour that we were there" (Amdrup 1902:92), a matter of three days.

Amdrup's party was stopped by impenetrable ice 97 km (60 mi) south of Kangerdlugssuaq, and their northernmost depot was put down at Nualik at 67°23', about 315 km (195 mi) from Ammassalik. At Nualik Amdrup found the ruins of a large house with the remains of thirty to forty Inuit bodies, a catastrophe of apparently fairly recent date. From Gustav Holm's report, it was known that in 1882 two umiaks had left the Ammassalik district and travelled northward, of which nothing had been heard since. Amdrup's discovery disclosed their fate. Death had come to them suddenly, but the cause was not at all evident. Amdrup built a cairn at Nualik, left a record within it, and took possession of the land for the king of Denmark.

Amdrup returned to Ammassalik on August 18, fifty-three days after setting out. He had travelled about 630 km (390 mi). The expedition left Greenland on September 3, 1899, and arrived in Copenhagen on September 12.

Lieutenant Amdrup began the second half of the Carlsberg Fund Expedition in 1900. *Antarctic* left Copenhagen on June 14 with Nikolaj Hartz and Christian Kruuse, botanists, Henrik Deichmann, physician and geologist, Søren Jensen, zoologist, Doctor Otto Nordenskjöld, geologist, Lieutenant J.P. Koch, geodetist, E. Ditlevsen, artist, petty officer N.A. Jacobsen, sailor and mechanic Søren Nielsen, and sailor Ejnar Mikkelsen. Four of this party – Kruuse, Nordenskjöld, Koch, and Mikkelsen

AGGAS, THE
BOAT IN WHICH
AMDRUP VOYAGED
FROM KAP DALTON
TO AMMASSALIK
– THE MOST
DANGEROUS COAST,
1900
COURTESY ARCTIC
INSTITUTE,
DENMARK.

– would later achieve renown on their own polar expeditions. The expedition objectives in 1900 were: (1) to land Amdrup and a boat crew in 69° N, or a bit farther north; (2) to investigate the regions around Scoresby Sund, in Davy Sund, and in Kejser Franz Joseph Fjord (while in Scoresby Sund they were to overhaul and complete Ryder's depot at Kap Stewart); and (3) to carry out scientific investigations in the Ammassalik district.

Antarctic met the pack ice on June 29 and was forced to try for a passage farther north, where it reached the coast at Lille Pendulum Ø. It managed with difficulty to reach Kap Dalton, 110 km (68 mi) southwest of Scoresby Sund, where on July 18 Amdrup landed.

There the ship's crew built a small house and provisions depot. It was the point of departure for Amdrup's journey in a small boat south to Ammassalik along the unknown coast. The house and depot would serve as a refuge for Amdrup if he could not reach Ammassalik and was forced to retreat to Kap Dalton. Once the house and depot were established, the ship left to continue investigations in the Scoresby Sund area and in Kong Oscar Fjord.

Amdrup, with Jacobsen, Nielsen, and Mikkelsen, set out on July 22 for Ammassalik, 730 km (450 mi) to the south, in a boat 5.6 m long, 1.4 m wide, and with 0.26 m of freeboard (18.4 x 4.6 x 0.75 ft). Their boat had been especially designed and built for the journey. It was seaworthy, light, and strong so that it could survive in rough seas, carry a good load, and be readily hauled out on land or ice. This small boat – Amdrup called it *Aggas* – carried four men and 1,659 kg (3,650 lbs) of supplies through the ice and icebergs off one of the most dangerous and unknown coasts in the world.

They left Kap Dalton in spite of a stiff northeast wind and steep seas because time was precious and they could not afford many delays, but *Aggas* proved to be an excellent sea boat. They travelled in bright sunshine through scattered ice floes and passed great headlands separating bays or fjords with productive glaciers at their heads and filled with sea ice and icebergs. It was an imposing coast of sharp mountain peaks with "pillar formations, needles or spikes that stood side by side along the crests, not unlike the teeth of a comb" (Amdrup 1902:209). They passed a bear on an ice floe who, wrote Amdrup, "showed his surprise at the unexpected sight by raising himself on his hind legs and turning his astonished head from left to right until he suddenly ... dove into the sea, as he probably had found that we were perhaps not wholly trustworthy" (Amdrup 1902:211).

They were stopped on July 24 by unbroken ice north of Kap Ryder, but by walking across the ice and climbing the 445-m (1,460-ft) height of the cape they found that navigable water lay beyond. The next day they were able to proceed, passed Kap Coster, and landed at Kap Beaupré. Kap Coster rises 945 m (3,100 ft) straight from the sea, and birds nest there – but only a few, perhaps 50–100 pairs, because this seemed to be a hard coast even for seabirds.

On July 26 unusually thick fog set in and they had to grope their way close in along the face of Stor Bræ, not knowing whether its overhanging front might at any moment drop ice blocks onto their heads or into their boat. It took four hours of rowing to pass the glacier face. The fog persisted as they arrived at Kap Savary, 730 m (2,400 ft) high and very steep, where the current runs very strong. On this day they met almost no ice at all. Fog – "this raw, cold, damp ice fog that wrapped up and shut the land from us" (Amdrup 1902:218) – continued for three days until the 29th when, in excellent, bright weather, they passed Kap Grivel and Kap Vedel, each 600 m (1,944 ft) high. The currents here too were very strong, and only with great labour at their oars could they reach the shore. Amdrup named the coast from Barclay Bugt just north of Kap Ryder to Kap Vedel the Blosseville Kyst to commemorate the French explorer lost in the vicinity in 1833.

Their journey from Kap Dalton to Kap Vedel had generally enjoyed favourable, or at least passable, ice conditions. But from a height of 150 m (500 ft) on Kap Vedel, Amdrup saw that the prospect ahead "was all other than promising.... Farther westward there was not a drop of water to be seen among numerous icebergs which lay as a belt along the coast" (Amdrup 1902:221). On their descent, unarmed, Amdrup and Jacobsen encountered a bear. They kept it at bay with a whistle until Nielsen and Mikkelsen arrived with a gun, "freeing us of unpleasant consequences" (1902:221).

They pressed on in spite of the poor ice conditions which they found became worse the farther they went. They had to return to Kap Vedel, but only after a struggle through tight-packed ice that was set in dangerous motion, grinding and crushing, by an offshore swell working its way through the ice belt. From the top of the cape Amdrup counted 300 icebergs among the ice floes.

From this point, Amdrup reported, began the difficult part of the journey. Amdrup could see that a broad belt of ice lay between them and the coast. He feared that a storm from the land could set the whole mass of ice moving seaward and prevent them from reaching the coast and thus cause the expedition to fail.

They reached Kap Johnstrup, 400 m (1,300 ft) high and one of the steepest and most jagged headlands on this coast, fairly easily. But the ice became ever thicker as they approached, but could not reach, Kap Ravn, 762 m (2,500 ft) high; progress became impossible. Amdrup climbed one iceberg after another trying to get a view of the prospects ahead. But such efforts "were not wholly harmless." Because some of the bergs were calving or capsizing, they were forced to proceed with great care. While Amdrup climbed a berg, the boat lay some distance off so that it might not be caught by an overturning or calving berg. The channels between bergs and ice floes were filled with crushed ice masses and only slight progress was made with each oar stroke. They spent the night on a large ice floe in still, clear weather. The following day they again worked through ice floes that were set in motion by the strong southwesterly current. Again they were stopped by the ice off Kap Rink. And then "came ice's faithful companion, fog which enclosed all in its clammy covering" (Amdrup 1902:228). They were once again among icebergs. "One iceberg after another rose from the fog, first revealing itself with expanding, dark, quite ghostly contours. So it sprang dark blue from the fog, gradually as it came nearer, until it finally majestically slid crushing along our ice floe to then vanish again" (Amdrup 1902:228). Some of the bergs actually projected over their floe as they passed by. The ice motion continued the next day and when the fog thinned at noon they found themselves still in the middle of a collection of large icebergs. Thick fog returned and they spent the next night – their third – again on a floe. When the fog vanished the next day, August 5, there was revealed "the monotonous but mighty and majestic coast, wild and crevassed, with steep mountain edges and numerous glaciers" (Amdrup 1902:230). At last they succeeded in reaching the land at Kap Garde. While they were making observations, a little white bear approached. Amdrup ordered him off with "a good loud shout" and the bear obeyed "at a gallop the best he knew." With continuing clear weather they arrived at Kap J.A.D. Jensen, described by the *Sailing Directions Greenland and Iceland* (Lighthouse Press 1998:85) as "an imposing vertical basaltic mass about 1,000 m [3,300 ft] high." It "was everywhere inaccessible," wrote Amdrup (1902:232). They could not land on the steep shores and were forced to spend yet another night on an ice floe. Amdrup kept the first watch, but with the accumulated fatigue of the preceding days he fell asleep while sitting for a moment. In that moment a bear crept up on the ice floe. Amdrup awoke and shouted. The bear was barely twenty paces from the sleeping bags when Jacobsen shot it dead.

On August 6 in "wonderfully sunny weather" they passed 1000-m (3,280-ft) high Nuna isua ("the end of the land") and Kap J.C. Jacobsen. Nearby they found a small island on which they could sleep on dry land for the first time in days and where they could dry their clothes, footwear, and sleeping bags. The next day they passed Kap Irminger and approached Mikis Fjord, where the terrain changed dramatically. Here the land had a more "friendly" appearance. Glaciers were greatly reduced in size and numbers, and the mountains were no longer the high, sharp, peaked, jagged basaltic ramparts that are found farther east and north. Instead, the land, though still high, had a more rounded form of granite and gneiss. "The slopes faced the southwest and must on this barren region be considered as especially fertile" (Amdrup 1902:237). Just beyond Mikis Fjord they came upon the entrance to Kangerdlugssuaq, the great fjord 74 km (46 mi) long, in which they found plentiful signs of Inuit of the past. Everywhere on the coast from Kap Dalton to this point there was "not the slightest trace that Eskimos had traveled or lived there. But here were found not less than eight house ruins, six camp sites, eleven fox traps, a bear trap, and several graves. From the condition of the houses, it appeared clear that they had not been occupied at the same time" (Amdrup 1902:240). Several of the houses apparently were very old, and one was quite new, very carefully constructed, and very well preserved. They felt that hunting must be excellent in the great fjord because they saw numerous seals, several bears, and many bear tracks.

On August 9 they tried to penetrate farther into the fjord, but found it much encumbered by ice of all sizes. It was a calm, quiet, warm day and the air was filled with the sound of water running off ice floes and

INUIT HOUSE RUINS FOUND BY AMDRUP IN KANGERDLUGSSUAQ
COURTESY ARCTIC INSTITUTE, DENMARK.

waterfalls from icebergs. "A rustling sound blended with a sound as if small whispering was heard continuously." And often calf ice "suddenly just exploded and dissolved into nothing but small pieces" (Amdrup 1902:242), probably because of the sudden expansion of cold air bubbles in the ice from the warmth of the air. One had to keep one's distance from such exploding ice pieces. Indeed, the ice could be dangerous. Amdrup (1902:242–43) described a spectacular sight:

> At a relatively short distance we watched on this day a large iceberg calving followed by capsizing and nearly complete dis-integration. With a short, dull boom it suddenly loosed a large piece from the top which fell with a great splash into the water. The large, heavy, motionless iceberg was suddenly in motion and

began to pitch violently but majestically up and down, raising on each pitch a part of its blue-green bottom out of the water while the iceberg's chalk-white upper part disappeared in the waves. The violent motion loosed large pieces from the iceberg's underside. They came rushing up with furious force smashing and pulverizing ice around it … and wilder and wilder became its motion. More and more pieces broke loose until finally the berg went completely around under deafening noise of ice that was smashed and crushed. The berg pitched up and down. Soon it seemed that it would disappear entirely, while surf, frothed and foamed, beat around it; soon it heaved high up from the water, and waves retreated as foaming water fell down the berg's blueish sides. So it boomed again; dissolution continued, and of the mighty colossus soon was found nothing other than a large expanse of scattered, ground masses of ice clumps and calf-ice pieces. But still long after continued the sighing, wailing sound across the ice. It is the sound of ice floes that are pitched up and down with the swells after the calving had gone.

On leaving the fjord on August 10, Amdrup's party passed the largest iceberg they had seen, 915 m (3,000 ft) long and 45–60 m (150–200 ft) high. They had a hard struggle through ice floes grinding and crushing against each other. Frequently they had to pull their boat onto the ice to avoid disaster. The boat made progress only when the floes separated for a moment before coming together again They landed on Nordre Aputiteq, a 90-m- (300-ft-) high island on August 11. It was bright and clear weather, and from the top of the island they had a wonderful view along the coast. To the north, beyond Kap Hammer and far inland from the coast, they could see a very high mountain which was rediscovered in 1930 (Apollonio 2003) and later named Gunnbjørnsfjeld, the highest mountain in Greenland.

Ice, winds, rain, and fog kept them on Nordre Aputiteq for several days. Ocean swells from offshore swept in on their landing place, and they had to frequently remove their gear and boat farther away from the sea. "It was a grand sight to look out across the tight ice masses south of us. The mighty icebergs and extensive floes pitched up and down and crushed with violent power against each other, and here on the island ... swells hurled great ice pieces up on the point. Woe to the ship that found itself out in ice in such conditions" (Amdrup 1902:248).

They spent their time examining an Inuit ruin, apparently the northernmost house of people then still living in Ammassalik. Many bones of seals, bears, and narwhals suggested that hunting had been excellent by the island. While waiting, they shot a bear that came ashore. It was a welcome addition to their food supply in view of the uncertainty of their progress toward their supply depot.

Amdrup and his companions were able to leave Nordre Aputiteq on August 16, but in thick fog. Ice floes and icebergs in great number lay everywhere along their route to the south. Once more it was a difficult and dangerous passage through ice blocks set in motion by ocean swells. Channels through the ice opened and closed incessantly among floes that pitched up and down. A pitching floe could easily come down upon the boat and crush or sink it. Again they had to spend the night on an unstable ice floe.

On August 19 they reached Nualik, where in 1899 they had established a provision depot. The worst of the ice was behind them. For the rest of the journey through known regions they made steady progress and on September 2 reached Ammassalik, where they were welcomed "with open arms" by the Danish missionary Peter Ruttel and the trader Johan Petersen with their wives.

Meanwhile *Antarctic* had left Kap Dalton on July 21 and entered Scoresby Sund, where it anchored in Hurry Fjord. It remained there for ten days while various investigations were carried out. From there the ship proceeded to Davy Sund with landings at several points along the way. It then left to take on more coal in Iceland, and arrived on September 11 in Ammassalik, where Amdrup with his companions were found. They returned to Copenhagen on October 4.

Amdrup's boat journey with his three companions was a dangerous, difficult, and most successful expedition, carefully planned and conducted very nearly as planned. They experienced much dense fog, and frequently had to haul their boat onto the floes to escape pressure from the ice. The weather was generally winter-like, and landings on the steep shores were often dangerous and in places impossible. Nevertheless, they obtained good scientific results, particularly from examination of Inuit graves, and they came home with not large but significant collections of geological, zoological, and botanical specimens.

MYLIUS-ERICHSEN – TRIUMPH AND TRAGEDY, 1906–8

The last few years of the nineteenth and the early years of the twentieth centuries were the time of the great, classic polar explorations. The public's attention and imagination were captured by the expeditions of Belgium, Britain, Germany, Australia, Sweden, Norway, and France to the Arctic and Antarctic. All contributed significantly to geographical and scientific knowledge. The climax of this era, in publicity if not in useful results, came with the races to the North and South Poles. Denmark was not idle at this time. Its quiet explorations of Greenland, begun 170 years before, had continued with steady if unspectacular progress. Denmark launched its largest expedition up to that time to complete the task of defining the geographic limits of the great subcontinent of Greenland. There were still long stretches of unknown coast in the northeast.

Ludwig Mylius-Erichsen conceived the expedition. He had led an expedition to Northwest Greenland in 1902–4. Mylius-Erichsen proposed that the northeast coast – which from 77º N reached by Captain Koldewey to Kap Bridgman visited by Peary was unknown, and was in fact the last unknown coast in Greenland – should be investigated. He intended to fill the gap from Kap Bismarck, Koldewey's furthest north, to Peary's Kap Bridgman and to Navy Klippe. He would then possibly pass through Peary Channel to Northwest Greenland and thus complete the outline of Greenland.

The plan called for two years of investigations. The first year would be focused on finishing the survey of Northeast Greenland. With that work accomplished, Mylius-Erichsen proposed to take his ship in the second year southward into Kejser Franz Joseph Fjord, where the explorations would continue. The work would be completed with a possible attempt to cross the inland ice sheet to the west coast. It was called the Danmark Expedition to Greenland's Northeast Coast, 1906–1908.

The expedition was planned with the aid of a committee of distinguished Greenland authorities, including Garde, Holm, Ryder, and

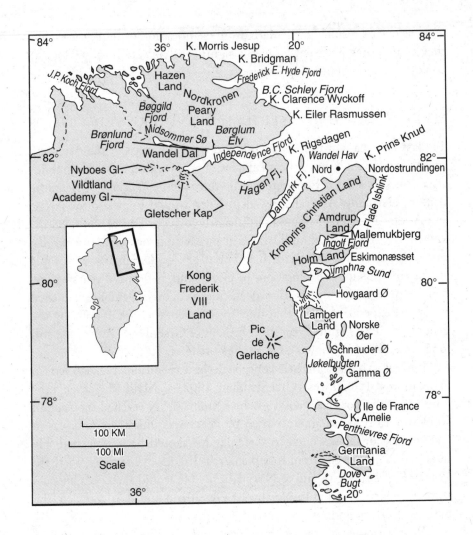

DOVE BUGT TO KAP MORRIS JESUP

Amdrup. Amdrup wrote the official history of the expedition. The expedition consisted of twenty-eight persons, with an unusually large staff of scientists and specialists – six cartographers, two meteorologists, two zoologists, one botanist, one geologist, one hydrographer, one ethnologist, one physician, and two painters. There were an ice-master for getting their ship, *Danmark*, safely through the ice, two mates who assisted the cartographers, two engineers, two stokers, three Greenlanders, and three sailors. To accommodate the large scientific staff, the scientists had agreed to do some of the sailors' duties when the ship was at sea. The captain of *Danmark* was Lieutenant Alf Trolle, who in later years became an admiral. They left Copenhagen in June 1906 and boarded the West Greenlanders, one hundred dogs, and additional supplies at the Faroe Islands and Iceland. Their goal was Kap Bismarck, about 77° N, where Captain Koldewey on his sledge journey of 1870 had discovered a safe harbour.

The Danmark Expedition had reason to hope that their vessel could carry them to an even higher latitude from which they could begin their exploratory journeys. Only the year before, 1905, the Duc d'Orléans had reached a new record high latitude along that coast (Wandel 1928). He had purchased the steam bark *Belgica* for a hunting expedition in the Arctic. *Belgica* was commanded by Lieutenant Adrian de Gerlache, who in 1897–99 had passed the first winter south of the Antarctic Circle aboard that vessel. On July 27 the ship reached the Greenland coast at Kap Bismarck, from whence it was able to follow open coastal water northward. The Duc's party discovered and landed on Ile de France, where they left a depot with a record. Then they continued north while the Duc shot all the polar bears they could approach. They reached 78°16' N, nearly 166 km (103 mi) north of Kap Bismarck, on July 31. They were able to map the coast from that point south to Kap Bismarck, connecting to the survey of Koldewey in 1870. Undoubtedly, Mylius-Erichsen hoped to be able to repeat the Duc's success in sailing northward.

The Danmark Expedition met its first ice on July 31, and the next day they met unexpectedly severe ice. Soundings showed they were then on the edge of the continental shelf. They surmised that the current and ice were concentrated on the shelf and dispersed in deeper water. After several days of searching, they found an opening in the ice and steamed in. Progress was slow, advancing on some days merely a kilometre or so.

LUDWIG MYLIUS-ERICHSEN
COURTESY ARCTIC INSTITUTE, DENMARK.

While stopped in the ice one day, they all left the ship to test equipment on the ice. The door to the main cabin had by accident been left open, "and the consequences were dreadful" wrote Trolle, the captain (1909:42). "All our hundred dogs had rushed into the saloon and the galley, and when we returned we were met by a scene of the wildest disorder. Although the grate in the galley had been burning hot, the dogs had jumped on it and had devoured everything they could find – soup, meat, and gravy. Most of them had already finished their meal, and were now making themselves comfortable in the different cabins."

Danmark reached clear water next to the land on August 12, having taken thirteen days to manoeuvre 225 km (140 mi) through the ice. It was a beautiful day and the sea was like a mirror reflecting Store Koldewey. Before they were stopped by impenetrable ice, they were able to steam northward as far as Ile de France (77°30' N), where they landed a large depot of provisions. They retreated to Kap Bismarck "with the most fortunate and extremely favourable result, that a small bay was found on the south side of Germania Land, which seemed excellently suited to serve as a winter harbour" (Amdrup 1913:65). They named it Danmarkshavn, and there they secured *Danmark* for the winter. The harbour lay just north of Lille Koldewey, which Amdrup (1913:80) described as "a single, enormous, reddish, smooth rock" rising straight out of the sea.

They had two motor boats with which they explored inner fjords of the large Dove Bugt west and southwest of their harbour and within which they hunted walruses for dog food. They built workshops on shore for the use of the scientists and they began the magnetic and weather measurements that continued without interruption for nearly two years into the summer of 1908. Then they began their journeys. Sledge trips in the fall of 1906 established depots 145 km (90 mi) farther north. As the several parties returned from depot-laying, they undertook surveys and geological explorations of parts of the unknown land. Late in October Aage Bertelsen, an artist, and Henning Bistrup, the chief mate, explored Mørkefjord, a small, very narrow, steep-walled fjord in the northwest corner of Dove Bugt. Amdrup, the expedition historian, wrote (1913:89):

DANMARKSHAVN,
1906–1908

COURTESY
ARCTIC
INSTITUTE,
DENMARK.

An attempt was made to climb the hill at the head of the fjord. But the hill became steeper and steeper, the higher they climbed and the attempt had to be given up before reaching the top. In their endeavour to climb the steep sides, it was necessary to remove their mittens to get a good hold, and the result in the low temperature –21° C [–6° F] was, that Bertlesen had his fingers very severely frozen. In the course of the night the wind rose to a raging storm. The original intention had been to make another attempt next day to reach the top; but it was now given up and as soon as there was enough light, the party began the homeward journey.

Bistrup wrote (Amdrup 1913:89):

> Such a journey as that of October 31st, in a piping storm down a river of glassy ice, I have never experienced. It was simply a marvel, that we got through at all. We took a whole day to transport our two sledges and dogs about 2 miles [3.2 km] from the tenting place to the mouth of the river. Bertelsen, whose fingers had been frostbitten in climbing the hill, now got his one foot slightly crushed between the sledge and stones, on using it as a fender when the wind took command and drove him and the sledge right across the river. We were obliged to unspand the dogs and crawl over the ice, dragging them after us until they could get foothold on stones or snow; as soon as they came on the glassy ice, they lay down flat and refused to move.… It was a tough day. When we were raising the tent, it blew so hard we could hardly stand and it was not easy, for example, to get our sleeping bags up to the tent. This was also blown down on the top of us when we at last got it up, but we had no energy left to raise it again and as there was just room as it was, we let it stay.

The powerful wind practically blew them out of the fjord, but when they reached Monument Fjeld the wind dropped completely and they went on with excellent travelling.

In the dark period of November and December, after continuous snowstorms of nearly two weeks, the Danes travelled among the archipelagic complexities of Dove Bugt and 205 km (127 mi) south to check on depots at Shannon Ø and Bass Rock laid down by an American expedition (which otherwise had nothing to do with East Greenland) in 1901. On their way south three dogs escaped their harnesses and disappeared. One dog was recovered at that site on their return several weeks later. Two dogs returned to the ship nearly six weeks later. Apparently they had managed to survive by digging into the snow to a bear that had been shot and cached on Store Koldewey. The surveyor Johan Koch got into trouble travelling in the darkness of November. His party was close to their goal of Germaniahavn, where *Germania* had wintered in 1869–70. Amdrup wrote (1913:94):

> The strong, northerly wind, however, rendered the steering of the sledges very difficult, as they were driven before the wind over the smooth ice. In the intense darkness (it was just about midnight on November 21), they could see only some few meters in front and Koch all too late discovered an open channel right in his way. The dogs swerved round the edge of the opening, but Koch could not stop the sledge. He had just time to jump clear when it toppled over into the water. Koch ran back immediately and stopped G. Thorstrup [the second mate] and Wegener. All three turned to the very risky work of salving Koch's sledge. G[ustav]. Thostrup's practical sense, however, soon got them out of the difficulty and the sledge was got out without further mishap. It is hardly necessary to add, that the party did not continue their journey after this accident.
>
> They camped for the night on the nearby shore. On its return to the ship, this party was able to travel over 315 km (195 mi) in five days in the darkest month of the year and at about –30° C (–22° F) with full loads on their sledges. This was an average speed of 63 km (39 mi) per day.
>
> One day they travelled about 83 km (51 mi). This was quite exceptional travelling, and it may have given them unrealistic

expectations about their travel capabilities on the main northern journeys.

Exploration continued throughout the dark period, and during the two years two hundred journeys in all were undertaken by the expedition into the interior of the country by way of fjords and lakes, and onto the inland ice. During February of 1907 depots were laid even farther north than before.

The long exploratory journeys to the north began on March 28, 1907, when the main sledging parties, with ten sledges in all, left the ship. Mylius-Erichsen and J.P. Koch led the two main divisions, and they were accompanied by supporting parties. In Jøkelbugten the travelling was very difficult because there the inland ice came right down to the sea and its forward pressure cracked and buckled the sea ice. Several sledges were completely broken in the difficult ice, and repairs took a long time. Beyond Lambert Land they frequently met and shot bears. It was difficult to restrain the very hungry dogs while they cut up the bears. Amdrup wrote (1913:115–16):

> The sledges were turned sideways, so that the dogs could not easily set them in motion towards the bear. The result was as bad as could be imagined. One team succeeded in setting their sledge in motion and this stimulated the other teams to such an extent, that soon all the sledges bore down on the bear at full speed, where the feast and fighting at once began. As the dogs were still harnessed to the sledges, there arose an indescribable confusion; traces and harness were terribly mixed up and a quantity of the harness was dyed with blood and dirt. G. Thostrup's team nearly missed sharing the booty, as the sledge on the way to the bear stuck fast in a fissure. Afraid that his dogs would get nothing to eat, Thostrup ran up and slipped off all the harness; he was probably the one that came off best and cheapest from the general scrimmage and confusion.

Again off Hovgaard Ø the ice was very bad, and the sledges were badly damaged and an odometer was broken. At Mallemukbjerg on Amdrup

Land they found open water caused by strong currents sweeping by the perpendicular cliffs, a warning of difficulties to come by that mountain. Here the first supporting party returned to the ship. After the sea froze, the northbound travellers continued.

The travellers had found no signs of indigenous habitations from Kap Amelie to Mallemukbjerg, a distance of over 250 km (155 mi), but a few kilometres farther north at Eskimonæsset they came upon distinct signs of an entire settlement such as snow knives, darts, and pieces of sledges and kayaks. They found a second such site before they left Amdrup Land. At each site they made a cache of the artefacts to be collected on their return. Two days later, on April 26, G. Thostrup and Alfred Wegener, the second support party, began their return to the ship. The two returning parties mapped the coast as they travelled south, the first party, Bistrup and Karl Ring, surveying the seaward islands and the second, G. Thostrup and Wegener, the coastline of the mainland.

By now, Mylius-Erichsen and Koch realized that the coast was not as they had expected to find it. According to Peary's map of 1892, it should have been trending northwest toward Peary's Independence Bay, toward Gletscher Kap and Navy Klippe. Instead the coast was trending farther east, increasing the distance by several hundred kilometres that they would have to travel if they were to achieve their objectives. On April 28 they travelled eastward along a high ice cliff that formed the southern shore of Erik S. Heinig Land, which is almost entirely covered by inland ice. Farther north they could see that the ice gradually sloped down to the sea. Provisions began to grow scarce, but they were fortunate here to shoot a bear. The next day they passed the easternmost corner of Greenland, where the sloping inland ice merged almost imperceptibly with the sea ice. At last the coast began to trend to the northwest and west, and here they made a very small depot. Mylius-Erichsen, Niels Høeg-Hagen, and Jørgen Brønlund went west toward Gletscher Kap and Navy Klippe. Koch, Berthelsen, and Tobias Gabrielsen went north to reach Kap Bridgman.

Koch and his party found the travelling across the sea ice of Independence Fjord toward Peary Land to be difficult and laborious over very rough ice; they did not reach the land until May 7. They were short of food for men and dogs and were uncertain whether they could reach their goal of Peary's cairn at Kap Bridgman. But in two days they killed eleven muskoxen that saved them from starvation; their dogs were by then nearly worn out with hunger. They reached Kap Bridgman (83°30' N), 890 km (550 mi) north of Danmarkshavn, through snowstorms and fog. There they built their cairn and flew the Danish flag. On their return they found, like Peary, that Frederick E. Hyde Fjord was fogbound and they passed it by. Bertelson and Koch now were ill, suffering from loss of energy, sore gums, giddiness, and constipation, all as a result of the purely muskox diet. While hunting they lost five dogs. They were probably killed by chasing a muskox over a 500-m cliff. The dead muskox was found at the base of the cliff along with one living dog. The other dogs were not found.

Koch and his companions arrived back on the south side of Independence Fjord on May 27, and to their surprise they met Mylius-Erichsen at Kap Rigsdagen at the southeast corner of the fjord. Mylius-Erichsen reported that while travelling west they had discovered Danmark Fjord, one of East Greenland's largest fjords, and travelled into it, not realizing it was not taking them toward Gletscher Kap and Navy Klippe. The diversion cost them almost a month of time and added nearly 300 km (186 mi) to their journey. While in the fjord, on May 17, they found muskoxen. According to Brønlund's diary, "In less than 5 minutes we had killed them all, 14 musk oxen" (Amdrup 1913:202).

They had retraced their steps out of Danmark Fjord and encountered Koch returning from Kap Bridgman. They then realized the country was not at all as Peary's map had led them to believe. Mylius-Erichsen and Koch discussed what should be done now that it was late in the season and their supplies diminished. Koch thought that he had seen the head of Independence Fjord. At first Mylius-Erichsen decided that they should return to the ship. A day later he changed his mind, thinking that in two or three days he could reach Navy Klippe and that hunting would sustain them. He had, after all, shot twenty-one muskoxen within Danmark Fjord. With that prospect, on May 28 Mylius-Erichsen travelled west while Koch's party sledged south.

Koch's return journey was affected by deep snow and slow sledging, by fairly good hunting whereby they got a seal, a walrus, and a bear, and by sledges damaged by rough ice. Their passage was difficult and scarcely free from danger. They encountered a large amount of open water along the coast, and at Mallemukbjerg the icefoot had been washed away; thus they were obliged to proceed on a sloping snow-field ending in a 30-m- (98-ft)-high snow declivity to the sea. Here Tobias Gabrielsen (the experienced West Greenland dog driver) drove all three sledges.

They reached the ship on June 23. They had travelled over 2,000 km (1,240 mi), and Koch noted (Amdrup 1913:139–40):

> It was first and foremost Tobias who procured the game which made it possible to bring this long journey to a happy ending; on his shoulders rested all the hard work during a great part of the journey; his certain judgment of the difficulties of the journey, his hardihood and dexterity as driver several times saved us from long detours and considerable delays, and perhaps even on a certain occasion averted a catastrophe. To all of us he was a good comrade, always amiable and helpful.

While the main parties were in the north, the rest of the expedition was busy laying depots for the use of Mylius-Ericksen and Koch on their journeys. In addition they made surveys and explorations throughout Dove Bugt and occupied hunting camps to insure food for the dogs during the second winter. The hunting success was not great; six walrus, one muskox, eight bears, sixteen seals, and 200 kg (440 lbs) of salmon. It was not sufficient for the dogs.

Mylius-Erichsen had not returned by the time summer thaws, melted ice, and flowing rivers made travelling impossible. It was clear that he could not return until the cold of autumn again made sledging practical. The original plan to move the expedition to Kejser Franz Joseph Fjord was therefore abandoned. In any case, the ship couldn't leave Danmarkshavn. Amdrup wrote (1913:162) that

> ice conditions were on the whole less favorable this year [1907] than in 1906, when just at this time, the 17th of August, the ship had sailed into Danmarkshavn in almost open water and anchored there…. But in 1907 at the same time of year the pack-ice was laying along the land in an immovable belt several kilometers broad, which would have barred the way completely,

had the *Danmark* tried to leave the harbour, while the winter ice was unbroken over the greater part of Dove Bay.

In anticipation of the second winter, they began to establish a second weather station inside Mørkefjord, near the inland ice, for comparison with the observations at the ship. Several journeys were necessary to carry in the materials for a small house and the weather station. The expedition had been equipped with the luxury of an automobile, Trolle (1909:52) reported, "but its motor was so feeble that it was of no great help to us. It was only used once on the smooth autumn ice of 1907 to draw in some building material for a meteorological station 40 miles [65 km] from the ship, but on its return it stuck in the snow, and there it stands." The Mørkefjord substation began to function in November.

As soon as autumn freezing began, Thostrup, the second mate, and six sledges went to search for the missing men. The sledges broke through thin ice and dogs and men barely escaped being drowned. Travel overland on thin snow covering rough ground was very difficult, and travel over the inland ice, which was necessary where the sea had not frozen, was hazardous because crevasses were not yet safely bridged by snow. Several dogs were lost in crevasses 60–90 m (200–300 ft) deep. Open water stopped the rescuers on October 17 at Mallemukbjerg. They could not know it but they were then close to Mylius-Erichsen and his companions, who on October 19 were stopped on the north side of Mallemukbjerg by the same open water. Thostrup and his party had to return having found no trace of the lost party. They had been gone two months, travelling in the heart of winter, in bad weather, and with only the moon and stars to light their way through rough ice. Three of the dogs died of exhaustion on their return.

Koch and Tobias Gabrielsen left the ship on March 10, 1908, on a new attempt to locate Mylius-Erichsen. They found Jørgen Brønlund's body at the depot on Lambert Land about 270 km (170 mi) from Danmarkshavn. With him were his diary and survey sketches by Høeg-Hagen, but Koch could not find the diaries or the survey records of Mylius-Erichsen and Høeg-Hagen. Brønlund's diary tells the story of the disaster. When Mylius-Erichsen, Høeg-Hagen, and Brønlund parted from Koch on May 28, they journeyed westward but soon found themselves in a new fjord, not

Danmark Fjord and not Independence Bay. It was named Hagen Fjord. This new diversion led them once again away from their goal.

Amdrup, writing in 1913 after Mylius-Erichsen's fate had been learned, considered why Mylius-Erichsen had been misled into Danmark and Hagen Fjords and away from his goal – Peary's Gletscher Kap and Navy Klippe. Amdrup wrote (1913:214):

> To understand why Mylius-Erichsen first took Danmarks Fjord and then Hagens Fjord to be Independence Bay, it must be remembered that on all his charts from these regions round here Peary states that from Academy Glacier the coast bends almost in the direction S.E., whereas according to what has been found out by the Danmark Expedition, it turns on the contrary almost in the direction N.E.
>
> As the entrances to Danmark Fjord and to Hagen Fjord lie farther north than the Academy Glacier and as Mylius-Erichsen was entitled to suppose from Peary's chart, that he would come to Academy Glacier from a point S.E. of the glacier, it was quite natural that Mylius-Erichsen steered into these fjords which, as far as he could see, first went southwards and then turned towards the S.W. Mylius-Erichsen, who was each time of opinion that he found himself in Independence Bay, thus assumed that this bay would go farther south than Academy Glacier and that it would at the same time turn west and north-westwards up to the glacier; in other words that it would describe a curve between the mouth of the fjord and Academy Glacier. In this way everything would fit in with Peary's charts.
>
> This mistake on Peary's chart thus became of extremely fateful importance to Mylius-Erichsen and his companions. For it was owing to this long journey into Danmark Fjord and Hagen Fjord, that their retreat was begun too late and had to be given up on account of the comparatively sudden melting of the snow. And we know that their enforced summer in the north led to their death.

Mylius-Erichsen's party had been hopelessly misled by Peary's map. They did reach Gletscher Kap and they were able to retreat as far as Danmark Fjord, but then the summer thaw made it impossible to travel farther. There they found very few muskoxen and only a few hares and geese. Walking over bare, stony ground wore out their shoes and boots. Brønlund wrote in his diary (Trolle 1909:60): "No food, no foot gear, and several hundred miles to the ship. Our prospects are very bad indeed."

They spared their dogs as long as they could, but eventually were forced to shoot and eat them. They travelled inland to the head of Danmark Fjord when colder weather and new ice made travelling possible, but still they found no muskoxen. A few hares were eaten raw. They decided to make their return to the ship by travelling back the way they had come, around the northeasternmost corner of Greenland and then down along the coast, using depots of supplies as they went. At last they came to Mallemukbjerg on Amdrup Land. There they found open water against the steep coast. They could not pass the open water and so they went inland onto the ice on October 19, the day the sun disappeared, with four starving dogs and one sledge. Their hope was to pass over the inland ice and around the open water off Holm Land to the depot on Lambert Land. Lieutenant Trolle wrote (1909:60): "it is wonderful that these three men should have succeeded in covering a distance of about 160 miles [258 km], barefoot over ice and snow, in twenty-six days, or about 6 miles [10 km] a day." And Amdrup wrote (1913:218–19):

> The journey home over the inland ice must have been terrible. The cold up there must have been felt intensely by the emaciated and weakened travellers, who doubtless had to use their provisions sparingly and who, for protection, only had a tent without bottom, poor sleeping bags and miserable foot-gear.
>
> The last especially has determined their fate. All have most likely been severely frostbitten and thus with the general weakness from want and suffering and the sickness resulting therefrom has led to their death rather than the lack of food....
>
> Their goal was the depot on Lamberts Land. Here they knew they would find provisions, petroleum and clothing. But by this

time they were completely exhausted and both Mylius-Erichsen and Hagen died just before they could reach the depot.

Mylius-Erichsen and Høeg-Hagen died from starvation, exhaustion, and exposure a few kilometres from the depot. Brønlund was able in the moonlight to walk on frozen feet to the depot where he knew that his body and his diary would be found. There he wrote a few lines and died. Brønlund had struggled far enough to insure that a record of the party would be recovered and their fate revealed. His last words were: "I perished in 77° N lat., under the hardships of the return journey over the inland ice in November. I reached this place under a waning moon, and cannot go on because of my frozen feet and the darkness. The bodies of the others are in the middle of the fjord. Hagen died on November 15, Mylius-Erichsen some ten days later" (Trolle 1909:61).

Throughout the second winter, 1907–8, the expedition continued its business of observations and journeys to investigate the country. A notable journey was made to Ardencaple Fjord west of Shannon Ø. It had been discovered by Captain Clavering, and Lieutenant Payer of Koldewey's expedition had tried to enter it in 1870, but deep snow prevented travel within. Hakon Jarner the geologist, Tobias Gabrielsen, and Hendrik Olsen made the journey in 1908, leaving *Danmark* on April 15 with two sledges and twenty-two dogs. They were also to go to the depot on Shannon Ø to collect dog food and to leave notices for ships that might arrive during the summer. The route was marked by alternating deep snow and excellent going, and by a number of bears which they shot; five were shot in less than twenty-four hours. At the entrance to Ardencaple Fjord they found three old Inuit winter houses. At first they encountered heavy going in deep snow, but then the surface improved and in the interior of the fjord there was smooth ice. They found two branches, Bredefjord and Smallefjord, and they studied the geology thoroughly. They returned to the ship on May 27 with excellent results.

Winter in the vicinity of Kap Bismarck was long and severe, but when spring came the seasons changed abruptly. The snow partly evaporated even at –7° C [20° F], and began to melt in the ravines. Lieutenant Trolle (1909:55) wrote of the meltwater: "Running under the glaciers it formed the most fantastic ice-grottoes, where the light was broken into all the colours through crystal-like icicles." Then in one day all the snow melted. The rivers were suddenly full, flowers were in bud, and butterflies were in the air. "It was a lovely time … the birds came nearly all on the same day, most of them even on the same hour. One day we had only the ordinary ptarmigan and the raven; the next we had the sanderling, the ring plover, the goose, the eider duck, and many others."

Bears must have been plentiful, for *ninety* were shot during the whole expedition. But muskoxen were scarce, and wolves even more so. They shot five wolves which they found to be very thin and hungry, and those five apparently were all there were for they saw no more. They found foxes on the land and walruses and seals in the sea. Hares were very plentiful, and in April and May they were very tame. They found many salmon in a lake.

The Danes found no living Inuit, but tent rings, meat caches and even some winter dwelling places were found everywhere along the coast as far as Danmark Fjord.

Lieutenant Trolle wrote (1909:52): "The land of King Frederick VIII is a beautiful mountainous country, in many places very much like Norway – the same picturesque valleys, the same deep fjords, with steep mountains as high as 2,000 feet [610 m] on both sides, which have inspired our two painters, [Achton] Friis and Berthelsen, numerous islets and rocks intersected with sounds. Everywhere there were traces of glaciers from the ice period."

Danmark got through the ice on July 21, 1908, and arrived back in Copenhagen on August 23. The Danmark Expedition was the least known and least publicized of all the great polar endeavours of the time, and it was one of the most successful in results; fifty-one reports were published as a result of its work. A number of its members returned to Greenland over the years.

Captain Johan Peter Koch and Doctor Alfred Wegener returned to East Greenland in 1912–13 on an expedition known as the Danish Voyage of Investigation. (It was also apparently known as the Danish Expedition to Dronning Louise Land and across the Ice Sheet of North Greenland 1912–1913.) Koch the surveyor and Wegener the meteorologist of the Danmark Expedition had conceived a plan to study snow and ice conditions on the inland ice sheet. The inland ice had been crossed several times after Fridtjof Nansen's first crossing in 1888, but the previous parties, except for a Swiss expedition in 1912, had crossed the ice as rapidly as possible. The purpose of Koch and Wegener, like the Swiss glaciologists, was to study the ice sheet itself and to take the time necessary to do so. They intended to spend a winter near the edge of the ice sheet making meteorological and glaciological observations and then to cross the inland ice to Upernavik, making observations along the way. They were accompanied by Captain Lars Larsen and an Icelander, Vigfus Sigurdsson. The expedition had sixteen Icelandic horses for transport of twenty tons of equipment and supplies, including six tons of compressed hay for the horses. It was Sigurdsson's job to take care of the horses.

The expedition sailed from Copenhagen aboard *Godthaab* and reached Northeast Greenland at Kap Storm a little west of Danmarkshavn on July 22. There the ship left the four men, sixteen ponies, and twenty tons of materials to get on as best they could. All sixteen ponies broke loose and six were never recovered. Koch had planned to spend the winter in Dronning Louise Land, but it was a very difficult task to transport their materials across the sea ice, the land, and Storstrømmen, the great ice stream that separates Dronning Louise Land from the coast. (During the struggle to do so Wegener fell and broke a rib.) Koch and Wegener described[5] the edge of Storstrømmen at Borgfjorden where they met and climbed it:

> Like a mighty wall of marble 40 meters [130 ft] high the perpendicular cliff of the glacier rises from the fjord. The sharp edges, prominent corners, and carved niches, the many small angles and bays and capes, and tongues, that alternate with long straight lines, looked as if they were fashioned according to the grotesque ideas and fancies of a humorous architect. Now one sees, as in a new marble quarry, a half-finished roughly hewn wall; now there meets the eye a smooth, bright surface which shines with the luster of a high polish; then again one perceives the humor of the master in baroque snow garlands, whose icicle fringe and tassels sparkle in the sunlight. Now the wall is a uniform white, like purest alabaster; now it is colored a pale brownish yellow or bluish gray; now the delicate colors occur

---

5 Quoted by Mecking in Nordenskjöld and Mecking 1928:272–73.

in the form of broad bands like streaks in agate. It takes hold of one, it is disconcerting, this mighty wall whose foundation is sunk 200 meters [656 ft] deep in foamy fjord water. It appears so unshakably firm, so eternal and unchangeable, that the mind can scarcely grasp the fact that it is the source of all the icebergs that cover the fjord, that from its front at the bottom of the sea the ice blocks detach themselves and are hurled to the top with such buoyancy as to shatter the ice cover of the fjord and make it surge up and down far and wide. A cobweb-like network of fissures still testifies to this surging motion kilometers away.

In early October they had to erect their prefabricated house on Storstrømmen itself because they could go no farther that year, and they spent the winter there. They called their house *Borg* (The Castle). They were able to make their glaciological measurements through a hole in the floor of their castle. During the autumn Koch fell 12 m (40 ft) into a crevasse where he broke a leg. Larsen rescued him, and in three months Koch's leg had healed. All but five ponies were shot; the five survived the winter well in a snow-covered stable.

In his fall into the crevasse Koch had lost their only theodolite, essential for finding their way hundreds of kilometres across the ice sheet. During the winter Koch contrived to make an effective substitute. They left their winter house on April 20, 1913. On the first forty days of the journey there were only two days of good weather and for twelve days they were unable to travel. For much of the way they faced headwinds and blizzards. Every day they had to dig into the snow to provide shelter for the ponies; each hole gave Koch an opportunity to make glaciological measurements. The ponies became snowblind and the last had to be shot just as they reached the western edge of the ice sheet early in July. Koch and his colleagues safely reached the settlement of Prøven (Kangersuatsiaq) near Upernavik in Northwest Greenland on July 16.

When the tragic news of the deaths of Mylius-Erichsen, Høeg-Hagen, and Brønlund reached Copenhagen in the fall of 1908, Ejnar Mikkelsen immediately laid plans to recover the diaries, maps, and records that J.P. Koch had not found with the body of Jørgen Brønlund. Mikkelsen had the support of his former chief, Captain Amdrup, of Gustav Holm, and other distinguished Danes.

Mikkelsen had obtained a sea captain's licence just before his participation on the Amdrup expedition of 1900. Since his return from that expedition he had participated in 1901–2 in the unsuccessful American Baldwin-Ziegler Expedition on Zemlya Frantsa-Iosifa that had hoped to reach the North Pole. He had led a small expedition in 1906–8 that travelled for sixty days out over the sea ice of the Arctic Ocean looking for an island reported to lie north of Alaska. He had found no land.

Mikkelsen's supporters in 1908 raised the funds for his search for Mylius-Erichsen's records. He bought a small, 40-ton sloop, *Alabama*, and had it partially rebuilt and strengthened and fitted with a 16 h.p. motor. He enlisted a crew of six and set out from Copenhagen on June 20, 1909. Their first stop was the Faroe Islands, where they were to pick up fifty dogs Mikkelsen had ordered from West Greenland, the home of the best sledge dogs. Mikkelsen found that twenty-three dogs had died and the rest were dying from disease. He had the miserable job of shooting them all on the deck of *Alabama*. His only option then was to go to Ammassalik and buy more dogs, even though the reputation of east coast dogs was not good. *Alabama* reached Ammassalik on July 29, having sailed through fog and ice. New dogs were purchased and Mikkelsen returned to Iceland to make repairs to his sloop's motor, damaged on the passage through the ice to Ammassalik. He arrived in Iceland on August 4. There his engineer had to be replaced and Mikkelsen was fortunate to recruit Iver Iversen, an engineer from a Danish naval vessel.

By August 17 they again met the ice off the coast of Greenland. Getting through the edge of the ice would be, Mikkelsen wrote (1913:19),

> a nasty piece of work ... the wind was blowing half a gale,
> right on to the ice, with a heavy sea running and the spray

dashing over the ice-floes, that ducked and dipped and hacked at each other, crushing and being crushed…. Sea after sea broke over *Alabama*, the railing was under water half the time, the dogs howled with fear, the wind tore shrieking through the rigging – all was noise and confusion as we dashed with furious speed towards the ice.

In spite of the uproar and the turmoil and after a solid, bone-shattering crash against the ice, *Alabama* passed the ice edge and broke through to ice-infested but navigable water beyond. At one point, in fairly open water, "the water was filled with an immense amount of large seals, which continually popped their heads out of the water; I once counted more than twenty at the same time" (Mikkelsen 1922:7). In the next few days the sloop received more than one good squeeze from ice pressure, and at one point Mikkelsen expected to see it crushed, but by August 25 they had reached an anchorage at Shannon Ø. They tried to sail northward to Danmarkshavn through open water next to the shore, but they soon found that the ice pressed in to the shore; it was impossible to get farther north. They secured their vessel in its winter harbour on Shannon Ø on August 27.

Mikkelsen began the sledge trip to Jørgen Brønlund's grave on Lambert Land on September 25. He was accompanied by four colleagues, two of whom – Lieutenant Vilhelm Laub of the Navy and the mate Hans Olsen as a support team – would turn back on October 2. Iversen and Lieutenant Christian Jorgensen of the Army would go to Lambert Land with Mikkelsen. "All goes well at the start, the dogs dash ahead at full speed, wild with joy, howling and barking and snapping at each other, all from pure excess of high spirits" (Mikkelsen 1913:30). But the trip north in the fall of the year was a very difficult journey. The north wind blew cold in their faces, and the sea ice was thin and in many places unsafe. Mikkelsen wrote (1913:31):

> There are stretches where young ice and old ice have frozen together, broken up and frozen together again, making a frightful chaos of heavy old ice-blocks with thin, young ice piled up between, water hidden by a thin coating of ice, and slush that looks safe enough to the eye, but will not bear the weight of a

ALABAMA IN ICE, 1909
COURTESY ARCTIC INSTITUTE, DENMARK.

dog. We are in constant danger of going through the treacherous covering of ice, and that means a nasty ducking.

Mikkelsen was the first to break though. More than once the ice broke under them, and as the wind blew the ice would break up; more than once they found themselves adrift on loose floes in open water. There were days when the gales prevented them from travelling. Deep snow slowed them down and exhausted them. A dog died on October 11 as they reached the old expedition house at Danmarkshavn, where they stayed to rest the dogs for four days. They then had "splendid" ice for two days, followed once more by very rough ice, gales, and deep snow. Two more dogs died as they laid a depot on Orlean Ø. The sun had now disappeared, and they travelled by twilight and by moonlight when the sky was not obscured by storm clouds. They struggled onto Lambert Land on October 30 and stayed until November 3, looking in the vicinity for any traces of Mylius-Erichsen, but without success. There was nothing more they could do that autumn in the increasing darkness. Their long, cold, difficult journey had been in vain.

They were 465 km (290 mi) north of *Alabama*, and now they had to travel home in darkness, fog, and snowstorms. One dog ate another; four dogs died that day from hunger and exhaustion. They returned to the house at Danmarkshavn on November 22 intending to rest there for three days. Deep snow fall and fierce winds kept them there for six days. Soon after their start again on December 2, Lieutenant Jorgensen suffered frostbitten feet which incapacitated him for the rest of the expedition. It was mid-December before they got home to *Alabama*.

They set out on their long journey for the north on March 4.

> ... a lovelier morning than that which greeted us as we came
> up on deck no one could desire. The sun – which is still too much
> of a novelty as yet to be regarded as part of the daily scheme of
> things – shines clear and dazzling in a perfectly cloudless sky,
> the snow-hills stand out clear and sharply defined, and far away
> in the distance we can see the high picturesque mountains of
> the continent, bathed in sunlight, sharp and distinct in the clear
> frosty air (Mikkelsen 1913:64).

Mikkelsen's goal now was Danmark Fjord, in which, it was known, Mylius-Erichsen had spent the summer of 1907. There Mikkelsen hoped to find records of the lost explorers. He was accompanied by Iver Iversen, who would go all the way with him, and by Laub, Olsen, and Georg Poulsen, who were the support party and would return to *Alabama* after five weeks. They covered 160 km (100 mi) in thirteen days and were then amongst islands of Dove Bugt, where they planned to ascend Storstrømmen, the great ice stream that would be their route up to the inland ice and then on to Danmark Fjord. They shot a bear in Dove Bugt whose flesh revived the dogs. The passage onto Storstrømmen was not easy. Very rough ice, deep snow, and strong winds were the story, and they had to relay the heavily loaded sledges, crossing the terrain three times to make progress. And farther along the ice stream the winds had stripped the snow and polished the ice so that there was hardly any traction for the struggling dogs and men. Slowly they ascended the glacier stream toward the inland ice. Mikkelsen wrote (1913:96):

> From where we are now we can see out over Dove Bay with its many islands, and the peak of the Devil's Cape standing up sharp and steep in the air, while far away in the distance can be seen the heights of Koldewey Island. It is a splendid view, and in this calm, clear air, even distant land appears quite near. The sun is shining on the dark, naked land, lending it a wealth of color not its own.... Dove Bay is mild and pleasant in comparison with where we are, but soon this also will disappear, and we shall be surrounded by ice on all sides.

Sledge runners split on the sharp ice, causing delays for repairs. On April 6, Mikkelsen built a depot of supplies on the ice in the event he and Iversen might return that way. Farther on they came upon deep and wide drainage channels for the meltwater of summer; the channels caused detours and delays while they searched for ways around them. The support party turned back on April 10, leaving Mikkelsen and Iversen with a hundred days of food to carry on alone. A few days later Iversen's sledge dropped into a crevasse. "The sledge was sunk through in a wide crack, and is only held by the bow and the ends of the uprights at the stern, which are resting on either side of a yawning abyss" (Mikkelsen 1913:123). It was recovered only with much labour; they were fortunate that it had not been lost. Crevasses were a constant danger for the rest of their journey on the ice.

As they journeyed north, even though they were on the inland ice, land was often in view, nunataks to the left or right as they passed along the edge of the ice sheet. Gales kept them idle and in camp for four continuous days in late April, and a day later two dogs died – worn out by the struggle against the wind. But when the wind changed from the northerly gales blowing in their faces, they were able to rig a sail and made good progress. Crevasses became more frequent; some were more than 7 m (25 ft) wide. One dog broke through a snow bridge, slipped from its harness, and was lost in the depths. Iversen's sledge broke through three times that day.

Mikkelsen wondered (1913:148) who would have thought that the weather would hold them "stormbound for fourteen of April's thirty days ... half the rest would be full of difficulties due to wind, bad ice, fissures, and all sorts of other misfortunes, and, finally ... the total distance covered in April would amount to only 108 miles [175 km] in a straight line." The month of May would have to be better.

The weather moderated somewhat, and though they were at an altitude of 1,100 m (3,600 ft), they were now on a rolling but generally descending slope of the ice. They were travelling where only Mylius-Erichsen, Høeg-Hagen, and Brønlund had ever been before them and where few if any have been since. As they reached the top of an ice hill,

> we for the first time can see the whole of the land of which we caught a glimpse yesterday. It is high country, stretching away north and east, wild and mountainous, and furrowed by deep fjords. Fifty miles [80 km] or more away we can see the steep slopes of Lambert Land, while behind us the pyramid of the Pic de Gerlache and the steep peaks of the other nunataks rise sharply above the inland ice.
>
> We can see far and wide over this desolate land, so imposing in its utter lifelessness, a great white surface, hard as glass and yet plastic and ever slowly moving, which only the highest mountain-top can pierce.... It is a beautiful and imposing sight,

but so oppressively silent, that one feels an impulse to cry aloud, to strike the dogs until they howl, only to break the silence which broods over all we see, as it has done and will do for thousands of years. But the sledges glide forward once more, and the air resounds with our shouts and the barking of the dogs; for a little space waves of sound roll out across the virgin surface where silence hitherto has reigned supreme (1913:153–54).

A gale held them in their tent for two days, but they got underway on May 7. "It is still blowing hard, and right in our faces; the snow is driving high, but we have had worse weather, and we bend to our hauling-straps, shielding our faces as far as possible from the wind and urge on the unwilling dogs" (Mikkelsen 1913:155–56). The next day, May 8, was calm and the travelling for a change was very good and they saw their goal – land around the interior of Danmark Fjord. Their job now was to find a way off the inland ice and down to the land before them. The edge of the ice where it met the land was a sheer cliff 30 m (100 ft) high.

It took two days to find a way off the inland ice. While they were searching on the first day, the remaining dogs left at their camp broke loose, entered the tent, and raised havoc. Worse, they ate one-quarter of all the remaining dog pemmican, a serious loss. By May 13 they were off the ice on which they had been struggling since March 24 – seven long weeks. "It is impossible to describe the intoxicating delight of this feeling of safety with which one steps out over firm, solid earth – the lurking horror of those hidden cracks now nothing but a nightmare passed" (Mikkelsen 1913:170). Then they found and shot two muskoxen – much-needed fresh meat for dogs and men.

They were able to sledge easily over a frozen lake and left five muskoxen undisturbed as they passed by. From a hill they found that the lake would lead them to Danmark Fjord: "Only a poet could paint in words the long narrow lake, lying among the high, steep hills, and Danmark Fjord with its dark sheer cliffs, and loveliest of all, the fresh, pale green of the nearer hills – a color so faint and fine as to seem an effect of light – a part of the spring one feels and hears all around" (Mikkelsen 1913:179).

Danmark Fjord is 160 km (100 mi) long. On their fifth day of travel on its ice, Mikkelsen and Iversen found what they had come so far to recover.

In a cache on the shore, stuffed in a shot cartridge, was a report by Mylius-Erichsen. It was dated September 12, 1907, and it described their summer spent in Danmark Fjord. Mylius-Erichsen and his companions had been prevented from travelling by open water, but had some success with hunting ptarmigans, hares, and eight muskoxen. They had killed seven dogs to feed the remaining dogs and themselves. They had over 136 kg (300 lbs) of meat on their sledge. Their plans at that date were to proceed eastward to the outer coast and then southward using depots laid the previous spring. Mylius-Erichsen's note said, "By shooting bears we hope to reach the ship safe and sound in about five to six weeks" (Mikkelsen 1913:187). They did reach the outer coast but, as J.P. Koch had learned from Brønlund's diary, were stopped by open water at Mallemukbjerg. They then tried to return to Lambert Land by crossing the edge of the ice inland from the mountain, a journey that was fatal to them from hunger, exhaustion, and exposure to wind and cold. Because their footwear was nearly worn out, they must have suffered severely frostbitten feet.

Mikkelsen and Iversen now had only seven dogs remaining and their supplies had been greatly reduced, so here they abandoned one sledge. The snow was getting soft on the fjord and they found it tedious going. And as they travelled toward the northern end of Danmark Fjord, they found how barren the land became compared with the vegetation at its inner end. Here were few signs of game anywhere.

They found a second cache on May 26 near the site of Mylius-Erichsen's summer camp, a barren and desolate spot. This cache contained a record of Mylius-Erichsen's explorations after they left J.P. Koch on May 28, 1907. It recorded that on the first of June 1907, they had reached Peary's Gletscher Kap where they discovered that Peary Channel "*does not exist*" (emphasis in original). From there they returned to Danmark Fjord, having discovered Hagen Fjord and Brønlund Fjord along the way. This report was dated August 8, 1907.

Mikkelsen and Iversen were also disturbed to learn that Peary Channel does not exist. Based on Peary's report they assumed that it did exist and, like Mylius-Erichsen, had considered returning by way of the channel to West Greenland; they had counted on a sea-level channel and they thought it might be a less difficult route than going back south along the east coast of Greenland. It could mean that they might return to Denmark sooner. The next day they sledged as far as Kap Rigsdagen, their north-ernmost point. From there began the long, long journey, 890 km (550 mi) by way of the east coast, back to *Alabama*. They had twelve days of food for their seven dogs and forty-five days of food for themselves. Their first goal was the northernmost depot of the Danmark Expedition. It was 166 km (100 mi) away and it took thirteen days to reach the site. It was slow going because of deep, soft, wet snow that exhausted dogs and men. By the third of June the snow was slush, and on that day Mikkelsen realized that he was ill with scurvy. They had good travelling along the ice of the easternmost corner of Greenland, along Kronprins Christian Land, but Mikkelsen was losing his strength and had to ride the sledge. They found very little food in the Danmark Expedition depot left there three years before, but just beyond they came upon a flock of geese and Iversen killed two. Six days later they reached another depot on Amdrup Land that had not been touched. It held 45 kg (100 lbs) of dog food, and there Iversen killed another goose. It was badly needed; it was now three weeks since Mikkelsen had been able to stand without assistance. Now they were wading through meltwater on the ice, a distance of nearly 16 km (10 mi). Farther south on Holm Land they found many remains of indigenous tent rings with bones of whale and walrus several hundred years old. They shot and wounded a bear, but they could not chase it in the soft snow and they lost it; the bear escaped to open water. They tried to cross Dijmphna Sund to Hovgaard Ø, but the travelling over ice flooded with melted snow was so bad that Iversen was up to his waist in slush. They had to return to Holm Land, where they waited eighteen days until the water drained from the ice. The rest helped Mikkelsen and the five remaining dogs. Iversen hunted every day in terrain that seemed to promise game, but he never got more than a gull or two. While hunting one day he found an-other depot from the Danmark Expedition with food for two men for two weeks, fuel, and dog food. A soldered tin contained clean clothes, cigars, cigarettes, and preserved gooseberries. There was a list of depots farther south, every thirty or fifty miles. "We are almost beside ourselves with joy" (Mikkelsen 1913:227). Indeed, their prospects looked bright. By now Mikkelsen was recovering, but they lost two dogs during the delay; one was so weak it had to be shot and the other drowned. On the eighth of July they were able to move on, hurrying south before the melting ice should break up and move out to sea. Off Hovgaard Ø there were lanes of open water to be crossed by ferrying on pieces of ice. Once the sledge fell in, some equipment, including their theodolite and botanical and geological samples collected earlier, were lost, and everything was soaked with salt water. Open leads in the ice and fog slowed their journey. So bad was the travelling that it took eight days to travel the 56 km (35 mi) to the next depot, and there they found much of its contents spoiled. Again they were forced to wait until the travelling improved. Three weeks went by without improvement. Rain came in downpours as heavy as any thunderstorm. Hunting on land was almost completely unsuccessful, and seals that they shot at the ice edge sank for lack of fat at that season. They wounded one bear which escaped in fog. "The very name of Hovgaards Island will remain in our memory for all time as synonymous with cold and hunger, hardship and disappointment" (Mikkelsen 1913:253). They had only 3.2 kg (7 lbs) of pemmican remaining, and the two remaining dogs were little more than skeletons.

They started south again on August 6, "And now," wrote Mikkelsen (1913:254), "the real fight begins."

They made a boat of their sledge by wrapping it in sailcloth which enabled them to float it over meltwater channels, the men wading. "We ourselves gradually develop into nondescript amphibious creatures" (Mikkelsen 1913:258). On the third day they travelled only 3 km (2 mi) in ten hours of work. They reached Lambert Land on August 15, "utterly exhausted with cold and hunger" (Mikkelsen 1913:260). But then Iversen shot twelve ptarmigan. On they went, only to have their sledge capsize in water and again soak everything. Now Iversen was ill and becoming weaker, but could not ride the sledge and had to walk because the two dogs could no longer pull the sledge. Nevertheless, Iversen continued to hunt and got a hare. The last two dogs were killed and the men ate them while they crossed to Schnauder Ø, where they expected that a large depot of food awaited them. It had taken them twenty-three days to reach the island from Hovgaard Ø, only 93 km (58 mi) to the north. After a long search they found a case of supplies, but only one of the five they expected to find. Nevertheless, Mikkelsen wrote (1913:279):

Now at last we feel sure of being able to complete the long and toilsome journey home – it is not far now to the northern depot, and there are no less than four more depots between there and Danmarks Havn, Our troubles are over now – the rest of the trip cannot be so difficult, for the frost must soon be here, and then the ice will be safer, and the going better, while for the present we have food enough to last us for a good rest here, until we have got back our strength for the last stage of the journey.

They shot five ptarmigan and started on. Colder weather froze the water and travel was much drier and easier. "Even the surface of the inland ice … is now covered with innumerable sparkling ice crystals, and the sledge runs twice as easily as before" (Mikkelsen 1913:282).

Southward from Schnauder Ø the travelling was good over long stretches of level ice. Mikkelsen and Iversen trudged toward the next depot, the first of four between them and Danmarkshavn 226 km (140 mi) away. Their spirits were high with better travelling conditions and food in hand. "We look around again at the surrounding country … it is in truth a splendid panorama, especially in the early morning when the sun is just up, and it throws its warm red glow over the great hills about the Pic de Gerlache.… All is beautiful around us"(Mikkelsen 1913:282).

The depot gave them food, not all of it spoiled and "quite good enough for sailors," said Mikkelsen (1913:290), sufficient for eight days with the next depot only 26 km (16 mi) beyond. They enjoyed the warmth of a fire from broken-up packing cases and indulged in the food. But the next depot was empty, nothing but empty cans scattered about. Now they met open water again and were obliged to abandon the tent and sledge on thin sea ice. They found the next depot on September 9. It too was empty. And they were 130 km (80 mi) from Danmarkshavn

They left every non-essential item behind at the depot, even their sleeping bags. They carried only their diaries, films, guns, some fuel and their stove, 1.1 kg (2.5 lb) of food, and a pair of stockings each – "things which we thought were absolutely indispensable." These they strapped in bundles on their backs. The sea ice now was much too thin to cross over bays. They had to follow every twist and turn of the coast, skirting steep cliffs and creeping over the glare ice of glaciers. Again they wounded a bear that escaped. They found no other game. The depot at Kap Amelie had no food – the third that they found empty. "It is hard, indeed, when one is starving, to find a stock of good provisions used mainly to feed dogs." But then Iversen shot four ptarmigan.

A gale arose just as they were to cross Skærfjorden, the last body of water separating them from Germania Land with Danmarkshavn at its southern end. The gale broke up the new sea ice of Skærfjorden, forcing them to wait through the night while new ice formed. It was very cold, their clothes were damp, and they had no sleeping bags or tent while the gale blew all night.

In the morning they began the crossing and for five hours made good progress. But open water forced them onto a rocky islet and the gale began again. There they stayed for forty hours. And there they cached their diaries, and started on again with only a bit of food, a gun and some shot, and stockings. The ice was very thin. They tested every foot of the way with an ice spear that went through the ice with ease. They were on that thin ice for seven hours before they reached the safety of Germania Land. There they ate their last bit of pemmican. The last depot at Kap Marie Valdemar, 16 km (10 mi) farther along, was empty except for three small cans of meat extract. They built a fire of packing cases and ate the extract and tried to rest.

The next day, September 17, they hoped would see them to the house at Danmarkshavn. It was a very long walk, starting in darkness and stumbling over the rough, rock-strewn shore. The sun rose and set and still they stumbled on. They stopped to rest, but the pain in Iversen's legs forced them on; he could not rest. At last in the darkness they came on a cache that held two cans of soup and a can of peas. These they ate, warmed with a packing-case fire. "One would scarcely believe that a little dish of soup and a mug of peas could have such a marvellous effect on a worn-out system" (Mikkelsen 1913:307). When the sun rose, they started on again, Mikkelsen occasionally supporting Iversen weakened with pain.

> After five hours' painful trudging we reach the last range
> of hills, and there far down below us lies a little cluster of sheds
> – Danmarkshavn.... We say but little, just sit there in silence,

drinking in the picture of the little hut, reddish-brown in the warm sunlight, with green plains stretching away on every side, a sweet oasis in the icy desert, with food and warmth and kindly shelter.... By eleven o'clock on the morning of the 18th of September we have reached it – the journey is at an end! (Mikkelsen 1913:307–8).

The journey thus ended was certainly one of the most remarkable of polar travel, for difficulties encountered and overcome, and for endurance exhibited. Mikkelsen and Iversen had been travelling for almost eight months, and they had accomplished their purpose – they had recovered records of Mylius-Erichsen and Høeg-Hagen and Brønlund.

They rested at Danmarkshavn for nearly a month. The weather in the meantime was very bad, but by October 15 it improved and they started north to try to recover the diaries they had cached on the islet in the middle of Skærfjorden They made poor progress for seven days and then had to give it up. They would try again in the spring. They returned to Danmarkshavn on October 25 and stayed there while storms raged and snow fell until November 5. They began the last stage of their journey – about 158 km (98 mi) to *Alabama* and their colleagues. They found their own depots along the way, but they had to lie up in a storm for five days. It was November 25 before they reached their goal on Shannon Ø. But there they found no warm shelter and no shipmates – only darkness, cold, and silence. *Alabama* was a wreck on the shore, and a rough house had been built from its timbers. Their colleagues were gone.

They learned later that the sloop had been crushed by ice pressure during the previous spring. The crew had salvaged all the supplies they could and piled them ashore. They had torn wood from the wreck and built the hut. They furnished the hut as best they could, and when a sealing vessel had appeared in late July, rather than stay and diminish the supplies that Mikkelsen and Iverson would need if they returned that way, the crew had left Greenland.

Mikkelsen and Iversen spent their second "winter of long and weary days" in that hut. On April 25, 1911, they started north once again to recover their diaries from Skærfjorden They reached Danmarkshavn in ten days and eventually arrived at the rocky skerry and their cache. It was torn to pieces; a bear had been at their cache. By digging about in the snow, however, they found a roll of film, a notebook, and most of the diaries. They spent the day digging, but, save for a few pages, they could not find one of Mikkelsen's diaries. On the 16th of May they began the long trudge home again. They spent the summer in a little house on the southeast corner of Shannon Ø where they could watch the sea ice break up and might first spot a ship. To add some variety to the monotony of their lives they adopted some young hares and looked after them. No ship came, and when great flocks of birds flew south they returned to their winter house by the wreck of *Alabama*.

During the autumn they killed muskoxen and made plans to move 680 kg (1,500 lbs) of meat and their rowing boat down to Bass Rock about 33 km (21 mi) south of Shannon Ø and near the Pendulum Øer visited by Clavering in 1823 and Koldewey in 1869. Two huts had been erected on Bass Rock in 1901 and stocked with provisions as a fallback position for the Baldwin-Ziegler Expedition, on which Mikkelsen had served. Mikkelsen and Iversen hoped to sledge their boat over the ice to Bass Rock, spend the winter in the huts, and then the following summer try to follow the coast down to Ammassalik, a very long and dangerous small boat journey. Mikkelsen's boat was *Aggas*, the same boat in which Amdrup and Mikkelsen had sailed in 1900 along the Blosseville Kyst.

It was a heavy load – sledge, boat, and meat – and it was slow travelling over rough ice and in darkness. The boat was too heavy for only the two of them to move across the ice and it had to be left on the ice, but Mikkelsen and Iversen reached Bass Rock on November 20. There they found a note that the crew of a sealing vessel had left in the hut the previous summer while they had been waiting on Shannon Ø only 33 km (21 mi) away.

The third winter was "a barren existence." They returned to Shannon Ø to collect more muskox meat, and while they were at their winter house a bear tried to break in. "There in the doorway, with its forepaws on the threshold, is the bear staring open-mouthed and dribbling in astonishment at the strange cave which it has broken into" (Mikkelsen 1913:365). Iversen shot, and the bear retreated and sank to the ground, dead.

They returned to Bass Rock with 272 kg (600 lb) of meat and equipment on their sledge. And there they waited. On July 19 a ship came. The Norwegian sealer *Sjöblomsten* found them and took them to Ålesund. The captain, Paul Lillenaes, received a reward of 10,000 crowns offered by the Danish government for information about Mikkelsen and Iversen.

Ejnar Mikkelsen and Iver Iversen were received in Denmark with mixed feelings. Mikkelsen gave a long series of talks throughout Europe and enjoyed strong support from the Royal Geographical Society in England. But he made remarks that were considered critical of the Danmark Expedition. He did not receive the Danish Royal Geographic medal, as had been expected, and he was not invited to ceremonies unveiling a memorial to the Danmark Expedition. After a time he did receive a grant from the government of 1000 crowns (about $150) and Iversen received 600 crowns.

RASMUSSEN – SEARCHING FOR THE SEARCHERS, 1912

Knud Rasmussen was born in Greenland, the son of a Danish missionary. His grandmother had Greenlandic blood. He spoke the Greenlandic language fluently and at age nine he had his own dog team. After higher education in Denmark, he spent his life studying the Inuit and Greenlandic people and exploring Greenland and other parts of the Arctic. He had served with Mylius-Erichsen's expedition to Northwest Greenland in 1902–4.

When Robert Peary made his last expedition to Northwest Greenland in 1909 and thus ended his trading activities of nearly eighteen years, Knud Rasmussen realized that the polar Inuit would be left without the tools and weapons of civilization to which they had become accustomed and upon which they had become largely dependent. Rasmussen, with the assistance of a private committee and private funds, established a trading station on North Star Bugt in the Kap York district in 1910. He called it Thule – the farthest, the northernmost place. It was to be the physical and financial base for a series of explorations that Rasmussen called the Thule Expeditions.

Rasmussen first planned an expedition to survey and make proper maps of the north coast of Greenland. But in the summer of 1911 Rasmussen at Thule learned of the concerns in Denmark over the fate of Ejnar Mikkelsen and Iver Iversen, missing then for over a year. He (1915:287) "considered it our unquestionable duty as comrades to extend our original plan by the addition of a relief expedition on his behalf." Rasmussen also hoped to explore Peary Channel as a possibly practical route to Northeast Greenland that would facilitate his survey of northernmost Greenland. He did not know, in 1911, that Mylius-Erichsen had found that the channel does not exist.

Knud Rasmussen therefore set off in 1912 across the ice sheet toward Danmark Fjord, about 1,150 km (715 mi) away. His party consisted of four. Peter Freuchen was the manager of Rasmussen's Thule station. Freuchen had served on Mylius-Erichsen's Danmark Expedition of 1906–8. Uvdloriaq and Inukitsoq were highly skilled hunters and sledge drivers. They were the first Inuit known to have crossed the ice sheet.

The start of the expedition was assisted on April 14 by thirty-five drivers and sledges with 350 dogs hauling heavy loads up the approaches onto the inland ice sheet. The last supporting parties left Rasmussen's party on April 19. The ice cap surface was good for sledging, and Rasmussen's party reached the eastern edge of the inland ice on the twenty-fifth day after its ascent of the glacier. Their average speed was 62 km (38.5 mi) per day. The eastern edge of the ice sheet where Rasmussen came upon it was a steep wall 20 m (65 ft) high; everything had to be lowered by walrus-hide lines the travellers had brought with them. It took twelve hours, and while they laboured at the job a gale was blowing strong enough to lift dogs on the line. Two dogs were blown over the ice edge and into an ice fissure where they disappeared.

The first job was to find food for their fifty-three dogs. Freuchen, however, had to be left in camp because he suffered severely from snow-blindness as they came off the inland ice. The other three began to hunt across the country. Rasmussen wrote (1915:305):

> It was a queer feeling, starting off in this fashion into a great unknown country, to be swallowed up by the gloomy monotony of the hills. There is a solemnity about these wastes which makes a deep impression on the mind. Hour after hour one walks, a man unspeakably alone, without sound or sight of any living thing, yet with every sense alert to hear and see and find – until at last the strain within and pressure from without

create a tension so great that one starts at the noise of one's own footsteps.

After five long days of fruitless hunting, at last they found and shot nine muskoxen, about a week's food for their dogs. During this time the hunters had wandered day and "night" (in fact there was twenty-four-hour daylight) and without sleep for up to forty hours. Rasmussen had left his diary in camp. Freuchen in camp was blindfolded and in darkness the entire time; the party lost track of time and were unsure what day it was. Only when they returned to Thule in the autumn could they correct their journal entries.

Having found food, they then had to find their way down to Danmark Fjord. It was no easy task. The route lay over a waterfall 180 m (330 ft) high. "This waterfall, frozen now, of course, was a most magnificent sight … falling in 4 sections, each of which was practically passable by lowering sledge and dogs. The whole of the fall lay between the steep walls if ice and rock, like tall close-built houses on either side of a street" (Freuchen 1915:351). Their route then was across rough, stony country. It was 150 km (93 mi) to the sea ice of the fjord, and they didn't reach it until May 31, twenty-one days after they descended from the ice edge. The journey down this valley, much shorter than the distance across the inland ice, had taken almost as long. Dogs and men were exhausted when they reached the shore, but on the fjord the sea ice was firm and level and sledging was easy. Further, they found muskoxen grazing along the shore and seals sunning themselves on the ice. The abundance of food and easy travelling restored the party.

They reached the site of Mylius-Erichsen's summer camp on the shore of Danmark Fjord on June 4. Freuchen recognized a number of items as belonging to the Danmark Expedition, but of course they found no record because Mikkelsen had removed it in 1910. Unfortunately, Mikkelsen had left no record of his own visit. From this Rasmussen concluded that Mikkelsen had not reached Danmark Fjord. Only a year later did Rasmussen learn that Mikkelsen had in fact been there. Rasmussen then wrote (1915:317):

In thus neglecting to leave a copy of the reports which he found, together with a brief indication of his own recent and intended movements, Ejnar Mikkelsen acted imprudently. If he and Iversen had subsequently perished – a possibility which had to be considered – no trace of them would have been left, in addition to which, Mylius Erichsen's reports would have been lost altogether.

It will thus be understood that we had good reason for supposing that Ejnar Mikkelsen has never been in Danmarks Fjord at all.

Rasmussen passed out of Danmark Fjord and travelled west along the south coast of Independence Fjord toward Hagen Fjord. Hunting was poor in this area. "The coast here was wild and desolate; a barren, melancholy place. It was newly formed land, all clay, without vegetation or game" (Rasmussen 1915:317). They therefore crossed Independence Fjord to Peary Land, where, Rasmussen wrote (1915:317):

> ... we found ourselves suddenly as it were transported to another quarter of the globe. We sighted musk ox even before reaching land, and our first impression, as soon as we had crossed the ice limit up on to the shore, was one of fertility and life. It was a real delight to see, not clay, nor rocks, nor gravel, but earth; mould, dotted everywhere with red blossoming saxifrage. Along the river banks were tracks of musk ox, hare and lemming, and in the air above, the skuas shrieked a welcome.
>
> From the moment we started off along the coast of Peary Land, it was like new life to ourselves and the dogs. Save for one or two short spells of ill luck, we now found abundance both of musk ox and seal....
>
> We were now in the midst of the Arctic spring, and it cheered our hearts to see it. This was real country, with food abounding in case any unexpected obstacle should bar our progress round by the northward, and force us to winter here (1915:320).

Peter Freuchen wrote (1915:359):

> We were now in an ideal hunting country. In the immediate vicinity of the tent, three herds of musk ox were grazing, hare and ptarmigan abounded, and seals lay out on the ice basking in the sun, so that we could get as many as we wanted…. while farther inland, towards the rocky heights the country rose somewhat, with big hills … with a rich growth of Arctic willows, and consequently affording good feeding grounds for musk ox.

Close to the mouth of Brønlund Fjord they found ancient tent rings at several places, but no winter houses in spite of searches in all directions. Rasmussen carefully measured the tent rings, which he considered "one of the most interesting discoveries of the expedition." Thirty-five years later those rings would be thoroughly investigated by the Danish Peary Land Expedition with most interesting – even startling – results.

The weather was now fine and clear, and the sea ice of Independence Fjord was covered with meltwater lakes. By the middle of June crossing the fjord was so difficult that Rasmussen's party gave up the idea of looking for Mylius-Erichsen's cairn at Gletscher Kap. They believed that he could not in fact have landed at the cape because the mass of great ice fragments and blocks from Academy Gletscher packed along that shore was "absolutely impassable."

At the head of Independence Fjord they also found that Peary Channel does not exist. That meant Rasmussen and his party could not pass through it to the north coast, as they had planned, and from there travel back to Thule. Therefore they had to make their way again up onto the inland ice. With the approaches to Academy Gletscher apparently impossible, their only alternative in that land of precipitous cliffs facing the fjord was by Nyboes Gletscher. But its terminus "ended abruptly in an unscalable precipice." By exploring the land north of the glacier they found that they could pass over the ground and gain access onto the glacier farther inland. The overland route involved climbing over a "hill" 800 m (over 2,400 ft) high and traversing 32–40 km (20–25 mi) of bare ground. Every piece of equipment, including the sledges, had to be carried on their backs. It took them two weeks. Once they had reached an accessible edge of the glacier, they left all their equipment and went hunting in an adjacent valley. "The valley seemed like a revelation of summer spread over the land, with its wealth of lovely yellow poppies" (Rasmussen 1915:323). They hunted there for fourteen days, shot seventeen muskoxen, and rested the dogs. But the weather now had turned to rain and fog and remained so for most of the rest of their days in that land.

It took them three days to ascend Nyboes Gletscher, with very bad weather and many difficulties from streams full of running meltwater. One stream was in fact a river with swift water over a very slippery bottom. It took them a day to cross it.

Rasmussen reached the plateau of Vildtland on July 15 and set up a camp next to the inland ice. Hunting there was unexpectedly good. Within fourteen hours the hunters had shot eleven muskoxen. The animals were fearless and grazed within sight of their camp every day. Rasmussen now was suffering from pains in his legs, like Iversen and Mikkelsen, from wading in cold water. The pains were so bad that he discussed the possibility of remaining with Inukitsoq in Peary Land for the winter and returning to Thule with the light of the spring when presumably his legs would be restored. His companions refused to consider leaving him for the winter. While Rasmussen rested, Freuchen and Inukitsoq went off to look for Peary's cairn on Navy Klippe overlooking Academy Gletscher. They returned two days later with Peary's record, which made no mention of his "discovery" of Peary Channel.

Rasmussen delayed their departure for home until August 8 because of bad weather. In the meantime his legs began to improve and within a week of their ascent of the inland ice he was able to walk with the aid of a stick. In the three weeks they had camped on Vildtland they had killed thirty muskoxen. They began the long journey over the ice to Thule with ample food for their remaining twenty-seven dogs, who were now well rested and in excellent condition. They shot one muskox on the day of their departure for a final feast for the dogs.

The journey over the ice was often marked by poor sledging, as is to be expected in the autumn, and by spells of rain, snow, or fog., but they travelled fast, averaging 43 km (27 mi) a day. They came in sight of the west coast on September 4, but because they had lost a day in their reckoning, their navigation was in error and they struck the west coast north of Inglefield Bredning rather than south of it. This caused a seven-day detour, during which Freuchen suffered badly from leg pains. They arrived in Thule on September 14. Eight dogs survived the expedition.

KOCH AND THE CIRCUMNAVIGATION OF PEARY LAND, 1921

Peary Land, the northernmost land in the world, was "circumnavigated" and surveyed for the first time in 1921 by the Danish geologist and geographer Lauge Koch. Koch was a nephew of J.P. Koch who had reached Kap Bridgman on Peary Land in 1907. Lauge Koch had accompanied Knud Rasmussen in 1917 when Rasmussen carried out his plan for the survey of northernmost Greenland that had been delayed by the search for Ejnar Mikkelsen and Iver Iversen. In 1920 Koch made his base at Robertson Fjord on Inglefield Land in Northwest Greenland. His plan was to continue the mapping of North Greenland begun with Rasmussen and to connect that survey with the mapping accomplished by Mylius-Erichsen's expedition in 1907; that is, to travel around the northernmost point of Greenland and part way down its northeast coast. He would return to his base at Robertson Fjord by way of Independence Fjord and across the inland ice. Lauge Koch started on March 19, 1921, with the help of nineteen drivers and sledges and 200 dogs carrying 1,500 kg (3,300 lbs) of pemmican, 1,500 kg of walrus meat and 400 litres (100 gals) of kerosene. He had clothing, footwear, and ammunition for two years. His expedition consisted of himself with three Inuit. His route at the beginning was northward along the channels and basins between Greenland and Ellesmere Island in Canada.

The supporting Inuit and sledges returned at intervals along the way as the loads were reduced. Koch and his companions and assistants rested and hunted for two weeks at Fort Conger, two small huts on Ellesmere Island, remnants of the Greely expedition of 1881–83. All the supporting Inuit turned back at 82° N on the Greenland shore near the northern end of Robeson Channel. Koch then went on with Nookapingwah, Etukussuk, and Inuiterk, three sledges, and thirty-two dogs. They had bad travelling as far as Beaumont Ø, but then conditions improved and on May 5 they passed the farthest point Knud Rasmussen and Koch had reached in 1917. Koch and the Inuit reached Kap Morris Jesup, the northernmost point of Greenland first reached by Peary in 1900, on May 13, where they examined Peary's cairn on the cape but found no record. Here is a small mystery. Peary's cairn had been visited in 1909 by Donald MacMillan, George Borup, and five Inuit, members of Peary's final Arctic expedition. MacMillan wrote that the cairn contained Peary's record and a self-registering thermometer. MacMillan (1934:225–26) made an effort to preserve the record's container from corrosion "and possibly prolong its preservation for a number of years." He also carefully replaced the thermometer "to await the explorer in the future." Nearby, MacMillan wrote, he and Borup built another cairn and in it placed their own record, including a note on the tidal observations they had made there. Kap Morris Jesup and the two cairns remained unvisited until Lauge Koch arrived there twelve years later. But Koch mentioned only one cairn and found neither the records nor the thermometer. Whose cairn did he find, and what happened to the records of Peary and MacMillan?

Koch sent two Inuit off to hunt and lay in supplies, while he and one companion continued the survey of the north coast. Koch a day or so later rejoined his hunting Inuit, who had seen no muskoxen (even though Peary had found them while travelling along that coast in 1900), but had shot one wolf. The dogs were now beginning to suffer from hunger. Lauge Koch arrived at Kap Bridgman on May 21, and there they found the cairn built by his uncle, J.P. Koch, in 1907. This completed the preliminary survey of the last remaining part of the Greenland coast. Since passing Kap Morris Jesup Lauge, Koch and his companions had travelled in a snowstorm and in fog that lasted for almost two weeks. They passed by Frederick E. Hyde Fjord and B.C. Schley Fjord, but were unable to explore or survey them because of the thick fog. Hunting had been poor and the last of their pemmican was eaten. Dogs began to collapse, some had to be shot – half of them were lost at this time – and the men helped to haul the sledges. Men and dogs were exhausted when the sun finally burned away the fog, and at a distance Inuiterk saw nine muskoxen. The fog again rolled in from the sea, but they decided to track the animals without waiting for clear weather. Twenty-four hours after they were first seen, Etukussuk found and shot the muskoxen. Koch wrote (1926:87): "At one stroke our situation had changed. The successful hunt had saved the dogs and with that the life of the expedition. We had lost sixteen dogs, but we had sixteen left whose lives we were certain to save." The Inuit – "one half naked and smeared with blood" (Koch 1923:107) – celebrated with an ancient tribal hunting ritual.

While the dogs rested and fed, Koch examined the area for fossils. He found a great many, and Nookapingwah, after hunting inland, returned to camp with a handful of fossils "which I immediately saw originated from the carboniferous. I was very surprised that carboniferous fossils occurred in this place" (Koch 1926:87).

They passed around the eastern end of Peary Land and then entered Independence Fjord on June 1 just as the snow began to melt under the twenty-four-hour sunlight. Even with the softening snow, travelling conditions remained good to excellent. They were now on the south shore of Peary Land, and here the coastline changed from the low, clay foreland they had followed from Kap Bridgman to vertical cliffs rising 400 m (1,300 ft) from the sea. Seals appeared on the ice and wolves became quite common. Apparently the wolves were well fed; they took no notice of the travellers. Summer had arrived in Peary Land, and one day they saw ringed plovers, arctic gulls, brant geese, ptarmigans, a snowy owl, and snow buntings. On June 9, Koch and his companions entered Jørgen Brønlund Fjord, known to them to be rich in game from the report of Knud Rasmussen's expedition of 1912, and Koch paused to hunt seals and fatten the sixteen remaining dogs. While two Inuit hunted, Koch and Etukussuk travelled on to the head of Independence Fjord and found the farthest cairn and a well-preserved report of Mylius-Erichsen. On their return to Jørgen Brønlund Fjord they climbed to the highest point in the vicinity to complete the survey of Independence Fjord. Koch wrote (1923:108):

> All Peary Land was laid bare before us like an enormous map. To the north high torn mountains with numerous glaciers, the highest peaks hidden in clouds; to the south big inviting valleys; and to the west the big lake in an enormous canyon, surrounded by ragged hill-slopes.
>
> Far into the country the canyon turned northwards and vanished from our sight. Like a flash it struck me: This is the Peary

Muskoxen in northernmost Greenland
Courtesy Arctic Institute, Denmark.

Channel. This must be the great depression seen by Peary from the ice-cap twenty-eight years ago.

From his later observations from the ice sheet, Koch was persuaded of the correctness of this conclusion. "Peary thus was fully justified in believing that this depression meant a channel, and it is most admirable to see the approximate correctness with which he indicates its course" (Koch 1923:108). Koch named the depression the Wandel Dal. The polar historian J. Gordon Hayes pointed out, however, that Peary mapped his channel in quite a different position from that of Koch's Wandel Dal. Wandel Dal is located north of Heilprin Land and Adam Biering Land, but Peary mapped his channel as south of Heilprin Land. Further, Peary mapped the channel as entering Independence "Bay" immediately north of Navy Klippe and Academy Gletscher. Wandel Dal drains into Jørgen Brønlund Fjord, which joins Independence Fjord almost 65 km (40 mi) northeast of Navy Klippe. Hayes (1934:185) characterized Koch's identification of Wandel Dal as Peary Channel as "a gallant attempt to champion a lost cause."

On Midsummer's Eve, Koch and the Inuit began their ascent of Academy Gletscher, by which they would reach the inland ice where lay the route for their return to the west coast. The approaches to the glacier were obstructed by huge pressures ridges in the sea ice; the glacier had squeezed the sea ice against the land. And the land was impassable. "On one side we had almost vertical sandstone mountains about 1,000 meters [3,300 ft] high, in front of which there lay large sharp-edges blocks, on the other side the very crevassed glacier formed a high wall" (Koch 1926:107).

And further, Koch wrote (1923:108), "The condition of the glacier was far from favourable. Creeks and rivulets crossed our course, and several times we had to hoist our sledges over vertical ice-fronts or over steep hill-slopes where beautiful cascades splashed down. In crossing lakes we had to use the [seal-skin] floats which we carried for the purpose, and with our skis and snow-shoes we paddled across."

They enjoyed calm and clear weather on their ascent of the glacier, and halfway up they decided to take a day or so of rest while Koch surveyed the glacier. On June 29 they reached the edge of Vildtland, which, from Rasmussen's experience, offered the hope of muskoxen.

They spent over two weeks hunting on the open ground of Vildtland at the top of the glacier and at the edge of the ice cap, but with little luck; they shot many hares but only one muskox. They began their crossing of the inland ice on July 18 with the minimum of food. "Our nourishment consisted of raw frozen hares and coffee 'sweetened' with tooth-paste" (Koch 1923:109). It was a long, difficult, and hungry journey homeward. A food cache that they hoped to find on Warming Land had not been laid because of an epidemic among the Inuit. Their dogs were reduced from ten to four. The next depot was 300 km (186 mi) away. They got among crevasses. When the men and the few remaining dogs were exhausted and starved a strong gale with a following wind saved them. They sailed their sledge the last 48 km (30 mi) to their next depot at Kap Forbes on Washington Land. Shortly after, they met Inuit hunting in the area who restored them with fresh food. There they remained for three weeks before travelling the last 484 km (300 mi) to Robertson Fjord. Two hundred days after they began their journey they returned on October 2 to Koch's base. He brought back four thousand Cambrian, Ordivician, and Silurian fossils. Lauge Koch had completed his work and all had returned safely from a very arduous but productive journey.

MIKKELSEN AND THE FOUNDING OF SCORESBYSUND, 1924

Following his return from his search for the records of Mylius-Erichsen, Ejnar Mikkelsen began work on a plan to transfer some East Greenlanders from the Ammassalik region, where animal resources were no longer sufficient to support the growing population, to the Scoresby Sund region. A treaty between Denmark and Norway on the rights of the hunters of the two countries in East Greenland provided that hunting territories in the vicinity of permanent Greenlandic settlements would be reserved exclusively for Inuit. Mikkelsen believed that the establishment of a new settlement "as far north as possible" was imperative if the hunting options for indigenous people were to be preserved.

The Danish government was reluctant to initiate a new settlement. The government had always had to subsidize the costs of its Greenland colonies, and it apparently felt that the remote Scoresby Sund location would entail great expenses unlikely to be offset by possible revenues from local products. Mikkelsen, working with the Scoresby Sund Committee, a private group supported by public subscriptions and the *Ferslew Press Syndicate*, undertook the experiment in colonization.

On July 10, 1924, the wooden steam-powered barkentine *Grønland* left Copenhagen for Greenland. It carried the materials necessary to build a settlement on the shore of Scoresby Sund and for the support of a dozen Inuit families for three to four years. It also carried the supplies for twenty-two men for sixteen months in case the vessel should be caught in the ice. They loaded fuel and four ponies at Iceland, the ponies to carry the loads on shore. Fine weather in the North Atlantic favoured the heavily laden vessel. The ship met pack ice when they were in view of the mountains of Greenland. *Grønland* reached open coastal water only twenty-two hours later, in contrast to the thirty-three days that it had taken Lieutenant Ryder to cross the ice belt, and Mikkelsen entered Scoresby Sund fourteen days after leaving Copenhagen.

The ice had not yet broken up within Scoresby Sund, but stretched fast and solid from the north shore across to the south shore. The ship entered a small bight between the fast ice and Kap Tobin. Rapidly moving pack ice squeezed the ship against the ice edge, came in hard against the stern, and threw *Grønland* on her beam ends. With a sharp crack of the ice, the pressure relaxed and the ship arose again, but the ice pressure had destroyed the rudder and rudderpost. In spite of the damage the ship was saved, and the crew was able to secure it in a protected refuge next to the land.

Mikkelsen had expected to use the ship, now crippled, to explore for the best settlement sites in the great fjord region. Now he found that within walking distance of their anchorage-in-distress was perhaps just the situation he had hoped for. Numerous ruined huts, tent rings, and stone fox traps showed that in ancient times people had lived there in great numbers. Nearby was an excellent harbour – they called it Amdrups Havn – with a broad level plateau for the settlement, protected by mountains from north winds and open to the sun in the south. Upland lakes fed by glaciers provided a river that ran through the plateau and could never run dry. "I decided to establish the center of the settlement here" Mikkelsen wrote (1927:216), "and in all my later travels along the coast of Scoresby

Sund, I never saw a more likely spot." The ship could be tied up alongside the shore. The cargo was unloaded along a gangway directly to the land.

On their approach to Scoresby Sund, they had found "immense" numbers of seabirds, seals wherever they went, bears along the edge of the ice, and schools of narwhals – a very rich community of animal life of the sea. And as Mikkelsen took the motor launch to look for additional house sites along the shores of the sound, he found large numbers of walrus wherever he went and many bears and seals and large flocks of geese and ducks. Mikkelsen (1927:216) called Kap Stewart a "splendid, fertile spot with grass waving in the gentle breeze, butterflies flitting from flower to flower, and bees humming as at home on a warm summer day. Even a beehive, small, but filled with delicious honey, was found." Heather covers very large areas, as do blueberries, dwarf birch, and willow. The botanist found over ninety species of flowers, including potentillas, saxifrages, and arctic poppies. Grasses 30 cm (12 in) high were abundant. Not surprisingly, Mikkelsen found large numbers of muskoxen while returning to the ship. The geologist found coal seams at Kap Stewart and later at Kap Hope.

The reconnaissance found a number of dispersed sites suitable for houses. Then began the business of towing barges, heavily laden with building materials, to the sites between large ice floes that were swept back and forth by the strong currents. Materials for four houses were delivered to Kap Stewart, for two houses to Kap Hope, and for two to Kap Tobin. At the same time, construction proceeded with the houses and warehouse at Amdrups Havn.

By now it was early September and snow fell. "The leaves of the willow turned yellow, the birch deep red – a splendid sight but a warning" (Mikkelsen 1927:220). Seven men were to remain for the winter to complete the buildings at Amdrups Havn and to construct houses at the other sites. The rudderless ship only awaited a favouring gale to open the close-packed ice beyond the sound.

"The gale came – a howling norther: now or never we had to try the most hazardous task I had ever undertaken." Mikkelsen, a licensed sea captain, wrote (1927:220–21):

GRØNLAND IN
AMDRUPS HAVN,
SCORESBY SUND, 1924

COURTESY ARCTIC
INSTITUTE,
DENMARK.

Conditions were about as bad as they could possibly be. The new ice was thick. Of steering gear we had none except a large oar on our quarterdeck, by means of which we hoped to be able to control our vessel in open water; but it had never been tried, and in pack ice it would of course be absolutely useless. We went slowly, as in the beginning we had to steer our vessel exclusively by means of the propeller, and it took six hours to reach Kap Tobin, where in a large channel of open water we proved our 30-foot [9 m] oar useless and let it slip overboard.

They were soon caught in the ice and held for three days. Finally a narrow channel opened. By judiciously ramming the ice they managed to steer a course, bouncing the bow one way or the other, assisted by the crew jumping onto the ice and checking the vessel around by means of a long line attached to the jib-boom. During one day over eight hundred manoeuvres were recorded in the engine room log. Nine days after leaving Amdrups Havn they reached open water and steered their way with sails alone southward in a gale. In a port in northern Iceland they rigged a crude jury rudder – good for fair weather only. The vessel made a port in Norway by good luck, and there Mikkelsen hired a tug to tow the ship to Denmark.

The wintering party at Scoresbysund received their first visitors in the next year, 1925, when the French explorer Doctor Jean Charcot arrived on August 1 on *Pourquoi-Pas?*. He found that the Danish geologist, Bierring Petersen, had died during the spring, but the other six Danes had completed the construction of all the buildings, including the eight dispersed on the building sites at the three capes. During the winter they had discovered warm springs of 62° C (144° F) on Kap Tobin, the overflow of one of which kept open water even in winter along the shore. Here were found seals and walrus, bears and foxes, and numberless birds in early spring.

Ejnar Mikkelsen arrived again at Amdrups Havn on September 2, 1925, on the repaired *Grønland*, now renamed *Gustav Holm*. On board were ninety colonists, young and old, from Ammassalik. "They lost no time in getting their large umiaks into the water and to shore where they ran about, shouting, laughing, rolling themselves in the luxuriant grass, taking possession of the land.... The daily routine had begun, and the settlement was transferred to the representative of the Danish government: our work was done" (Mikkelsen 1927:223).

Mikkelsen visited the Scoresbysund settlement once again in 1926 as a guest of Doctor Charcot on board *Pourquoi-Pas?*. The first year of colonization had been darkened by four adult deaths from influenza, an infection brought from Ammassalik the previous year, but the illness had long passed by the time the ship arrived. The colony manager, Johan Petersen, the West Greenlander who had been interpreter with Gustav Holm and with Lieutenant Ryder's expedition to Scoresby Sund, was enthusiastic over the future of the new colony and reported that salmon, trout, arctic cod, halibut, and angmagssat (capelin) swarmed in the waters. The Inuit had discovered huge rookeries that promised an unlimited supply of birds and eggs. Even in winter open water was found close by Kap Tobin and not far from Kap Hope and Kap Stewart, and there good hunting was possible. Johan Petersen recommended that the government send one hundred more settlers from the west coast of Greenland to Scoresby Sund. Thus was established the second settlement of recent times on the east coast of Greenland.

Settlers at
Kap Tobin,
Scoresby
Sund, 1925

Courtesy
Arctic
Institute,
Denmark.

KAYAKERS AT SCORESBYSUND, 1925
COURTESY ARCTIC INSTITUTE, DENMARK.

International Interest 3

WORDIE AND THE FIRST PROBES INLAND, 1926

After World War I, Oxford and Cambridge Universities began a series of expeditions to the sub-Arctic and Arctic regions. They were usually but not always summer ventures. James Wordie, a geologist at Cambridge, had been with Sir Ernest Shackleton in the Antarctic in 1914–16, had drifted on the pack ice after Shackleton's ship *Endurance* had been crushed in the ice, and had survived a winter on desolate Elephant Island. In 1923 Wordie tried to reach East Greenland but failed, when within clear visibility of the Greenland coast, because of very adverse ice conditions. His ship had passed into a region of "extremely heavy" ice floes. When pressure began, the ship was lifted bodily onto the ice. "It was a position of considerable danger," wrote Wordie (1927:248), who from his *Endurance* experience would know. The vessel was released later when the pressure relaxed. His further efforts to reach the coast that season were unsuccessful.

Wordie tried again in 1926 on the Norwegian vessel *Heimland* with a crew of ten and a scientific party of eight – Wordie as geologist, two surveyors, an archaeologist, a radio expert, and three assistants. *Heimland* entered the pack ice on July 8 and found a way through without much difficulty, but was forced to lay to in the ice three times because of very dense fog. The ship reached open water on July 11, and it then steamed across 65 km (40 mi) of "land," or open, water, a remarkably wide stretch of ice-free open water along the shore. When the fog lifted, Wordie's party found themselves on the south shore of Lille Pendulum, about 74°36' N. They were a bit early, in the middle of July, for the ice to clear from the great fjords, so they began pendulum observations at Sabine Ø on the site at which Captain Edward Sabine had made the same observations in 1823 and Captain Karl Koldewey in 1869. These observations, requiring many swings of the pendulum over hours and days, were to determine the force of gravity and from that the actual shape of the Earth.

Sabine Ø is almost exclusively of volcanic origin, and thick masses of volcanic ash are found on the mountain called Hasenberg by Captain Koldewey. Wordie's party found fossil tree trunks within the ash; the trees had the appearance of having been charred and scorched. They speculated that hot ashes had descended on and destroyed the Tertiary forest. Wordie (1927:229) wrote: "The presence of these trees is but one more instance of the temperate conditions and rich vegetation in the Arctic in the older geological periods. Today the vegetation is barren in the extreme.... Later we were to find a more luxuriant growth on the mainland; here, however, the but slightly weathered volcanic *debris* had served to drain away all moisture, and the opportunities of plant growth were extremely meagre."

While the pendulum observations were underway, the ship voyaged through Clavering Strædet. On an excursion ashore, Augustine Courtauld found a note left by Doctor Copeland from the Koldewey expedition on the same day of the month, July, fifty-six years earlier. Wordie's party visited the hut and cache on Bass Rock at which Ejnar Mikkelsen and Iver Iversen had spent the spring of 1912, and then returned to Sabine Ø to rejoin the two physicists making the pendulum observations. The observations had been barely completed when the scientists, sheltering in an old Danish hut, were struck by a violent wind: "[T]he wind blew incessantly with gale force or more for seventy hours," wrote Gordon Manley (Wordie 1927:263), "and then dropped suddenly when, much to our delight, the ship arrived.... We decided that the party on the ship were not going to be heroes rescuing marooned members of the expedition, so we welcomed them very quietly, and when they came into the hut, much to their astonishment, we made them all sit down, after wiping their feet [the physicists had passed the time during the gale in cleaning the 'appallingly dirty' hut], and gave them afternoon tea!" Manley (Wordie 1927:263–64) observed that

> the storm was remarkable for the way in which it arose and
> blew for nearly four days incessantly with either rain or sleet;

sometimes with snow driven hard from the northeast. Apparently such storms are typical of the northeast coast of Greenland in that latitude, but farther south the weather is much more unsettled in the ordinary way, subject to the prevailing Icelandic depression. Farther north the weather is prevailingly fine except for these remarkable storms.

Heimland then steamed south around Clavering Ø. The region had been surveyed by Clavering on the south in 1823 and on the north by Koldewey in 1870, but on the west side of Clavering Ø, where the two earlier surveys did not quite meet, Wordie's party found a new fjord, Granta Fjord, leading off to the west. "It proved a region of great beauty, the mountains in the outer part descending steeply to the shores of the fjord, but receding again near the head to form a wide terraced valley which led due west to the great Jordanhill Glacier" (Wordie 1927:231). While Wordie was investigating the inner waters around Clavering Ø, the surveyors were mapping Loch Fine, discovered by Clavering. The archaeologists, D. McI. Johnson and his assistant J.H. Bell, meanwhile, were plotting where tent rings and winter house were found and where they were not found. They were in fact extending farther south the archaeological investigations of the Danmark Expedition, and excavated sites reported by Scoresby, Koldewey, and Nathorst. Clavering Ø was rich in sites but Granta Fjord and Loch Fine were not. Johnson and Bell found "huts of apparently all gradations of age ... from recent ones in good condition to the very old ones." "Tent rings were commonly found in groups of thirty or forty," and were particularly numerous on Hvalros Ø and on Bass Rock. They found a kind of structure not previously described. These usually occurred in pairs, took the form of a mosaic of carefully laid stones, and resembled the floor plan of a conventional winter house, but they were rather small, measuring only about 1.8 m (6 ft) long and about 1.4 m (4.5 ft) wide in front, where there appeared to be an entry, and barely 0.9 m (3 ft) wide in back. Their significance remained doubtful to the archaeologist. The artefacts found apparently contained no surprises, with the exception of three harpoon heads fitted with rough *iron* blades. The archaeologists did not speculate on the source of the iron. Johnson surmised from the evidence that the Inuit had arrived in the region from a single migration from the north around Greenland, apparently the last of several southward migrations as indicated by earlier Danish conclusions from the Danmark Expedition.

By early August ice had cleared from Kejser Franz Joseph Fjord, Wordie's principal objective, and *Heimland* was able to enter. Wordie's party was only the third to enter the great fjord, preceded by its discoverer Koldewey in 1870 and by Nathorst in 1899. Wordie the geologist noted (1927:232) that this great fjord system did not appear to be the consequence of any breaks in rock types or planes of weakness: "It cuts across Tertiary lavas, Devonian sandstones, Silurian limestones and Archaean gneisses and schists entirely unaffected by the changes of rock types.... Examination ... rather suggests a system of drowned valleys, but not of tectonic origin." In the inner reaches of the fjord, over 160 km (100 mi) from the sea, they enjoyed uninterrupted fine weather with abundant sunshine and surprisingly luxuriant vegetation. The same conditions were reported by Koldewey and by Nathorst, and they appear to be normal for the interior of the fjord. Arctic willow and birch grew 38–46 cm (15–18 in) high. Wordie found that the flora gave the region a softer tone and colour than one would expect in such high latitudes. The colour was limited only by the minimal precipitation.

Wordie's goal was an investigation of Petermanns Bjerg well inland from the head of Kejser Franz Joseph Fjord and first seen by Ralph Copeland and Julius Payer in 1870. They had called it a "monstrous pyramid of ice," and they estimated its height at 3,350 m (11,000 ft). It was thought in 1926 to be the highest mountain in Greenland. Wordie hoped for a possible ascent. He attempted an approach over Nordenskiöld Gletscher at the head of Kejser Franz Joseph Fjord, but the climbers quickly found that this was impractical. On August 5 Wordie's climbing party of six made another attempt from Kjerulfs Fjord. By the second day they had the peak clearly in view and estimated its height in excess of 3,050 m (10,000 ft), but found that to reach it would take more time than was available. It was at least 32 km (20 mi) from their camp, with two intervening ridges, each of 1,830 to 2,135 m (6,000 to 7,000 ft) in height. They climbed lower peaks and from them found "the view to the west of interest. There is here no ice-cap, as one would expect; mountains and valleys follow one another as far as the eye can see over a distance of probably 80 miles [130 km].... Perhaps someday these will attract the mountaineer, and if they do he will be well repaid for the difficulties and dangers of reaching his playground" (Wordie 1927:234). They left the inner reaches of the fjord with great regret.

The ship steamed into Moskusoksefjord to connect the expedition's survey in July of Loch Fine with Nathorst's map. In this region they found no shortage of game. "Musk oxen, for instance, though concentrated in certain more suitable localities, are on the whole extremely abundant." Here Wordie (1927:237) voiced a plea for their protection.

> Though we saw them in large numbers – between two and three hundred in all – we nevertheless felt certain that there is danger of their rapid extinction unless measures can be taken either to protect them altogether or at least to ensure that they are only killed for fresh meat. It is their misfortune never to have been hunted and to be extremely tame as far as man is concerned. The danger would not perhaps be so acute were it not that in recent years it had become profitable to sell young calves in Europe and America, and to capture two calves generally means the destruction of a herd of say fifteen adults. There are several records of sealing sloops from Denmark Straits, which have gone out of their way to visit East Greenland merely to round up a herd of musk oxen and capture the young ones. I hope therefore that the Danish Government, who have now the sovereignty in this part, will do all they can to safeguard this most interesting European mammal – an English native in Glacial times.

Wordie's party now passed south along the outer coasts of Geographical Society and Traill Øer, the maps of which were unchanged since Scoresby's and Clavering's time. In fact no exploring or mapping party, except for Lieutenant Ryder's in 1891 which was wrapped in heavy fog, had passed along that coast since Captain Clavering over one hundred years earlier. Wordie's surveyors fixed positions and corrected Scoresby's map of 1822. They found that what Scoresby, held by pack ice to a position well offshore, had plotted as capes were in fact high mountains standing well back from the coast. Wordie's coastal survey was brought to a close on August 22 by ice drifting from the northeast and the threat of a gale.

Lauge Koch
Courtesy Arctic Institute, Denmark.

Heimland passed down the coast of Liverpool Land in heavy rain, holding as close as possible to the land to look in vain for any signs of the lost crew of the Norwegian ship *Anni*. She was a small brigantine that had wintered at Myggbukta (Mosquito Bay), a Norwegian weather station, in 1922–23 and had left there on August 15, 1923. Her crew of seven men had not been heard from since. *Anni* was most likely crushed in the ice, but there was some hope that perhaps some of her crew had reached the land. No trace of the lost vessel or men was ever found.

At Amdrups Havn in Scoresby Sund Wordie found the Danish geologist Lauge Koch erecting his house as a base for geological studies northwards from Scoresby Sund, the beginning of thirty years of work by Koch in the fjord region of East Greenland.

Heimland left Scoresby Sund on August 23 and passed through the pack ice in four hours. They had rough weather and gales on the voyage to Iceland and Scotland and reached Aberdeen only on September 8.

KOCH BEGINS THIRTY YEARS OF RESEARCH, 1926–27

When James Wordie met him at Amdrups Havn in 1926, Lauge Koch was beginning a scientific program that continued over many years until 1958. After his return from northernmost Greenland and his circumnavigation of Peary Land, Koch had proposed to the Danish government a detailed geological investigation of the fjord region of East Greenland. He was accompanied by a Danish geologist, Alfred Rosenkrantz, a specialist in Mesozoic animal fossils, and by Thomas Harris, an English specialist in Mesozoic plant fossils. Koch also was accompanied by two West Greenlanders, Tobias Gabrielsen and Karl Mathiassen. Tobias Gabrielsen had been a member of Mylius-Erichsen's expedition of 1906–8. The two Greenlanders had brought forty dogs from West Greenland for the sledge journeys Koch had in mind. Lauge Koch had also brought a large motorboat and materials to build a winter house. In the autumn of the year and the following spring and summer Rosenkrantz and Harris made a detailed survey of Jameson Land and Hurry Fjord from the motorboat and by sledge. They brought home eight tons of fossils. Among them were skulls and incomplete skeletons of small amphibians called *stegocephalians*.

The fossils were the first to prove the existence of land animals perhaps as old as the late Devonian period about 350–400 million years ago.

By the latter part of October ice formation allowed Koch to begin the first of the two long journeys of the expedition. He had several objectives for the journeys. The first was a geological investigation of the coast as far north as Danmarkshavn. Koch's investigation would be made easier by Nathorst's earlier geological reconnaissance and mapping and by the topographical mapping of Wordie's expedition in the summer of 1926. Wordie gave Koch a copy of the map Wordie's expedition had constructed. In addition to the scientific work, Koch planned to visit government-owned houses – really hunting camps – along the coast. There were eight between Kejser Franz Joseph Fjord and Danmarkshavn. If the camps were not inspected every five years the government of Denmark would lose possession under a 1923 agreement with the East Greenland Company, which had built them and later transferred them to the state.

The Danish East Greenland Company had been established in 1919 with subsidies from the Danish government. It was in part an indirect result of the Danmark Expedition of 1906–8 on which its principal founder, Hans Jensen, had participated. The company's business was fur trapping. In 1919, 1920, and 1921 wintering trappers worked from a number of stations between Danmarkshavn and Clavering Ø. In 1920 the schooner *Dagny* was crushed in the ice while trying to relieve the two northernmost stations. Two of the seven men at those stations died, and only five, suffering greatly from scurvy, managed the 260-km (161-mi) journey from Danmarkshavn to Sabine Ø in the spring of 1921. In 1923, the schooner *Teddy*, after relieving company stations, was crushed in the ice. Its crew, drifting on the ice, managed with great difficulty to reach Ammassalik. In 1923, also, *Anni* was lost without a trace. In 1924 the East Greenland Company was dissolved, its hunters were recalled from Greenland, and its eight stations were given to the government. It was Lauge Koch's job to inspect them.

Koch's third task was to estimate the "carrying capacity," the game conditions, of the land for possible settlement by Inuit from the southern coast.

Koch planned to travel in the autumn as far as the Norwegian radio station at Myggbukta on Hold with Hope which broadcast daily weather reports to Europe, the first such station established in Greenland. Myg-gbukta is about 334 km (207 mi) north of Scoresby Sund. Koch's autumn journey would be the first sledge journey along this route of which there is any record. It was viewed as a reconnaissance in preparation for a longer spring journey to Danmarkshavn.

Autumn sledge journeys can be difficult and discouraging. By the time the sea ice freezes enough to support travel, the days are short and rapidly getting shorter. Travel must begin each day before the sun can give much light and it may continue well after dark. The travelling party may then find itself stumbling in darkness through deep snow and over rough ice. Wind and snowstorms become more frequent and more violent, and the temperatures are steadily decreasing as the sun becomes lower and the darkness increases. One can look forward on autumn journeys only to ever darker, colder, and more difficult conditions.

Koch chose to travel north across Jameson Land via Hurry Fjord be-cause ice along the outer coast of Liverpool Land was undependable and intersected with open water. The journey across Jameson Land went well, but farther north as far as Kejser Franz Joseph Fjord the route was "ex-tremely difficult" because in the previous summer drift ice had been blown into all the north-facing fjords, making a very rough surface; "deep snow between the pressure ridges made sledging very irksome" (Koch 1928:5). Koch and his Greenlanders started with only ten days' provisions, expect-ing to hunt game along the way and to live off the land as Koch had done in North Greenland. They found no game at all as far as Davy Sund, about 177 km (110 mi) from their base. They were forced to consider returning, a bitter disappointment to Koch, but just as he gave the order to turn back they came upon ptarmigan and a muskox, and the next morning a bear came into their camp. In twenty-four hours they saw seven bears and killed three. Their journey was saved. They reached the Norwegian station at Myggbukta on November 8, twelve days after leaving Scoresby Sund, and remained there three days, hunting and geologizing in the vicinity.

One day while returning south from Myggbukta through Kejser Franz Joseph Fjord, Koch was collecting fossils on a mountain.

I went unarmed as I usually did when in North Greenland. Instinctively I felt I was being followed, but it was not until I was on my way back, and about 4 kilometers [2.5 m] from the camp, that I discovered that four[1] wolves were in pursuit of me. We reached the camp simultaneously. One of the Eskimo immediately shot one wolf, whereupon the others fled.... It was my tenth journey by sledge, so I ought to have known better than to walk about unarmed (Koch 1928:6).

But that did not end the events of the day. Koch and Karl Mathiassen

> drove towards the interior of the fjord. We had not travelled far when we sighted two bears that fled up on to a high iceberg, which we had to ascend to kill them. This iceberg was very large and extraordinarily beautiful. At the very moment we fired our guns, the sun shone on the highest mountain peaks, which lent to this large fjord a wonderful and impressive grandeur. Shortly afterwards Tobias arrived, we got the bears down the berg, loaded them on the sledges, and drove in to the shore to get the wolf and the bears skinned. About a hundred musk-oxen, which stood in silhouette against the flame-coloured evening sky, watched us with interest. In the afternoon I searched in vain for fossils (Koch 1930:249).

They arrived back at their base at Scoresbysund very late on November 23.

Koch had hoped to do some local travelling within Scoresby Sound during the winter, but "owing to weather conditions all such plans would have to be abandoned. Throughout the winter there was open water in the mouth of Scoresby Sound, and ice conditions were very varying, the open water at times extending even as far as ... Cape Stewart. The weather was mild, but extremely unsettled, and continuous storms and extraordinarily heavy snowfalls prevented longer journeys" (Koch 1930:253).

Lauge Koch began his second long journey with his two West Greenlanders, a Scoresbysund resident, and forty dogs on February 22, 1927. They started in deep snow, which they encountered throughout the

---

1 Koch says "three" wolves in Koch 1930. We may assume this is correct since this is a more detailed and "official" report.

journey all the way to Danmarkshavn, a distance of about 705 km (437 mi). Koch wrote (1928:6): "The words 'deep snow' might serve as a diary of the whole journey." Of conditions off Traill Ø, Koch wrote (1930:257): "All day we worked our way through the very soft snow, which in places was one and a half meters [5 ft] deep and with water underneath. When we made a halt, we had to cling to the sledges to avoid sinking waist-deep into the snow.... It was very exhausting for men and dogs, we advanced but slowly." Because of the difficult travelling, Koch had to pass a number of fjords he had hoped to enter and examine.

The weather in February had been "very unfavourable," but in early March, Koch wrote, "day after day was fine and calm." They travelled along the outer coast, that is, on the east side of Traill Ø, Geographical Society Ø, and Ymer Ø . Polar bear dens were frequently seen and they were usually inhabited by a female with a one-year-old cub. "The den is generally very small, there is only room enough for the bears to lie close to each other. The bear seems to stay in the den from the first days of December till the sun again appears. In the first part of February the bear makes short strolls in the neighbourhood, and in the last days of February or the first days of March the den is definitely left" (Koch 1930:256).

"We had expected to encounter high pressure-ridges opposite Traill Island and Geographical Society Island, but it turned out otherwise, the ice being quite smooth but covered with immense quantities of snow – often more than 1 meter deep and with water underneath" (Koch 1928:7). They reached the Norwegian station at Myggbukta on March 6 and stayed there to rest the dogs until the 10th. In the meantime the Greenlanders killed some muskoxen, which were numerous in the vicinity. The journey north from Myggbukta was frequently interrupted by blizzards, once for four days, as they travelled from cabin to cabin of the East Greenland Company. During the latter half of March the storm blew almost continuously. The house at Kap Borlase Warren was almost buried in snow and the roof had been torn off. Open water off Wollaston Forland prevented travel on sea ice along the outer coast, so they had to find a route inland across the forland. Fine weather returned in April. Their forty dogs consumed quantities of food, but hunting was good and they frequently found muskoxen or bears. One day on Hochstetter Forland Koch counted three hundred muskoxen. They arrived at Mylius-Erichsen's expedition house at Danmarkshavn on April 8. The house itself was completely buried in snow and they remained for less than a day. On their return, while storm-bound, they found a coal seam known to Tobias Gabrielsen from the 1906 expedition. The coal burned "extremely well" and soon they had a roaring fire in a cave, dried their clothes, warmed themselves, and cooked meat for several days. On the journey south they often encountered stormy weather until they reached Clavering Ø, but Koch was able to investigate the geology of a number of fjords and islands, and he made interesting collections of fossils at numerous locations along the journey. They saw three very large herds of muskoxen in one day on Hold With Hope. In one week and all within 193 km (120 mi) near Ymer Ø and south of Ella Ø – a "polar bear pathway" – they found forty polar bears. Koch examined the geology of Moskusoksefjord, Geologfjord, and Antarctic Sund. At Ella Ø he found numerous fossils. "This was a great surprise. It soon proved that it was a very important find I had made, since I could identify the fossils as Lower Cambrian trilobites, which had not hitherto been known from East Greenland" (Koch 1930:273). Koch went on to survey the geology of Geographical Society Ø, Sofia Sund, Ella Sund, Kempes Fjord, and Segelsällskapet Fjord.

Along the Liverpool Coast, about 113 km (70 mi) long, Koch and his Greenlanders found the travelling unexpectedly good. He wrote (1928:9) "this coast … with its alps attaining heights of some 2,000 meters [6560 ft], represents some of the most beautiful landscapes in Greenland." And there they had a curious experience.

> During the three days the journey lasted it was if the air was filled with millions of invisible larks singing constantly day and night. Naturally it was not larks, but small alp-birds, the sea kings [Little Auks], that hatch in millions on these cliffs. They were flying in great flocks toward the open water to search for food, but so high up in the air that the eye could not distinguish them; we could only hear their twitter. These twitterings are doubly thrilling here in the otherwise so silent Polar regions (Koch 1928:9).

They arrived back at Scoresbysund on June 1. "I must ... admit that the dogs as well as we ourselves were more exhausted than we knew; the hard work of travelling through the deep snow had set its mark on all of us." The Danish government vessel *Gustav Holm* anchored at Scoresbysund early in August 1927, and Koch's expedition returned to Copenhagen on August 20.

KOCH AND THE END OF RECONNAISSANCE, 1929, 1930

Lauge Koch had accomplished a reconnaissance of the geological structure of the east coast of Greenland from Scoresby Sund to Danmarkshavn in 1926–27. In 1929 he began a series of investigations to fill in the details. While previously he had worked alone or with just one or two colleagues, in 1929 he organized an expedition composed of seven geologists and a botanist who would operate to a considerable degree independently although under the general direction of Koch. Their field of investigations would be that surveyed by Koch in 1926–27 from Clavering Ø to Davy Sund.

The expedition was privately funded by a few Danish individuals living in England and by the Carlsberg and the Rask-Orsted Foundations. When Koch had those funds in hand, the Danish government lent the steam-powered barkentine *Godthaab* and the captain of *Godthaab* with fourteen officers and crew members. There were three "first class" motorboats and a number of smaller boats. *Godthaab* was provisioned with food, clothing, and equipment for wintering if the ship should be unable to leave Greenland in the autumn. There were enough camping supplies so that five field camps could be established simultaneously. Altogether, this was a far more expensive, larger, and more complex operation than Koch had previously undertaken. It initiated the series of large and complex Danish investigations that would characterize the 1930s.

Godthaab left Copenhagen on June 16 and after taking on coal in Iceland met the pack ice of East Greenland on July 1. The pack was dense and the ship proceeded only very slowly. They were icebound for thirteen days. *Godthaab* broke into open water along the coast on July 20 and proceeded to Clavering Ø, where all members went ashore. They spent several days in the vicinity of Kap Mary; ice prevented them from moving freely in the bay. Within a few days they found "a number of extremely well preserved Triassic fish remains" (Koch 1930:183). Ice then allowed the ship to steam into and anchor in Young Sund on the north side of Clavering Ø. There they met Norwegian hunters, and there Koch landed independent geological parties for several days. Koch wrote (1930:185) that "everywhere along the coast we encountered large flocks of geese." They enjoyed the fine, clear weather so often found in this part of the coast. Two Norwegian sealing vessels arrived and visited them. The Norwegians were on their way to hunt muskoxen in Loch Fine; James Wordie's warning about the threat to muskoxen had not yet been acted upon by the Danish government.

By midnight on July 26 all the geological parties were back on board *Godthaab*, and Koch directed the ship to the south side of Gael Hamkes Bugt for an investigation of the vicinity of Loch Fine. Again, Koch landed several scientific teams, and after two days one team returned to the ship with a large collection of fossils.

August 1 was a day of strong winds and rain. A motorboat took a geologist, Helge Backlund, and the botanist, Gunnar Seidenfaden, to the head of Loch Fine with the plan that they would walk overland to Moskusoksefjord, where they would meet the ship. Delivering them to the head of the loch was "a very cold and exhausting journey." On August 3 and 4 the ship steamed around Kap Broer Ruys and into Kejser Franz Joseph Fjord. Koch landed several parties and the ship anchored in Duséns Fjord on Ymer Ø. They found the fjord to be much longer than expected. It had been thought to be about 21 km (13 mi) long; in fact, it is 56 km (35 mi) long. Koch carried out a careful survey of the fjord while geological parties worked in other areas. Duséns Fjord is rich in vegetation and with numerous hares and several herds of muskoxen.

The Norwegian vessel *Veslekari*, on a scientific expedition, was seen north of Duséns Fjord, but the crew refused to give any information about the program of the scientists, an indication of rising tension between Denmark and Norway over the political status of East Greenland.

In the meantime, the geologist Oskar Kulling had found "extremely well preserved placoderms [ancient and primitive fishes] in the Devonian beds" (Koch 1930:189). *Godthaab* steamed into Moskusoksefjord to meet

Backlund and Seidenfaden, who had walked across from Loch Fine. The ship then steamed south into Antarctic Sund, landing geologists on Ella Ø and Ymer Ø, and then returned to an anchorage in Moskusoksefjord to clean its boilers. While there, Koch and the captain had a chance to visit *Heimland*, which was waiting as James Wordie, on his third expedition to East Greenland, and his party were climbing Petermanns Bjerg. The geologist Arne Noe-Nygaard had found an extremely well preserved fossil of a placoderm in a large block that required several men to carry on board.

Godthaab then anchored 40 km (25 mi) farther in Geologfjord, and Koch took a motorboat toward its head. Very strong winds developed during the return, and they had a wet, cold trip returning to *Godthaab*. The ship returned to Ella Ø and again met *Heimland* with all Wordie's party on board.

Godthaab sailed down Kong Oscar Fjord, where several geological parties were landed in the vicinity of Segelsällskapets Fjord. Ice prevented sailing farther south in Kong Oscar Fjord. On August 26 they returned north to Kejser Franz Joseph Fjord, where they spent several days investigating a number of locations.

September arrived with thick fog. In the next two days the various geological parties were collected and brought on board. The ship passed out to the mouth of Kejser Franz Joseph Fjord and landed parties at Duséns Fjord and Sofia Sund for a day. A day or so later landings were again made, and from Duséns Fjord they brought back large fossil collections of Devonian fishes. The expedition's work was finally completed on September 7. All parties were brought on board in thick fog and the ship departed from Greenland.

The next day was marked by snow and gale-force north winds. The day after that, September 9, the ship was stopped by the pack ice. Snow, north winds, and thick weather prevailed for the next eight days while the ship drifted south in the pack ice. On September 17, when they could see open water, they were struck by winds of increasing violence, even hurricane force, and by a fierce blizzard. In the turmoil of heavy seas and ice floes *Godthaab* took many blows; the ship's stern hit thick ice and split the rudder. Lauge Koch wrote (1930:202):

The darkness and the driving snow made it impossible to distinguish anything but our nearest surroundings, and the deck was so slippery that we had to use the greatest caution when moving from one place to another. As the ice floes became more scattered, the movements of the ship increased in violence, and the ship was trembling all over when she almost incessantly charged into the floes with a loud crash.... For the first time since my long journeys on the inland ice in my youth, I realised that very likely we should not escape alive.

By midnight of September 18 they were out of the ice, and after an easy journey they arrived in Copenhagen on September 27. This expedition had supported the largest staff of geologists that had ever worked in the polar regions.

Lauge Koch's geological and mapping explorations continued in 1930, again with *Godthaab*. He was accompanied by a scientific staff of five – two geologists, a botanist and cartographer, an ornithologist, and a meteorologist. Their area of investigation was the nearly same as in 1929. *Godthaab* passed through the ice rather easily in three days, July 1–4, and, after riding to two anchors in the face of a northerly gale off Kap Borlase Warren, the vessel entered Young Sund on July 6. It stayed there, or nearby, for about a month. As in 1929, geological parties were landed for a few days at a time at various points in Young Sund and then in Gael Hamkes Bugt. The ship went into Kejser Franz Joseph Fjord and Moskusoksefjord; in both fjords scientific parties were landed. On August 16 they went through Sofia Sund, between Ymer and Geographical Society Øer in an attempt to sail down Kong Oscar Fjord to Nathorst Fjord. Ice stopped them after a short distance into Kong Oscar Fjord, and the ship had to return back through Sofia Sund. They turned south outside the islands to find that the ice made it impossible to approach the shore anywhere north of Scoresby Sund. There a three-day gale forced them out to sea, and so, the season being late, they sailed for Iceland, where the scientists took a steamer for Copenhagen.

WORDIE – CLIMBING THE PEAKS, 1929

James Wordie returned to East Greenland in 1929 with a party of nine, again on *Heimland*. They made two attempts to penetrate the pack ice, the first on July 8 at latitude 71°30' N. Near the edge of the ice they encountered enormous numbers of Little Auks in rapid flight from pool to pool, or standing or lying breast down on the ice floes.

> There was a continuous twittering from the birds in flight, a contrast to the general stillness felt in the ice. None of us had previously seen Little Auks in such numbers on the pack edge.... Early each morning they arrived in almost countless flocks flying out of the west; the day was spent among the open pools near the ice edge; in the evening the birds flew westwards again, appearing as clouds on the eastern horizon, then passing overhead, and vanishing towards the west.... Later the Liverpool Coast came in sight, and I remembered how Dr. Koch had once told me that that region is one vast rookery of Little Auks. For their summer feeding therefore it appears they must make the daily journey to and from the ice edge about 60 miles [95 km] away, keeping however to the same latitude as their nesting sites on the Liverpool Coast. Latitudes 70° and 71° might well be called the Auk Latitudes in contrast to the Bear Latitudes, as Norwegian hunters denote 73° and 74° (Wordie 1930:481–82).

A passage through the ice at 71°30' N proved impossible, so after five days they struggled out of the pack and headed north to 74°20' N to try again on July 15. Ten days of fine weather followed, a sign that the pack was close and tight; looser, more open ice is often accompanied by fog. The crew of *Heimland* resorted at times to dynamite and ice chisels to free the vessel and to make any sort of progress at all. At one point "great polar floes, of a thickness and age undreamt of in the Antarctic, formed as it were an almost immovable framework; between them small floes, of a size hardly possible to edge and push with our limited steam power, in effect acted as a cement" (Wordie 1930:483). The pack began to move on July 29 and it squeezed and lifted the ship. A few hours later she was refloated, but the next day ice pressure again lifted her and bent the rudder thirty degrees. A third nip held the ship until July 31. The ship was squeezed again on August 2, but then the ice began to open, and they anchored in Mackenzie Bugt on August 4. Lauge Koch's ship, *Godthaab*, had been held in the ice for thirteen days at this time.

Wordie's principal object, as it had been in 1926, was the ascent of Petermanns Bjerg, then believed to be the highest mountain in Greenland. Because the season was now late, they wasted little time getting to the head of Kejser Franz Joseph Fjord and entered its side branch, Kjerulfs Fjord, early on August 6. Late that evening the climbers had established their first camp at 915 m (3,800 ft) above Riddar Gletscher. *Heimland*, meanwhile, carried two geologists, W.F. Whittard and M.M.L. Parkinson, on a survey of pre-Devonian rocks from Davy Sund to Hold with Hope, from 72° to 74° N. The climbing party, R.C. Wakefield, A. Courtauld, V.E. Fuchs, J.F. Varley, V.S. Forbes, and Wordie, spent the next several days above 2,134 m (7,000 ft), working their way westward across glaciers, past high peaks, and along rocky ridges, mapping as they went. By August 15 they were within striking distance of their goal. With the weather deteriorating, Wordie realized that the attempt on the peak must be made then or not at all. By that evening they had reached within 30 m (100 ft) of the summit, but the morning breeze had become a very strong gale, and if inactive the climbers became bitterly cold. Near the summit they were fully exposed to the gale and were on ice-glazed rocks "where the climbing was much more difficult." They found the summit height to be 2,942 m (9,650 ft), and took a round of photographs, maintaining themselves against the gale of wind in semi-crouched positions. In spite of the cold blast, none suffered frostbite. Below them lay a panorama of glaciers and mountains stretching west to the inland ice sheet. Wordie's party continued to survey this inland area while on their return to Kjerulfs Fjord, where on August 18 they found *Heimland* waiting for them, twelve days after they began their exploration. Wordie and his party brought back the first map of very rough country stretching over 48 km (30 mi) inland from Kjerulfs Fjord, a substantial achievement for twelve days of a strenuous traverse over mountains and glaciers.

James Wordie planned to visit the Norwegian weather station Myg-gbukta in Mackenzie Bugt, but ice prevented an approach. They therefore left for home on August 25. There followed a five-day struggle with sea ice. At times the ship was unable to move at all. They reached Aberdeen on September 9.

WATKINS AND THE AIR AGE, 1930–31

The British Arctic Air Route Expedition to East Greenland in 1930–31 came about because of growing interest at that time in the possibility of trans-oceanic aircraft travel. Aircraft did not then have the range for non-stop ocean routes and would be dependent upon intermediate refuelling facilities. An air route between North America and Europe, and particularly Great Britain, via Iceland was of especial interest. The east coast of Greenland was the least known part of that route. H.G. Watkins (he was known as Gino) was the organizing spirit and leader of a privately funded expedition to learn more about that region and to locate a possible aircraft landing site. He had earlier led a summer expedition to Edgeøya in Svalbard and a winter expedition to Labrador. He was twenty-three years old when he set out for East Greenland.

The principal objectives were (1) meteorological observations for a year on the coast and near the height of the Greenland ice sheet, (2) a survey of heights of the ice sheet, and (3) mapping of the coast for 160 km (100 mi) or more north and south of the Ammassalik area. The original hope had been to map the coast from Ammassalik northward to Kap Dalton not too far south of Scoresby Sund, a distance of 705 km (437 mi).

Watkins led thirteen well-qualified men, and the expedition was equipped with two de Havilland Gipsy Moth aircraft with both skis and floats, the first airplanes to be used in East Greenland. Watkins chartered the Norwegian sealer *Quest* to carry the expedition to Greenland and to assist with coastal surveys.

The expedition was fortunate to find a suitable site for its base about 48 km (30 mi) west of Ammassalik with relatively easy access to the inland ice; such access is very rare along that very rugged coast. After the first party departed to establish the weather station on the inland ice sheet, Watkins and the rest of the expedition set off in *Quest*, with an airplane on board (with its wings folded), to begin the coastal mapping northward from the base. The plan was that *Quest* would lay supply caches as it steamed north. It would also serve as a base at suitable locations for the aircraft which would make aerial photographs of the coast to supplement the survey. At its northernmost point, the vessel would land the four surveyors in a small boat with an outboard motor. The surveyors would then make their way southward back to their base, making their observations as they went. The boat would partially duplicate the journey made by Amdrup in 1900.

Quest started from Ammassalik on August 13 in ideal weather. On board were several Inuit families with all their possessions and dogs who were returning north to their scattered winter houses after the trading season at Ammassalik. Hundreds of Kittiwakes flew up and down the coast and settled in crowds on ice floes. At one point five whales spouted close to the ship. The Inuit were soon landed, and on the 14th the ship entered Kangertigtvatsiaq at 66°20' N, where they found cairns built by Amdrup. Watkins began the survey there where the scenery was magnificent. A huge glacier entered the fjord and needle-peak mountains reached up 1,800–2,134 m (6–7,000 ft) above the water. Hanging glaciers balanced precariously on steep hillsides and other glaciers reached the sea. The surveyor Spencer Chapman wrote (1933:30): "At the head of the fjord, away in the distance, was a superb pinnacled mountain reminiscent of St. Paul's Cathedral; this was Ingolfs Fjeld." On a glacial moraine their Inuit pilot and guide showed them the edible plant *Angelica sylvestris* about 0.6 m (2 ft) high and, wrote Chapman (1933:31), "a much-prized delicacy, having a powerfully aromatic flavour which I found very pleasant. There were also masses of black crowberries ... growing here, which were very refreshing to eat though a trifle insipid in flavour."

After completing the survey of the fjord, the vessel steamed north and sheltered from bad weather in a fjord previously unknown to Europeans with a salmon lake at its head. They named it Lake Fjord. It was the best place they had yet seen for an air-route base. The lake provided an ice-free base for Watkins' aircraft for the two days of aerial photography that were then needed to keep the aerial mapping current with the survey on the ground. Watkins and the pilot N.H. D'Aeth, flying at 3,050 m (10,000 ft), took oblique photographs of 240 km (150 mi) of coast.

While waiting for clear weather so that the flights could get underway, the surveyors worked among the ice floes of the fjord, triangulating across from shore to shore. Chapman wrote (1933:33), "The ice was so thick, however, that we were very soon in difficulties." There they found how difficult it would be to work among heavy and drifting ice in a boat leaking badly from blows by the ice. On occasion they had to haul the 4.9-m (16-ft) boat out on the ice to avoid being crushed. Finding camping places on the steep shores was difficult. Cliffs of bare rock fell at a very steep angle 600–914 m (2–3,000 ft) to the sea. "Often we would have to cruise along for several hours before we could find a suitable camp-site. Sometimes our tents had to be pitched on a precarious ledge a hundred feet [30 m] above sea-level" (Chapman 1933:35). Chapman wrote (1933:36–37):

> Steenstrup's glacier projected ... into the sea, ending abruptly in great blue walls of ice two or three hundred feet high [60–90 m]. Here the whole surface of the sea was covered with small chunks of brash-ice varying in size from three-inch cubes to pieces the size of a football – as well as the actual floes, of course, which were still present. This brash-ice stretched as far as we could see.... At last we ran out into comparatively open water and soon saw the cause of our troubles. At the top of a projecting tongue of the glacier was a huge green cave in the ice, and pouring from it with a roar an intermittent stream of small pieces of ice which splashed into the water a few hundred feet below. Presently, as we watched, a piece of ice as big as a house crashed off the glacier, sending out waves which made our boat rock like a cork. Then to our joy, for it was a spectacle far beyond the description of words, the whole roof of the cave crumbled in and, with a shower of debris and powdered ice, poured into the sea.

The surveyors waited at Kap Gustav Holm, perched 60 m (200 ft) above the sea on the only available flat ledge, to be collected by *Quest* when the flying from the lake was completed. It was there that the geologist Lawrence Wager found the southernmost fossils in sedimentary rocks in East Greenland.

Thick and dense ice and bad weather slowed *Quest* on its way to Kang-erdlugssuaq, but the vessel reached its entrance on August 23 and on the 24th entered the fjord, which was full of ice, the first vessel ever to do so. *Quest* managed to reach the head of the fjord, about 74 km (46 mi) from the sea. They found numerous glaciers entering the fjord along the way, but the glacier at the head of the fjord surpassed all the others in size. It was 4.8 km (3 mi) miles wide at sea level and continued for 3.2 km (2 mi) as a floating tongue of ice into the fjord. Watkins left a food cache at the head of the fjord, the forty boxes well weighted with heavy rocks to protect them from bears. Then the ship left the surveyors and went off to the nearby and ice-free Mikis Fjord, from which the airplane could fly.

The surveyors shot two bears while working in the big fjord. One bear was too heavy to pull ashore; Chapman had to stand knee deep in icy water while skinning the bear. They saw other bears that they did not hunt.

On the 27th the surveyors had a near disaster. A glacier less than a quarter kilometre away calved, and the resulting wave swamped the small boat tied to the shore. All their supplies and cameras were soaked. The following night the boat was tipped and filled with water and dumped the instrument box. After ten hours of searching the bottom of the sea, the box was spotted in 4.6 m (15 ft) of water. A cold dive recovered it and the instruments were dried and cleaned. "Courtauld took the theodolite to bits: and although he lost at least five small screws and springs, and had as many parts left over when he had finished, the instrument actually worked again" (Chapman 1933:46–47). When *Quest* returned to pick up the surveyors, they learned that on September 1 Watkins and D'Aeth had photographed a range of mountains, 96 km (60 mi) inland that they thought must be nearly twice the height of the 2,134-m (7,000-ft) coastal mountains. Although thought at the time to be a new discovery, it is likely that this was the "very high" mountain seen and commented on by Lieu-tenant Amdrup from Nordre Aputiteq in 1900.

The next day Watkins and D'Aeth, having completed the aerial photography, flew 483 km (300 mi) back to their base. Captain Ludolf Schjelderup, master of *Quest* and very experienced in the ways of the Arc-tic, strongly advised the surveyors against travelling back south in their small boat because of the lateness of the season and the severe ice. He offered to support the survey from his ship. Their return south on the ship was hindered by fog, heavy rain, a storm, and thick ice, but the survey progressed fairly well. Whereas it was previously thought that the ice cap came right down to the coast south of Kangerdlugssuaq, the surveyors found that there was in fact a belt of mountains up to 65 km (40 mi) wide. The mountains were highly glaciated and only the tops emerged above the ice. Farther south the surveyors found a series of islands that were low and snow-covered and difficult to distinguish from the mainland. They returned to Ammassalik on September 14.

Much of the work of the Watkins expedition involved ice sheet travel to establish and maintain the interior weather station, and two traverses to the west coast to record the altitudes and weather of the inland ice. In the summer of 1931 they surveyed and mapped the coast south of their base using two small boats driven by outboard motors. They had hoped to do this work in the winter and spring with dog sledges, but severe gales had broken the sea ice preventing the spring survey. Sea ice began to break up in June and Augustine Courtauld and John Rymill began the survey with a small boat, but bad ice not far from the base prevented any progress; thus they had to return after two weeks with very little accomplished. While waiting for the ice to clear, Watkins and D'Aeth flew down the coast and made a set of aerial photographs.

Watkins, Courtauld, and Percy Lemon were finally able to start the survey with two whaleboats and a kayak on August 15th under a brilliant warm sun and a cloudless sky. Because it was late in the summer and their base would be closed while they were away, they would continue south along the coast after completing their survey, pass through Prins Christan Sund, and return to England by way of West Greenland. Two days after their start they began the survey at Kajartalik ("a place having a kayak"). Lemon recorded the story of the journey in Chapman's book *Northern Lights* (1933:231).

> No place could have been more fortunately chosen than Kajartalik as an original base. The view in all directions was unobscured, and the weather was glorious.
> The country in these regions is barren to an almost incredible degree. Around our base the vegetation would have been described as scanty; a few berries and Alpine flowers growing

in small patches of sandy soil deposited beside streams or cracks in the rocks was all there was. On the coast between Isertok ["a muddy place"] and Umivik there is practically nothing.

The surveyors, mapping as they travelled, lived on the birds and seals that Watkins shot from his kayak, and stopped at Inuit villages either abandoned or inhabited. At Pikiutdlek ("a low place covered at high tide") the villagers forecast a storm which came on that night. Lemon wrote (Chapman 1933:232): "On the following morning the wind had died down, and we wanted to go. The natives assured us that the gale had not finished and our previous experience had shown us that although they were by no means infallible, they were usually right." The gale blew for four more days and left the sea with a litter of ice cakes which made boat travel impossible until the south-bound current cleared the ice. They were held at Pikiutdlek for nine days. "The delay was very annoying and tedious." On September 1, they reached Umivik, the finest place for seals they had seen. Watkins shot four in two days, while Courtauld and Lemon mapped the complicated islands and channels of Umîvik Bugt.

By September 8 they had completed the mapping of the convoluted coast in that area and had finished what they had intended to survey south of Ammassalik. Ahead of them lay 565 km (350 mi) of uninhabited coast they would have to pass on the way to their destination at Nanortalik, the nearest settlement on the west coast. They expected to complete the journey in ten days. They had left the ice behind them and found the coast "exceptionally beautiful, much broken up by small islands, and channels; and vegetation, between Umîvik and Tingmiarmît, is fairly prolific" (Chapman 1933:235). The weather soon changed to heavy rain, and then the outboard engines began to give trouble. Going around exposed headlands in small boats with unreliable engines and in bad weather was cause for concern. It was very slow going to get past Akornorniarmiut (referring to "people living between headlands") Ø, a place notorious among the Inuit for rough seas. The malfunctioning engines and leaking, overloaded boats forced them back. They had to lay up on a small beach in a leaky tent enduring torrential rain for three days. In the meantime Lemon repaired as best he could the leaking stern of the larger boat. They were able to leave only after six days and reached Tingmiarmît on September 18. The journey behind the islands to Tingmiarmît had been very beautiful; they found this one of the best parts of the coast, as had Holm and Garde fifty years earlier.

Beyond lay Puisortoq, the great glacier thrusting into the sea and dreaded by the Inuit because huge pieces of ice often broke off underwater and then shot to the surface like missiles. They were considered very dangerous for small boats passing by the glacier. The Inuit advised: "Do not speak, do not eat, until Puisortoq is passed" (Chapman 1933:241). While waiting for weather good enough to pass, Watkins' larger boat was blown ashore and damaged its stern against the rocks. Repairs were made after a fashion while the rain poured down without relief. They continued to try to get the engines to work properly. On their third attempt they passed Puisortoq and continued on until dark when they found a landing place as a storm was brewing. The following day Courtauld found and repaired the problem with the engines that had plagued them so long. They then had made 80 km (50 mi) without trouble when just north of Lindenow Fjord they unexpectedly met three Norwegian hunters spending the year on the coast. The leader, Ole Mortensen, was an old ship's carpenter, and he immediately began repairs of Watkins' battered boats. The party shared the Norwegians' small hut, luxurious quarters after weeks in leaking tents. The Norwegians were lonely and homesick, so said Lemon, and wanted Watkins to spend the winter with them. "It certainly was a depressing place, this narrow fjord, now covered with new ice, but they treated us with such kindness during our short stay that it seemed ungrateful to leave them" (Lemon in Chapman 1933:244). From there the journey was uneventful until they came to the entrance to Prins Christian Sund, the passage to the west coast. There they came across the first house of a West Greenlander. Lemon wrote (Chapman 1933:245): "The south-west coast of Greenland is completely different in character to the [east] side. At Narsaq, the end of our day's journey, we saw the first grass field and sheep grazing in it. The country-side here resembles the south-west coast of Ireland. The climate is much milder, with frequent rain and mist." The journey to Nanortalik was uneventful and they arrived at journey's end on October 7 with four litres (one gallon) of fuel remaining. They were warmly welcomed by Knud Rasmussen, who had preceded them down the coast from Ammassalik. Rasmussen called their trip "A distinguished achievement ... I have seldom seen an expedition with so little equipment and would hardly have believed it possible to make such a journey at that time of year" (Gabel-Jørgensen 1940:31).

BOYD AND A PHOTOGRAPHIC RECONNAISSANCE, 1931

Louise Arner Boyd was the daughter of a very successful mining engineer. She thus inherited an interest in land forms and geology, and she trained herself as a very competent photographer of natural terrain and geological formations. Louise Boyd travelled to Svalbard in 1924 and 1928 and to Zemlya Frantsa-Iosifa in 1926. She found that "far north, hidden behind grim barriers of pack ice, are lands that hold one spellbound ... one enters another world where men are insignificant amid the awesome immensity of lonely mountains, fjords and glaciers" (Boyd 1935:1). Inevitably, East Greenland attracted her, and in the 1930s she made four voyages to the great fjord region and farther north.

Each of her expeditions to East Greenland was fully documented by narratives complete with scientific reports and richly illustrated with her photographs and published by the American Geographical Society. Her comprehensive photographic work probably first fully awakened the outside world to the "awesome immensity" of the region's lonely mountains, fjords, and glaciers.

Louise Boyd undertook her first expedition to East Greenland in 1931. It was intended as a photographic reconnaissance in preparation for a more comprehensive scientific expedition planned for 1933. She chartered the Norwegian sealer *Veslekari* for the season as she did for each of her following three voyages. The ship was 38 m (125 ft) long and specially built in 1918 for the polar seas, reputedly the strongest of all Norwegian wooden sealers. Unlike most of her class, *Veslekari* had a curved bow that enabled her to ride up on ice floes and crush them under her weight. The vessel carried a crew of fourteen in 1931. Her captain that year was Paul Lillenaes, who had rescued Ejnar Mikkelsen and Iver Iversen from Bass Rock in 1912 (Kjaer and Sefland 2005). Boyd's party included six guests. She intended to visit every fjord in the Kejser Franz Joseph–Kong Oscar Fjord region.

Veslekari left Norway on July 1, visited Jan Mayen, and met the East Greenland ice on July 13. Boyd wrote (1932:534): "We had no fog and no rain after entering the ice, but brilliant sunshine. And further compensation lay in the beauty of the ever-changing scene; the varied sculpture of the great marble-like blocks of crystalline ice; the blue of the ice above, the deeper blues of the frozen pools on the surface of the floes and of the cracks in the ice, and yet another blue, sometimes deep purple, of the ice below the surface."

After four days crossing 226 km (140 mi) of pack ice the vessel reached the coast on July 17, the first in 1931 to do so. After a brief visit to the Norwegian radio station Myggbukta in Mackenzie Bugt, *Veslekari* followed the north shore of Kejser Franz Joseph Fjord to Nordfjord and on to Hoelsbu, a Norwegian hunting station in Moskusoksefjord, where the party spent several days. At the trappers' hut, Boyd wrote, they found a tame young muskox that followed the hunters about. There were in fact two tame young muskoxen, named Lita and Lensman, at Hoelsbu. One of the two resident Norwegian hunters, John Giaever, whose partner Otto Johnsen had tamed the animals, provided a more expansive account of the encounter (1958:184–85):

> Among Miss Boyd's companions were a very newly-wed couple, Swedes, ... The turtle doves, each with an apple, went off into the hills on a walking tour.... All at once the charmingly pastoral idyll was shattered by terrified screams and shouts issuing from the direction of the hills. It was our turtle-doves who came flapping in fright from out of the wilds, soaked in sweat and jabbering confusedly in two different languages at once. From the Babel it emerged that the two dears had been attacked by a couple of monsters, and poor darling Yulle had been well and truly butted in the expected place. They had come running for dear life, leaving a trail of binoculars, cameras, apples and walking sticks ... 'and thank God we're safe, and oh God, here they come, run for your lives, everybody'
>
> 'Moo.' And there, on top of the nearest hillock, a few yards away, stood the 'monsters,' Lita and Lensman, the latter still

giving black looks, but Lita darting long, loving glances at Otto and mooing affectionately.

And after the first surprised sight of these two Otto and I started to shake with mirth. Soon the company began to titter, then to laugh, and finally everyone including the turtle-doves were almost hysterical with merriment.

Louise Boyd (1932:536) found the extreme inner end of Moskusoksef-jord, beyond Hoelsbu, "ablaze with the purple-red of the largest mass of fireweed (*Epilobium*) that we saw anywhere." Farther on, in Kejser Franz Joseph Fjord, Boyd's expedition found a herd of muskoxen at Eleonore Bugt, and just beyond arose the Teuffelschloss itself, "the most colorful feature of all this 'colored country'" (Boyd 1932:543). They anchored at the west end of Ymer Ø and found quantities of flowers in full bloom and ptarmigan and many muskoxen. Similarly, they found many muskoxen and Greenland hares near the mouth of Isfjord. On July 30 they reached the head of Kejser Franz Joseph Fjord, 220 km (136 mi) from the outer coast. There "ice-covered summits towered from three to seven thousand feet [914–2,134 m] above the water, the walls of brilliant hue, the architecture of complicated and pleasing design" (Boyd 1932:543). Boyd wrote (1932:528):

> Mile-high walls of rock form much of the coast of East Greenland in the region of Franz Josef Fiord. A great plateau capped with ice here ends in spurs and scarps, and its border is traversed by some of the profoundest fiords known in the world. From the ice cap glaciers descend to the heads and to the foot of the walls of the fiords and show a variety of form and of glacial action probably unsurpassed. In many places the rock is brilliantly colored and presents an aspect even more striking than the colored rocks that form portions of the walls of the Grand Canyon of Arizona. Add a sea that is dotted with icebergs or fringed with pack ice on whose outer border are great floes that have come from the polar basin north of the Svalbard region, and we have a picture of such majesty and on so vast

a scale that no explanation need be given by any explorer for wishing to visit or revisit such a scene.

On a day of brilliant sunshine and an air temperature of 27° C (80° F), surrounded by icebergs and glaciers, they had a "most enjoyable dip" in the fjord. There also they found grass 46 cm (18 in) high, the tallest found anywhere along the coast, and an abundance of flowers. In nearby Kjerulfs Fjord they found willows of the same height, the highest they saw anywhere in the region. Boyd was able to make some corrections to existing maps. At the head of Isfjord she found two glaciers, not one, discharging into the fjord, and she found the fjord longer than previously mapped. She noted the possibility that these discrepancies from earlier observations could well have been the result of glacial retreat. *Veslekari* was the first vessel to reach the head of Isfjord, and later Lauge Koch named the land at the head of the fjord for her – Louise Boyd Land.

After visiting every branch of the Kejser Franz Joseph Fjord complex and landing at the extreme end of every fjord, they passed on to Kong Oscar Fjord. There they met the Norwegian sealer *Polarbjörn* with a scientific party led by Adolf Hoel. Narwhals were very numerous at the entrance of Rhedins Fjord, and blueberries in full bloom covered the hillsides. In the inner reaches of Kempes Fjord, also, Boyd made some corrections to the map. She found a previously undiscovered valley connecting Kjerulfs Fjord with Dicksons Fjord. The largest herd of muskoxen they had seen grazed in Duséns Fjord; they counted 274 in all. Boyd entered all the branches of Kong Oscar Fjord and landed at numerous points, visiting trappers' huts throughout the area. She completed her first visit to East Greenland with a stop at Scoresbysund, where they found the flyer Wolfgang von Gronau and the seaplane *Grønland Wal* en route from Germany to America, the first to fly over the Greenland ice sheet. Boyd visited the outlying settlements at Kap Stewart and Kap Hope within Scoresby Sund. Finally *Veslekari* sailed north to Lille Pendulum Ø and Bass Rock. They sailed for Norway on August 19, and were clear of the ice two days later.

Louise Boyd had taken several thousand photographs. She had acquired the knowledge and experience and the firm foundation for more detailed scientific work in later years.

While Louise Boyd and her party were at Scoresbysund, two Norwegian medical students, Arne Høygard and Martin Mehren, had descended from the inland ice sheet onto the Waltershausen Gletscher in Nordfjord visited by Boyd a few days earlier. The Norwegians had completed a purely sporting thirty-five-day, 1,050-km (651-mi) crossing of the ice sheet from Umanaq with two sledges, sixteen dogs and 550 kg (1,200 lbs) of gear. They returned to Norway on *Polarbjörn*.

Exploration, Research, Politics, Sovereignty

NORWAY IN SOUTHEAST GREENLAND, 1931

Norwegians for years and for several generations had hunted bears and muskoxen, and trapped foxes in Northeast Greenland, and in 1922 they had established the radio and weather station at Myggbukta, the first such station in East Greenland. Adolf Hoel had sent out the scientific expedition of 1929 encountered by Lauge Koch north of Duséns Fjord, and in 1930 Hoel led a scientific party to the region between Clavering Ø and Davy Sund. Land surveying and mapping and soundings of certain fjords were undertaken, and the expedition left materials for nineteen hunting camps in the Kejser Franz Joseph Fjord region. The Norwegian scientific work, including twenty-one oceanographic stations, was continued in that region in 1931, and in 1932 a radio station was established at Antarctic Havn at the southern end of Kong Oscar Fjord. Aerial photography using a Lockheed Vega aircraft was undertaken in 1932 from north of Wollaston Forland to the central part of Traill Ø. About 2,100 aerial photographs were taken. Archaeological, botanical, geological, and oceanographic work of the previous year was extended in the Clavering Ø and Kejser Franz Joseph Fjord regions. This work was continued in 1933. Much of this activity, of course, was intended to strengthen the Norwegian political position in East Greenland. The Norwegians did not continue their scientific expeditions after 1933, but annually thereafter sent vessels to supply the station at Myggbukta and their hunters in the region.

In 1931 two Norwegian hunting expeditions were sent out to establish hunting and radio stations in Southeast Greenland, a region that had not been visited by Norwegians since the Norse era. One expedition was led by Finn Devold and sailed in the sealing vessel *Heimen* of Tromsø. Devold's party included six trained hunters, including a radio operator. A geologist, a botanist, and a surveyor accompanied Devold for the summer. They landed first at Tingmiarmît and then moved to Skjoldungen, first visited and named by Wilhelm Graah in 1829, where Devold established a radio station which he called Finnsbu. The party built two other stations, each occupied by two hunters, and a number of small huts in the district.

The second party was led by Ole Mortensen and sailed in *Signalhorn*. Mortensen's expedition numbered only three men. They landed first at Kangerdlugssuaq, which Watkins had explored and mapped the previous year, where the Norwegians erected a hut. They quickly found that the fox trapping prospects were poor and so they moved far south to the area just north of Lindenow Fjord, where a house was built. It was there that Mortensen gave hospitality to Watkins, Courtauld, and Lemon on their boat journey down the coast, and there Mortensen repaired Watkins' damaged boats. Mortensen was drowned in February 1932, when he fell through ice in the fjord outside the station.

The two Norwegian expeditions – those of Devold and Mortensen – found the hunting and fox trapping to be very poor, the two expeditions trapping only fifty-six foxes altogether. Finn Devold found that poor ice conditions during the winter in the fjords made travelling very difficult. His station sent out weather information throughout the winter. Both expeditions were relieved by *Polaris* in July 1932.

In 1932 a new expedition was sent out with government support to erect three new radio stations in East Greenland for weather observations and broadcasts as part of Norway's contribution to the International Polar Year of 1932–33. One station was located on Hochstetter Forland on the northeast coast. In Southeast Greenland one station was erected in Kangerdlugssuaq and the second north of Lindenow Fjord. It was in 1932 that Norway declared its sovereignty over the country between 60°30' and 63°40' N to include several stations on the southeast coast; Finn Devold was required by the Norwegian government to hoist the Norwegian flag at Finnsbu. The government sent out an expedition in charge of Gunnar

Horn with a botanist and a hydrographic surveyor in *Veslemari*. The purpose of the expedition was to visit and investigate as much as possible of the territory that Norway claimed. Horn's expedition moved the wireless station near Lindenow Fjord to a better location a bit farther north where it was named Torgilsbu (after Torgils Orrabeinsfostre, the Norwegian who had been shipwrecked and survived on the coast 1,000 years before). During the winter the trapping was a complete failure in the districts of the two expeditions, one at Torgilsbu, the other at Devold's stations near Skjoldungen.

The Fishery Board of Norway dispatched *Heimland I* in 1933 for hydrographic and fisheries research led by Thor Iversen. Depths were measured with an echo sounder from Kap Farvel to the Blosseville Kyst and weather reports were broadcast four times a day.

In 1933, following the decision by the Permanent Court of International Justice awarding sovereignty of East Greenland to Denmark, *Signalhorn* collected the wintering party in Kangerdlugssuaq and closed that station. (Lawrence Wager later found the house destroyed, apparently by the wind.) *Signalhorn* then took on board the Devold expedition from Skjoldungen, terminating Norwegian activity in that particular district, but not at Torgilsbu.

The Torgilsbu weather station was occupied by three men in the following years, relieved each July by a supply vessel. A new building was erected in the summer of 1938, but the station was dismantled in the summer of 1940 after the German invasion of Norway.

NORWAY AND DENMARK ON THE BRINK: SOVEREIGNTY AND THE WORLD COURT

It was not an accident or coincidence that Norwegians and Danes increased their activities in East Greenland in the 1920s and dramatically so in the early 1930s. The question of who had sovereignty over East Greenland had become a matter of serious dispute between them. Each country attempted to strengthen its position in expectation that the issue would go before the Permanent Court of International Justice. Norway's claim was based only in small part upon the Norse colonization of West Greenland in the tenth century, an occupation that lasted five hundred years. Indeed, Norway had renounced its claim on that basis early in the nineteenth century. Norway largely based its claim on the proposition that East Greenland was *terra nullius*, that is, an unoccupied land distinct from either Norwegian or Danish activities that had occurred previously in West Greenland. Further, Norway noted that eighty-one Norwegian sealing vessels had been active in this region from 1889 to 1920. Norway also took the position that the presence of Norwegian hunters spending winters in Northeast Greenland since 1893, scientific exploration in the twentieth century, and the establishment of the Myggbukta radio station in 1922 confirmed its claim for sovereignty.

Denmark had exercised effective jurisdiction over West Greenland since 1721 and had gained international recognition of its sovereignty over Northwest Greenland in 1916. It had begun exploration of the east coast in 1829, established the mission and trading station at Ammassalik in East Greenland in 1894, and continued exploration in 1898 and later years. Norway, nevertheless, maintained that Denmark had never exercised effective jurisdiction over East Greenland. Each country had a plausible claim, but in 1919 the Norwegian foreign minister had advised the Danes verbally that Norway would not dispute Denmark's jurisdiction over East Greenland. He also said that Norway could not relinquish the fishing and trapping rights which Norwegians had exercised in East Greenland and adjacent waters for generations, but two years later Norway would not commit that position to writing. The two countries arrived at a *modus vivendi* embodied in a treaty, the Greenland Pact of 1924, focused primarily upon the rights of Danish and Norwegian hunters, that seemed to accommodate the interests of both. The establishment of the colony at Scoresbysund in 1924–25, which gave Inuit preferential hunting rights, appeared to the Norwegians to be an infringement of the rights of Norwegian hunters in that area. In 1930 Norway conferred police powers on some of her subjects in East Greenland, clearly implying a form of sovereignty. Denmark protested. The next year, 1931, Norwegian hunters raised the Norwegian flag over their station at Myggbukta. The government of Norway at first stated that the flag raising was entirely a private act. A few days later, however, Norway proclaimed that the occupation of parts of East Greenland by Norwegian hunters confirmed Norwegian ownership of what Norway called Eirik Raudes Land located between

71°30' N and 75°40' N. – from the northern end of the Liverpool Kyst to the northern part of Hochstetter Forland.

Denmark initiated the Three-Year Expedition in 1931, led by Lauge Koch, which in part had the purpose of examining possibilities for Inuit settlements where Norwegians had been hunting. Norway viewed this as a violation of the understanding of 1924 with Denmark and of well-established Norwegian hunting and trapping rights.

Denmark appealed to the Permanent Court on July 12, 1931. Norwegian hunters in the summer of 1932 occupied, and the Norwegian government claimed, lands between 60°30' N and 63°40' N in Southeast Greenland – that is, from Lindenow Fjord to about Kap Møsting. By this time, the question had become heated in the two countries and harsh words were spoken. There was even talk of war between Norway and Denmark. The court deliberated for nearly two years.

The question was complicated by the history of Norway, Denmark, and Sweden. In 1397 the three countries were united as one. Sweden later separated, but Denmark and Norway remained joined until 1814. Denmark was then forced to cede Norway to Sweden, but Iceland, Greenland, and the Faroe Islands, unquestionably Norwegian possessions at that time, remained, by Danish stratagem and Swedish oversight, part of Denmark. Norway remained united with Sweden until 1905, when it gained independence. Further, the issue of East Greenland itself now before the court was complex and significant for the international community. It was one of the weightiest cases to be handled by the court and had implications that went far beyond the remote east coast of Greenland. It set precedent for territorial claims over remote islands and lands not easily or effectively occupied or colonized by claiming powers. The judgment of the court was delivered on April 5, 1933.

The court's proceedings filled six large volumes, and the judgment itself required over 100 pages. The court ruled, in short, that Denmark had claimed and had sufficiently demonstrated effective sovereignty to have valid title to all of Greenland. Apparently the court attached considerable importance to the Commission for the Supervision of Geological Exploration in Greenland established by Denmark in 1878 (Jorgensen *in* Anon. 1978:122), which, by sponsoring such exploration on a systematic and sustained basis and reporting the results of a number of explorations in the areas claimed by Norway, had reinforced Denmark's claims. The court ruled that Norway's claim to Eirik Raudes Land was illegal and invalid. Norway accepted the decision with grace in spite of the intense feelings over the question. Norway retained hunting and trapping rights and the right to maintain its radio stations, under Danish jurisdiction and restrictions, in East Greenland.

KOCH AND THE THREE-YEAR EXPEDITION 1931–34

Intensive and sustained multi-year Danish explorations and scientific investigations in East Greenland began in 1931. They were organized within two independent expeditions. One was in southeastern Greenland, from Kap Farvel toward Scoresby Sund, under the general direction of Knud Rasmussen. The other was directed toward the area from Davy Sund at 72° N northward to Store Koldewey at 76° N and was organized by Lauge Koch. Both were part of Denmark's response to the Norwegian challenge to Danish sovereignty.

Koch's expedition was called the Danish Three-Year Expedition 1931–34 and was funded by private, foundation, and government monies. It was supported by two vessels, *Godthaab* and *Gustav Holm*, and after 1931 by two floatplanes operating from the vessels. Its object included cartography, geology, hydrography, zoology, botany, and archaeology. In the first summer, 1931, the priority was to build two permanent stations for winter activities, one on Clavering Ø at a site called Eskimonæs and the other on Ella Ø at the northern end of Kong Oscar Fjord. Two substations also were to be built, one in Nordfjord and the other at Kap Brown on the northern shore of Jameson Land between Nathorst and Fleming Fjords. The ships also were to carry supplies for Danish trappers and deliver them to several trapping stations.

The two ships left Copenhagen together on June 16 carrying twenty-four of the scientific party. At Thorshavn in the Faroe Islands, fifty-two dogs and two tons of dog food were taken on board, along with three Greenlanders who would drive dog teams from Eskimonæs and Ella Ø during the following winter. Both ships, although following different courses, met the ice edge on July 7. Within the pack, "the ice consisted of large unbroken ice fields separated by close-packed floes of thinner ice evidently formed in spring months. Fairly high and newly formed pressure ridges were found in several places, and often the ice packed, though slightly, around the ships" (Koch 1955:46). While the ships were within the ice the weather was "mostly clear and calm." *Godthaab* escaped the ice near Hold with Hope on July 29 and *Gustav Holm* farther south on August 3. Both ships were at Eskimonæs on August 5.

Altogether about fifty-five men were at first involved in unloading supplies and building the station at Eskimonæs. The work went on from August 5 until the 8th, when *Gustav Holm* departed for Ella Ø. The Eskimonæs house was essentially completed on August 12. *Godthaab* then went north with trappers' supplies to a camp on Hochstetter Forland, was back at Eskimonæs on August 17, and then left Eskimonæs on August 20 for Ella Ø.

On its departure from Eskimonæs, the crew of *Gustav Holm* had constructed a small house at Nordfjord. It was manned by three men. Ninety-five tons of supplies and coal were unloaded at Ella Ø, and house construction began on August 15 and was completed by August 28. The ship departed on August 22 for Fleming Fjord, where another small house was built at Kap Brown. The vessel departed on August 25 and reached Copenhagen on September 6. *Godthaab* arrived on September 8.

The ships had spent twenty-one and twenty-nine days in the pack ice; they could spend only thirty-two and twenty-four days on shore. Because of the "extremely unfavourable" conditions in the pack ice, time was short and priority had to be given to the construction of the two main expedition houses. Scientific work was therefore "not very comprehensive," but the archaeologist Helge Larsen discovered and began to excavate the site at Dødemandsbugt on Clavering Ø. It was the "largest ruined settlement hitherto found in Greenland" (Larsen 1934:6). The geologist Daniel Malmqvist investigated sediments from which traces of oil had been reported in the previous year. He measured Permian, Triassic, and Cretaceous beds in the vicinity of Clavering Ø, Carboniferous beds on the island, and Devonian sediments on Ymers and Traill Oer.

Gunnar Save-Soderbergh with Arne Noe-Nygard collected vertebrate fossils from the Devonian in the areas where Malmqvist worked, and Hans Frebold and Hans Poser collected "extremely good" invertebrate collections from those locations and from Hochstetter Forland.

Altogether sixty-five people had taken part in this expedition. Eight men were left to spend the winter at Eskimonæs and at Ella Ø.

The primary object in 1932 was aerial photography as a basis for cartography to provide a strong foundation for scientific work. For that purpose two aircraft – Heinkel low-wing monoplanes on floats – were lent by the Danish Navy to the expedition. Again two ships supported the work and ninety-five people took part. This year three Icelandic ponies were taken to carry loads for the geological explorations. The ships left Copenhagen on June 15, but not until July 17 was *Gustav Holm* able to reach Eskimonæs.

After visiting Ella Ø, *Gustav Holm* steamed north, leaving depots of supplies for Danish trappers at several points, and anchored off the west side of Hochstetter Forland. There a station called Kulhus was built near the coal seam discovered on the Danmark Expedition. Four men were left at Kulhus for the winter to carry on mapping triangulations to provide ground control for the aerial photographs in the region north of Clavering Ø. Zoological studies were also made. While the house was being built, the airplane took Koch on photographic flights for mapping the area from Clavering Ø north as far as Dronning Louise Land. The ship then went north to Bessel Fjord, where materials for a trappers' hut were unloaded.

In the meantime *Godthaab* had reached Eskimonæs on July 25 after two weeks in the pack ice. The ship carried supplies for the two main stations and for the small stations at Nordfjord and at Kap Brown on Fleming Fjord. Along the way she landed geological parties on the Winter Øer, on Strindberg Land in Geologfjord, in Duséns Fjord, on Gauss Halvø, and near Kap Simpson at the southern end of Traill Ø. The primary work of *Godthaab* in 1932 was oceanographic and marine biological observations. The vessel made hydrographic stations throughout the great fjord system and its numerous branch fjords, around Geographical Society and Traill Øer, and down to Scoresby Sund. The work consisted of oceanographic sampling of temperature and salinity at various depths, bottom soundings, bottom dredgings and bottom trawls, and various kinds of net tows for plankton and swimming organisms. In all, *Godthaab* made 134 hydrographic stations. The vessel left Scoresby Sund on September 3 after waiting out hurricane winds. *Godthaab* and *Gustav Holm* both arrived in Copenhagen on September 18.

During the summer Helge Larsen completed archaeological work at Dødemandsbugt. On the southeast coast of Clavering Ø, Larsen had found six settlements with ninety-three house ruins, and at Dødemands-bugt itself he found forty-three house ruins. He recovered about 2,400 specimens, representing 157 types of implements, as well as many worked pieces of bone, slate, wood, and baleen from the jaws of whales. Larsen concluded that this material represented not one culture, but a mixed culture, a fusion of peoples who had come from the south and from the north. The people from the south were of the Inugsuk Culture and moved north from the Ammassalik area at the beginning of the sixteenth century. They met people of the Thule Culture who had come from the north of Claver-ing Ø. The mixed culture lived there until the nineteenth century, when they disappeared. Apparently they did not die in that region for no human bones were found in association with the most recent house ruins. Larsen's guess was that the last of the people moved north where their trail disap-pears in the vicinity of Danmarkshavn.

An archaeological reconnaissance of the Ella Ø and the Kulhus areas was begun in the autumn of 1932. The aerial photography on this first summer of such surveys in Greenland was not entirely satisfactory because the film was not fully sensitive to objects at great distances. Nineteen men were left for the winter at Ella Ø, at Eskimonæs, and at Kulhus.

The Icelandic ponies on this and subsequent expeditions worked well, being quite able to carry loads if the ground was not too difficult. Koch wrote (1955:275) that "the ponies were very curious, and time upon time they tried to join a herd of musk-oxen. As a rule, however, the musk-oxen were frightened and ran away before the ponies reached the herd." In the period 1932 to 1938 a total of thirty-eight ponies were used in East Greenland. The ponies were not returned to Iceland. Some died in accidents, some ran away, and the rest were shot. Their bodies were used for food for sledge dogs.

The expedition in the summer of 1933 was the most active and most productive of this three-year (1931–32, 1932–33, 1933–34) project. It was favoured by unusually good ice conditions. *Godthaab* and *Gustav Holm* both passed through the ice zone in only one night, and they were on the coast of Greenland at Scoresby Sund by Midsummer's Day. One ship experienced no ice obstruction all summer, and the other was delayed only six hours on one occasion. They spent sixty-six days along the coast, a remarkably long time. Fog was fairly frequent on the outer coast, but the weather in the fjords was generally calm and fair, and this year the scientific personnel were not distracted by house building. The expedition consisted of 109 people, including ships' crews. There were four topographical mapping teams, seven geological teams, three zoological teams, three botanical teams, and an archaeological team. Two aircraft with their crews and four photographers provided ice reconnaissance for the ships and the aerial photographic cover for the mapping and for geological reconnaissance. Eleven Icelandic ponies carried loads for one of the geological teams that undertook explorations for gold mining on Clavering Ø. Because most of the people had previous experience on the east coast, their equipment had been perfected and their projects progressed efficiently. The expedition worked from Scoresby Sund in the south to Peary Land in the extreme north, a range of nearly 1,370 km (850 mi) of latitude.

The ships and scientists worked in the Scoresby Sund region – mainly on Jameson Land – in June and early July until ice broke up farther north. The two floatplanes flew photo lines throughout the region. The ice had improved by July 13 such that *Gustav Holm* started north for Eskimonæs and Ella Ø. On an ice reconnaissance flight, Koch and his pilot landed at Myggbukta, where they met the Norwegian vessel *Veslekari* with Louise Boyd's second Greenland expedition on board. *Gustav Holm* arrived at Eskimonæs on July 16. The geologists now worked in the vicinity of Clavering Ø. The ship then took supplies to Ella Ø. In the meantime the airplanes were completing the aerial photo lines in the region between the two stations.

On August 4 Charles and Anne Lindbergh arrived at Ella Ø on their flight across the North Atlantic, investigating flying conditions across Greenland for Pan American Airways. After visiting Eskimonæs they left for Ammassalik on August 6.

Gustav Holm started north from Eskimonæs on August 6, landing geological parties along the way. She arrived at Kulhus, which was to be closed, late on August 7. The ship then voyaged north and arrived on August 10 at Danmarkshavn, where supplies for trappers were unloaded. The ship continued on even farther north in unusually favorable ice conditions. On August 15, close to the Norske Øer off Lambert Land, she reached 79°05' N, 17°49' W, 258 km (160 mi) north of Danmarkshavn and farther north than had been reached by any other vessel. There was much fog on the voyage north, but Koch and his aircrew on August 16 made a long flight to the area west of Danmark Fjord. Later in the day they flew to Peary Land – the first flight to that remote land – returning to the ship just as fog shut in. The ship was back at Danmarkshavn the next day. The scientific parties boarded as it voyaged south and was back at Eskimonæs on August 20. The vessel departed on August 25 for Ella Ø. It reached Scoresbysund on August 28, collecting scientific parties as it came south. It had fifty-one passengers on board. Some of them were transferred to *Godthaab*.

While *Gustav Holm* had gone far north, *Godthaab* remained in Scoresby Sund, continuing to support, as she did in 1932, detailed hydrographic and marine biological investigations as well as geological parties and aerial photography by one of the aircraft. The vessel interrupted that work to sail for Ella Ø and Nordfjord on July 31, and she was at Ella Ø when the Lindberghs arrived. *Godthaab* was back at Scoresbysund on August 14. While the ship anchored at Hekla Havn, Lieutenant Ryder's winter site in 1891–92, a flight was made south to Kangerdlugssuaq, about 355 km (220 mi) away, first entered by Amdrup in 1900 and mapped by the Watkins expedition in 1930. During the summer all the planned flight lines between 72° and 76° N were completed, as was the trigonometrical survey in the area. *Godthaab* made oceanographic stations in Gåse Fjord, by Røde Ø, and in Øfjord all around Milne Ø. In all, 341 oceanographic stations were made. At Scoresbysund she received passengers from the crowded *Gustav Holm* on August 30, when the ships departed for Iceland. They arrived at Copenhagen on September 25.

1934 was the final year of this ambitious three-year undertaking, and only *Gustav Holm* took part in the expedition. Only one airplane was involved, and its job, because the aerial photography was essentially completed in 1933, was primarily that of ice reconnaissance for the ship. Five Icelandic ponies were carried to Greenland this year. Unlike the very favourable ice conditions of 1933, 1934 was a difficult ice year. There was so much fog and rain that there was not even one day when aerial photography would have been possible. The ship spent six days getting through the pack ice and suffered some damage among the very thick and close-packed floes. She arrived at Scoresbysund on July 23.

One geological party worked around the western reaches of Scoresby Sund, in those fjords originally explored by Ryder over forty years earlier. While steaming north from Scoresby Sund, the rudder of *Gustav Holm* was damaged in thick ice but could be repaired. On the way north scientific parties and supply depots were landed at several locations. The ship arrived at Ella Ø on August 1, and then proceeded farther north, leaving scientists on Gauss Halvø on the north shore of Kejser Franz Joseph Fjord and in Moskusoksefjord. With the help of reconnaissance flights the ship reached Eskimonæs on August 9.

The Danish administration had instructed *Gustav Holm* to take supplies for trappers as far as Danmarkshavn, but because of difficult ice conditions this task had to be abandoned. A reconnaissance flight had found that Ardencaple Fjord, Grandjean Fjord, Fligely Fjord, and Lindeman Fjord, all north of 75° N, were free of ice, but close-packed ice along the shore prevented the ship from getting far north from Clavering Ø.

The voyage south to Ella Ø was shrouded in heavy fog most of the way. After collecting geological parties in the area, the vessel started south on August 26 with wind and snow prevailing. Its passage was made difficult all along the way by severe ice. Navigation was further complicated by a hurricane that blew out of Scoresby Sund and by much ice within the sound. Not until September 10, very late in the season, was the ship able to retrieve the geological party that had been working all summer in the interior of Scoresby Sund. On September 13, in open water on the return to Denmark, the vessel shipped a heavy sea that completely destroyed the fore part of its bridge and did other damage. It arrived in Iceland on September 16 and in Copenhagen on October 1.

All but one of the scientists returned to Denmark this year; a botanist remained for the winter at Eskimonæs. The stations at Eskimonæs and Ella Ø served as police posts, with two Danes and two Greenlanders remaining at each one.

KOCH AND THE TWO-YEAR EXPEDITION, 1936–38

Lauge Koch led the Two-Year Expedition of 1936–38. Its purpose was exclusively geological exploration, and it was supported by *Gustav Holm*. In 1936 there were forty-seven ship's crew and expedition members, of whom sixteen were geologists and assistants, including two people in charge of six ponies. The expedition had no airplane in 1936. It arrived at Scoresbysund without meeting any ice offshore, and it reached Ella Ø on July 25. Supplies were delivered to Eskimonæs, to Sandodden, and to the Nanok hunting station on Hochstetter Forland.

Geological teams were set ashore at Kongeborgen on Kong Oscar Fjord, on Gauss Halvø, in Moskusoksefjord, and in Duséns Fjord. Vertebrate fossils were collected in a rich location on Gauss Halvø and Triassic fishes were found near Clavering Ø. Devonian sections were mapped in Moskusoksefjord, and Devonian and Carboniferous sections were investigated at Kongeborgen and in Duséns Fjord. Paleozoic collections were made on Ella Ø and in Duséns Fjord.

The expedition was singularly fortunate that it met hardly any ice along the coast, something that had never happened before. But there were heavy rains during the summer, and in the autumn many of the depots were destroyed by bears. The ship began her return on August 23 and the scientific parties were boarded along the way. The expedition of 1936 remained in Greenland for forty-seven days. It left the coast on September 7 and arrived in Copenhagen on September 22. Seven people remained for the winter at Ella Ø and at Eskimonæs.

In 1937 *Gustav Holm* was sent with an airplane to Southeast Greenland for aerial photography in July, and therefore she could not load Lauge Koch's expedition in Iceland until early August. Eight ponies with thirty-nine tons of hay were taken on board. The expedition had eight geological teams, and the ship left Iceland on August 5. Ice conditions were in extreme contrast to those of the previous year. Dense ice was found off the coast of Liverpool Land and progress to the north was not possible. The expedition had intended to establish a new station in Fleming Fjord, but because of the very dense ice that plan was abandoned and it was decided to erect the station in the interior of Scoresby Sund. The station was to be a base for the triangulation for the mapping of the interior of Jameson Land. The vessel reached the site for the station – called Gurreholm – on

August 10 and remained there with frequent rain until August 17. For the remainder of the short summer the ship struggled with heavy winds, snow, sleet, and ice in Scoresby Sund. She managed to reach the colony on August 24 after a week of difficult passage through the ice. The ship tried unsuccessfully to sail north from the colony to relieve the people who had spent the previous winter at Ella Ø and Eskimonæs, but that was impossible. It also tried to return to Gurreholm; that attempt also failed. All the supplies for the northern stations were unloaded at Scoresbysund, and the vessel left the colony on September 7 in thick snow and strong winds. She was jammed in the ice for nearly two weeks with little or no progress toward the open sea until September 21 when the ice scattered. She reached Iceland the next day and returned to Copenhagen on October 7.

Because of previous indications of the possibility of unknown land between Svalbard and Northeast Greenland, Lauge Koch planned a flight in May 1938 to look for it. The Danish Navy bought a Dornier-Wal flying boat and *Gustav Holm* was sent to Kongsfjorden, Spitsbergen, to serve as a tender for the aircraft. The two pilots, a radio operator, and Lauge Koch flew from Copenhagen on April 30 and arrived at Kongsfjorden on May 6. They tried to reach Greenland on May 7, but were forced to return by snow and fog. The aircraft reached the coast of Northeast Greenland at 81°05' N on May 10 and after flying south about 65 km (40 mi) returned to Kongsfjorden after a six-hour flight. They set off again in the evening of May 15 in excellent weather. They flew over much of Peary Land at an altitude of 2,500 m (8,200 ft) and took many photographs. Koch found no new land between Greenland and Svalbard, but he noted a number of corrections to the map of Peary Land. They returned to Kongsfjorden after a flight of eleven hours and thirty-five minutes, and the aircraft was back in Copenhagen on May 20.

After the flight to Peary Land, *Godthaab* supported Koch's expedition to East Greenland in 1938 with fifty-one people and six ponies. There were four geological teams and a zoologist in the scientific party. Because of the bad experience with ice in 1937 and the necessity to avoid spending the winter in Greenland, the ship carried an airplane for ice reconnaissance. The ship was held for eight days in the pack ice before she was able to reach open water along the coast. Geological parties were put ashore in Moskusoksefjord on July 30, at Kap Franklin, and in Scoresby Land.

Godthaab reached Ella Ø on August 2, arrived at Scoresbysund on August 11, and reached Gurreholm on the same day. That station was closed – its work of triangulation of Jameson Land had been completed – and the ship returned to the colony at Scoresbysund. Drift ice there pressed the ship on to the bottom in shallow water, but she was able to get off undamaged. *Godthaab* returned to Ella Ø, retrieving geological collections that had been cached along the way, and arrived at Eskimonæs on August 20. She left the coast on August 30 and arrived in Copenhagen on September 15. This was the last of Lauge Koch's expeditions before World War II.

RASMUSSEN AND THE LAST THULE EXPEDITIONS, 1931, 1932, 1933

Knud Rasmussen first saw the east coast of Greenland in 1904. "From the mouth of Prins Christians Sund," wrote Carl Gabel-Jørgensen (1935:32), Rasmussen's associate and chronicler of his last expeditions, "he attempted to force a passage up the East Coast in a row-boat. Ice and bad weather between them made progress impossible, but from the headland Aluk, Knud Rasmussen could see the gleaming mountains of the East Coast stretching far away towards the north, and inspired by the sight he resolved to visit again this part of Greenland's imposing coast." Rasmussen could not make another attempt to journey along the southeast coast for twenty-seven years. In the meantime he had established the trading post he called Thule in northwestern Greenland, and from there he had undertaken a remarkable series of long and difficult journeys across the inland ice, around Greenland's north coast, and across Arctic Canada to Alaska. He spent a few months in 1919 at Ammassalik collecting ethnographic material. He called these the Thule Expeditions, the most famous being the Fifth Thule Expedition across the top of North America and even, briefly, to Siberia. Being of part Greenlandic ancestry, Knud Rasmussen spoke the indigenous language fluently, and he collected and published many reports of Inuit legends and ethnological information.

The opportunity to return to East Greenland came in 1931 when he undertook a short reconnaissance of the coast from Kap Farvel to Ammassalik which he called the Sixth Thule Expedition, in anticipation of very extensive explorations in 1932 and 1933 – the Seventh Thule Expedition.

KNUD RASMUSSEN
COURTESY ARCTIC INSTITUTE, DENMARK.

The preliminary voyage of 1931 was made possible by revenues from Rasmussen's Thule station, and that of 1932 partly so. These expeditions, together with those of Lauge Koch farther north, were of course part of the concerted strategy of Denmark to assert and confirm its sovereignty and jurisdiction over East Greenland.

Rasmussen attributed the success of the 1931 journey to the unusually open ice conditions that prevailed that year. He had reviewed the ice reports for many years and believed that there had been a significant improvement. The two previous Danish expeditions along this coast – those of Graah in 1829–30 and of Holm in 1884–85, each travelling in umiaks – had reached their furthest points only after months of struggle through the sea ice. Rasmussen (1933a:385) found that in August and September "this ice-besieged coast ... was so free of ice everywhere that there was unhindered navigation for motor boats and fair-sized vessels."

"It is the drift-ice which characterizes the East Coast," wrote Gabel-Jørgensen (1935:32). "Ice-floes innumerable are borne southwards along the coast by the Polar Current. They lie along the whole length of the coast blocking every approach and forming a menacing dangerous barrier which in the course of time has repulsed so many attempts to reach the coast from seaward."

Rasmussen started from Julianehåb on August 19, 1931, in *Dagmar*, 11 m (36 ft) long and fitted with sails and a 35 h.p. motor. There were eleven people on that small boat as they set out. His goal was Ammassalik, 1,130 km (700 mi) from Julianehåb. In the course of the eight weeks of the expedition they would voyage a total of 4,032 km (2,500 mi). Knud Rasmussen wrote (1932:173–74):

> Even an old Greenland traveller who is accustomed to the country there cannot but be impressed with the East Coast, which, compared with the West Coast, is much more wild and colossal, apparently an inaccessible cliff coast with numbers of fjords, in which the shining inland ice tongues out and spreads quantities of calf-ice and icebergs out over the fairway. And between the fjords: sky-scraping promontories, glacier-shorn, wind-worn.... And lastly, stretches where there is not even land, but only glaciers such as Puisortoq ... all of

them landscapes that are brilliant in sunshine, sparkling with gorgeous colour, but terrifying in a storm.

The whole of this coast from Kap Farvel to Ammassalik consists of primary rock, and only here and there are small reefs with a haven that can provide shelter from the storms; otherwise the coast as a whole is open, with the Atlantic Ocean right in upon it. Under such conditions one has to hurry forward from harbor to harbor, and for preference in good weather. In July and August the weather seems to be quiet and fairly constant, especially in the fjords; but as early as September the northeaster, the most feared of all the winds, starts to blow and sets a tremendous swell in towards the coast.... The barometer falls are great and violent.

Rasmussen left the archaeologist Erik Holtved and two Greenlanders at a small house at Narssaq ("A level ground") in Lindenow Fjord on August 21. The voyage northward the next day was in clear, calm, "brilliant and beautiful weather." Rasmussen's party camped for a night in the wild alpine country of Tingmiarmît "in a small green-clad valley, where a variegated profusion of flowers covered the now deserted Eskimo huts" (Rasmussen 1932:174). Tingmiarmît is a land of calm weather; the northeast gales never penetrate this region. The valley is "engulfed by the sharp pinnacles which seemed to end high among the clouds – a grand but wild sight, because the landscape was chaotic in its lines" (Rasmussen 1932:174).

Gabel-Jørgensen wrote (1940:55) of Tingmiarmît: "As an experience the voyage surpassed even our wildest dreams. The coast is a thing of beauty, the culmination of which is the Tingmiarmît Fjord. From the base island the view all around the horizon was perfectly wonderful. The sea and the ice in the east, the inland ice in the south and west and the splendid alpine landscape with its pointed peaks together form a unique panorama full of novelty and change."

Farther along, Rasmussen stopped at Griffenfeldt Ø, barren and exposed to the fogs and winter ice of the sea. On the 24th, Rasmussen and *Dagmar* arrived at Skjoldungen Ø, where they met Norwegian hunters from Finn Devold's expedition. Rasmussen spent six days surveying the valley the Inuit call Eqalungmiut (Graah spelled it Ekallumiut).

Rasmussen (1933a:386) called it "a fertile, blossoming, and thicketed valley, lying oasis-like in the midst of calving glaciers and wild alpine heights." He wrote (1932:176) that this

> is the one oasis on the southern part of the East Coast – a fertile, bloom-carpeted and bush-grown valley in among calving glaciers and savage alpine crags. There was a baking heat, swarms of mosquitos and brilliant summer weather throughout our stay ... it seemed as if the earth actually overwhelmed us with this peculiar arctic luxuriance, consisting not only of flowers and greens, but also berries – black, lustrous crowberries that were crushed almost at every step, the soles of our kamiks becoming red with the flowing juice.

It was those berries that had saved Lieutenant Graah's life in 1830, one hundred years before, on his return from a year of desperate struggle and semi-starvation on that coast. Knud Rasmussen met two more Norwegian hunters, also members of Finn Devold's hunting expedition, in the valley of Eqalungmiut. Just north of Skjoldungen, Rasmussen's party discovered two large previously unknown fjords; so complex and difficult is the coast that Graah and Garde had missed both of them.

Rasmussen reached Ammassalik on September 1 after "a fantastically beautiful passage in utterly fairy-like moonshine, glassy calm sea, clear sky and still air." Gabel-Jørgensen (1935:33) wrote:

> The return voyage began on September 6 and was immediately followed by a serious accident which came within a hairsbreadth of costing the lives of the entire expedition. Off Umivik a tempestuous storm got up suddenly; big seas carried away the dinghy, smashed the rudder, and damaged the propellor. The boat was driven far out into Denmark Strait before the naval crew, under Captain Bangsboll's command, succeeded in making the ship manageable again. The boat was repaired from her own resources in Skjoldungen and the journey southwards continued on September 19.

Knud Rasmussen provided a more detailed description of the storm. At noon of September 11, as they approached the great glaciers of Colberger Heide, the wind came from the northeast and the waves suddenly grew higher. Glacier-calved ice forced them farther from the land, and the heavy seas and ice caused problems with the boat they were towing. The boat was swamped and the tow-line broke, but the boat was secured again with difficulty. Then the tow-line fouled *Dagmar*'s rudder and broke it off. A jury-rudder was rigged, and with sails and engine the captain, F. Bangsboll, manoeuvred farther offshore out of the ice. The boat in tow was swamped again and its tow-line caught in *Dagmar*'s propeller shaft and broke. The boat could not be recovered in the rough seas. At nightfall they were 40 km (25 mi) from land with an engine that could not be used, a useless rudder, and torn sails. For two days they lay to in a storm of force 11 or 12 (56–71 knots) that carried them 200 km (125 mi) south and 130 km (80 mi) from the shore.

On the afternoon of September 13 the wind dropped enough to allow them to rig a new jury rudder and cut free the tow line from the propeller shaft. Very early in the morning of the 15th they reached an anchorage at Skjoldungen where repairs could be made. Gales slowed the return south along the coast and they did not reach the Julianehåb district until October 2.

While Rasmussen was en route to and from Ammassalik, the archaeologist Eric Holtved excavated twenty-five houses in Lindenow Fjord and recovered more than two thousand artefacts for the National Museum in Copenhagen. Johannes Olsen made detailed magnetic observation at eighteen stations; thus that coast was better charted magnetically than any comparable coast in West Greenland. The inner part of Skjoldungen Fjord was triangulated and mapped; but this was primarily a reconnaissance journey and, wrote Rasmussen (1933a:390), "the experience of navigation in these waters gained on the Sixth Thule Expedition was prerequisite to the success of the Seventh Thule Expedition."

Knud Rasmussen's 1932 expedition, the Seventh Thule Expedition, numbered sixty-two members, including twenty-five Greenlanders from the west coast and Inuit from the Ammassalik district, "most of them with kayaks." It was a complex undertaking operating from a ship, *Th. Stauning*, which carried a seaplane on loan from the Danish Navy. Rasmussen's second-in-command, Captain Gabel-Jørgensen, wrote (1935:33), "[t]he effective use of the aeroplane on Watkins' ... Expedition had opened entirely new prospects: it was now possible to see beyond the first range of mountains – the extension of vision which had been the desire of every explorer had at length been realised. This freedom of movement both on the water below and in the air above made it possible to use the short summer much more intensively than hitherto."

"Our task was a complete exploration – topographical, geological and archaeological – of the stretch from Umivik to Kap Farvel" (Rasmussen 1933a:390). The distance is 600 km or nearly 375 mi in a straight line, the land area is 73 km (45 mi) wide, and the job had to be done in two months. The coast includes more than fifty large and small inlets and sounds. The expedition used seven large and small motorboats, and they travelled 20,000 km or over 12,400 mi. Of the eighty-one days in the field, forty-one were flying days in which 100 flights were made. The seaplane set a record for flying in Greenland for that time – 125 hours and 19,000 km (11,800 mi) in one season. The seaplane was used for aerial photography, the basis for mapping the coast. The photography, under the direction of naval Lieutenant Erik Rasmussen, was accomplished from six locations with *Th. Stauning* as base, and over 1,500 photographs were taken. Remarkably, the program went off almost exactly as planned, and because of favorable ice conditions, good weather, and skilful management, the planned work was concluded by September 2. The whole coast from Pikiutdleq north of Umivik down to Kap Farvel, the southernmost point of Greenland, was photographed. Ground control for the photographic mapping was secured by four surveying teams travelling by motorboats, each with a surveyor and two Greenlandic assistants. They occupied 137 stations and they obtained more than 4,000 triangulation intersections. Rasmussen (1933b:39) described their task:

> For the geodesists the days have been toil from morning to night. Every day up a mountain – perhaps not once but twice, for surveying, and high up among glaciers and the eternal snow in order to get a view over the great expanses.
>
> Much new land has been surveyed, many new fjords have been recorded, and over long stretches the map has been greatly altered, especially in the region and round about north

The Great Gletcher at the Head of Skjoldungen Fjord,
photographed from the air by The Seventh Thule Expedition, 1932
Courtesy Arctic Institute, Denmark.

of Skjoldungen, where Captain [*sic*] Graah's original map was lost in 1830, and where Holm and Garde did not get so far as to make supplementary triangulations in 1885.

The geologist Richard Bøgvad made collections at 500 places. The coast is granite and gneiss, and "there are none of the very interesting sedimentaries that we find farther north" (Rasmussen 1933b:39). They found no signs of mineral deposits.

Poul Nørlund found evidence of two Norse farms, the southernmost known, in the Kap Farvel district, but he found no additional Norse ruins on the east coast beyond that known as the Rolf Ruin in Lindenow Fjord, the only one known from East Greenland. The Lindenow ruin appears to be that of a hunting site rather than a Norse farm.

Rasmussen (1933a:393) noted that "the Eskimo archaeological work was extremely rich in its results, for this is a coast on which in former days there was a large Eskimo population." Two hundred house ruins were noted and Therkel Matthiassen excavated twenty-one ruins. The oldest dated back to the fourteenth century.

Rasmussen was particularly interested in the potential of the southeast coast to support new settlements. The expedition found excellent sealing all along the coast, but found no land game. With the exception of trout in some rivers, there were no quantities of fish. They found some sharks, but the biologists concluded that the waters were too deep and too cold to support codfish, which are plentiful off the west coast. Because the game is exclusively seal which may be migratory, they would be uncertain support for people.

Knud Rasmussen's program for 1933 was to extend the detailed mapping and investigations northward from Umivik to Kangerdlugssuaq and to make connection with Ejnar Mikkelsen's expeditionary work of 1932 on the Blosseville Kyst. The distance from Umivik to Kangerdlugssuaq is 630 km (390 mi), and the average breadth from the coast to the inland ice sheet is 97 km (60 mi). Rasmussen also hoped to make a reconnaissance of the coast from Kangerdlugssuaq to Scoresby Sund – a farther 525 km (325 mi) – in anticipation of detailed exploration in later years.

The Seventh Thule Expedition of 1933 was larger and with more objectives than that of 1932. Forty-five Danes, four Germans, one Englishman and one hundred Greenlanders and Inuit participated. There were seven motorboats, much better than those of 1932, and a schooner, *Nordstjernen*, not as good as *Th. Stauning*, to support the seaplane. The schooner carried the same aircraft as was used in 1932. The objectives were (1) aerial photography in conjunction with land surveying; (2) official inspection of the land, i.e., determination of the carrying capacity of the coast; (3) ethnological studies of the east coast Inuit; (4) geological; and (5) glaciological investigations; (6) fishery research; (7) zoological research; (8) botanical collections; (9) an artist's impressions of the land and the people; and (10) a motion picture of East Greenland and the Inuit. Many of the 100 Greenlanders and Inuit were involved in the motion picture production.

The expedition's members came from several directions. The surveyors travelling from the west coast in the motorboats had started up the east coast in the most beautiful summer weather, but ice blocked their anchorage in Lindenow Fjord and they were unable to leave the fjord for ten days. The expedition people were all gathered together at Ammassalik on July 22 when the seaplane arrived from the west coast. From Ammassalik the various groups, working from their seven motorboats, dispersed to their jobs. The aircraft flew 3,225 km (2,000 mi) and obtained five hundred stereoscopic pairs of photos. The coverage was extended beyond Kangerdlugssuak to Kap Daussy on the Blosseville Kyst. The surveyors carried their triangulations and ground control, supplemented by four hundred stereoscopic pairs of photos, from Umivik north to Kangerdlugssuaq and arrived back at Ammassalik by mid-September. They ended their journey at Julianehåb on October 3.

The marine biologists conducted fisheries investigations along the coast. "It is already apparent how remarkably the marine life varies from fjord to fjord along the coast" (Gabel-Jørgensen 1935:40). The poverty of conditions in Lindenow Fjord had been documented in 1932, "but as far north as Kangerdlugssuaq, particularly in Uttental Sund, a great richness of life was displayed, both seals and fish being plentiful."

Knud Rasmussen and his boat crew sailed from Ammassalik, bound for Scoresbysund in his new boat, *Kivioq*, on August 14. En route they stopped briefly at Tugtilik ("the place where the reindeer live"), where they visited a small British expedition led by John Rymill. *Kivioq*, on its

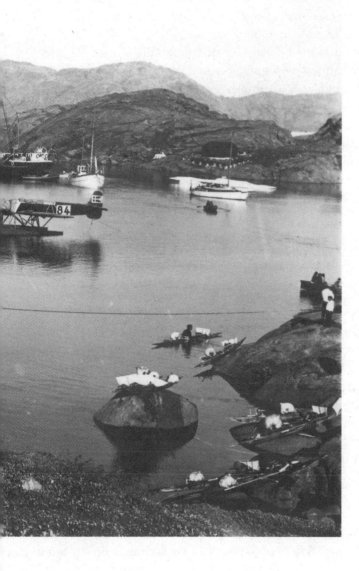

The Seventh
Thule
Expedition
Assembled
at
Ammassalik
with the
*Kivioq, Nor-
dstjernen,*
and *Dagmar.*
1933

Courtesy
Arctic
Institute,
Denmark.

cruise to Scoresbysund, encountered very little ice on the Blosseville Kyst and enjoyed calm weather – entirely unlike the experiences of Amdrup in 1900 and Mikkelsen in 1932. "Cape after cape was passed – there is something disquieting in the monotony of this coast – and … *Kivioq* sailed into Scoresby Sund in most beautiful weather" (Gabel-Jørgensen 1935:45). On its return the party picked up baggage from Rymill's party at Tugtilik and arrived at Ammassalik on September 3.

Rasmussen suffered food poisoning at Ammassalik. It was followed by pneumonia. The illness was undoubtedly exacerbated by the fatigue brought on by running such a complex expedition. When he left Ammassalik on October 10 he was seriously ill. He died in Copenhagen on December 21, aged fifty-four.

Knud Rasmussen received honorary degrees from the Universities of Copenhagen and Aberdeen. A number of locations in Greenland and streets in Denmark are named for him. He has been called "the symbol and the hope of a Greenland civilization to come" (Malaurie 1956:273).

MIKKELSEN RETURNS TO THE DANGEROUS COAST, 1932

Even after the successful establishment of the new colony at Scoresbysund in 1925, there was in Denmark still much controversy and opposition to the project. Because of his prominent role in founding the colony, Ejnar Mikkelsen had antagonized highly placed members of the government bureaucracy, including the director of the Greenland Administration. For several years he was excluded from Scoresbysund; indeed, access by him to any of Greenland seemed blocked by the Greenland Administration (Schledermann 1991). But in 1931 the dispute with Norway over the question of sovereignty of East Greenland became serious, and there is no doubt that by establishing the colony at Scoresbysund Mikkelsen had made a major contribution to the position of Denmark in its case for sovereignty, which it presented to the Permanent Court in 1931. Denmark, nevertheless, was faced with the necessity of greatly increasing its presence and activities in East Greenland. Ejnar Mikkelsen was the obvious person to lead an expedition to investigate the coast from Scoresby Sund to Ammassalik, that gap between the expeditions in 1931 and 1932 of Lauge Koch in the north and of Knud Rasmussen in the south.

So it was that in 1932 Mikkelsen returned to the Blosseville Kyst, along which he as a very young seaman had travelled in a very small boat with Gustav Amdrup in 1900. Apparently the region – and no more than its southernmost part – had been visited only twice in the intervening years. In 1928, 117 Inuit from Ammassalik had travelled north toward the fabled hunting region of the great Kangerdlugssuaq. A few of the hunters reached the southeastern entrance of the fjord, but most of the travellers wintered at Nualik, the peninsula about 111 km (69 mi) short of their goal where Amdrup had cached supplies in 1899. In 1930 H.G. Watkins' ship, *Quest*, had entered Kangerdlugssuaq, where his party had mapped the fjord and examined the geology. The coast from Kap Brewster just south of Scoresby Sund to Kangerdlugssuaq was in 1932 the least known of East Greenland.

Mikkelsen returned in 1932 on *Søkongen*, a typically sturdy Scandinavian powered schooner about 22 m (70 ft) in length that had been in service on Greenland's west coast. Mikkelsen's party included nine scientists and assistants and the ship's crew, a total complement of eighteen. They had two purposes. First, cartographers, geologists, and biologists would make the first detailed investigations of the coast at a number of locations, and, second, the ship's crew would erect a number of small houses at intervals to facilitate the passage of travellers between Ammassalik and Scoresby Sund. The overcrowded population with limited hunting resources at Ammassalik would thereby be encouraged to move to lands with better hunting opportunities. The houses would also have implications for Denmark's case before the Permanent Court for International Justice.

Søkongen found rather easy access to the coast, reaching Kap Dalton on July 10 after only a few hours of what Mikkelsen called "not really … ice navigation," passing the first of many icebergs along the coast. Mikkelsen seems to have found a naturally favourable passage to the coast in relatively ice-free water between a line of icebergs and pack ice to the north and pack ice to the south. The icebergs were grounded on a submarine bank and formed a dam on the north side of which the pack ice drifting from the north piled up. Pack ice crowded in again south of the open water behind the dam.

Kap Dalton was the site of Gustav Amdrup's hut and major supply cache in 1900, about 110 km (68 mi) southwest of the entrance to Scoresby Sund. It was the starting point for Mikkelsen's explorations southwestward to Ammassalik. While the crew of *Søkongen* repaired Amdrup's hut and cache, the cartographers, geologists, and botanists began their examination of the coast. As the vessel lay at anchor for a day or so at the various sites visited, an efficient routine evolved by which motor launches took the scientists back to fjords passed along the way or ahead to fjords not yet reached by the schooner. The areas surveyed were thereby substantially increased within the limited time available. Thus they passed slowly down the coast, some days in brilliant sunshine with the wonderful scenery of Greenland – the shining ice sheet in the distance, the dark, rugged, mountainous coastline, the drifting icebergs – displayed before them. More often, dense fog obscured the dangers of ice floes, icebergs, or headlands looming as shadows, all a threat to the ship, when great caution and vigilance were essential.

Contrary to Mikkelsen's expectations based upon his open boat voyage thirty-two years before, they were able to find anchorages safe from drifting ice in most of the small fjords with their steep mountain sides, one sign that the Blosseville Kyst is less hostile than had been thought – but it is not benign. The East Greenland Current carries immense quantities of ice floes and icebergs swiftly to the south. Off the Blosseville Kyst the current is constricted by Iceland to the southeast so that the current runs faster there and the pack ice becomes denser and is forced closer to the coast. Icebergs ground on shoals, the current flows fast around the steep headlands, and ice floes may jam against the icebergs and the shore. A ship following that coast could very easily and very quickly get into serious trouble.

The geologists found this coast to be of steep, rugged, basaltic mountains separated by narrow, branching fjords. Farther inland, away from the coast, the mountains consist of plutonic mineral-bearing rocks. The inland ice sheet is visible at the heads of the fjords from which icebergs were produced. Great lagoons are characteristic of the coast about Kap Dalton. Mikkelsen suggested that in the autumn of the year, when sea ice had left the coast, violent breakers rolled boulders, "some of them very large and rounded," alongshore to form the lagoons.

Amdrup's expedition in 1900 considered this coast the most barren of all those of East Greenland, but in 1932, when Mikkelsen was able to go into the interior of fjords, the botanists found that plants that could not flourish on the almost vertical mountains and in the raw, cold, foggy climate of the outer coast grew richer in abundance and in number of species. The gentler slopes and valleys and meadows around Scoresby Sund and farther north are not to be found on this coast; Mikkelsen's party found no traces of reindeer or muskoxen. Only signs of hares were found in the isolated places among the mountains and inland glaciers. Birds appeared to be abundant, unlike Amdrup's observations, nesting by the lagoons or lakes and on the inaccessible mountain sides. This is poor country for foxes, but *Søkongen*'s crew saw twenty-six bears on the coast and within Kangerdlugssuaq, where seals also seemed to be plentiful.

In Knighton Bugt Mikkelsen noted that the summer thaw of 1932 was at least two weeks earlier than in 1900. There the surveyor, Michael Spender, found two hot springs – too hot to hold one's hand in them.

The currents run very fast along the very steep coasts of Kap Beaupré, and navigational difficulties were compounded by very dense fog. Mikkelsen wrote (1933a:23):

> About 10 p.m. the fog was so dense that we ran against the huge ice foot of a small berg, before we had seen the berg itself; our speed was not great, but still we were badly jolted. Fortunately, it was an ice-foot which sloped gently upwards, and so we were able to refloat the vessel with a reversed engine without any damage being done.... With the strong current it was evidently more dangerous to lie made fast to the ice than to continue, and all through the night we therefore groped our way blindly, the ice being sometimes rather closely packed, and at other times so scattered that for some time we could not see ice floes around us.

They approached Kap Tupinier in very dense fog. "We were only able to see the actual foot of the promontory when about 500 m off the shore, and we now made our way laboriously in a westerly direction, between great quantities of ice and against such a heavy current that we were hardly able to head it" Mikkelsen 1933a:23).

The ship's crew built a house, 3.5 m by 3.5 m and 2 m high (11.5 x 11.5 x 6.5 ft) with a pitched roof for a spacious loft, at Kap Daussy, while the scientists investigated the surrounding country. There were quantities of wildfowl, particularly eider ducks, nearby, and a bear was shot near the house site. For four days the carpenters and the naturalists had good working conditions with fine weather. Just beyond the cape the voyagers got among masses of pack ice swirled about by the currents among grounded icebergs. The schooner was pressed toward the land close on the starboard side. The crew struggled with the ice for four days trying to find a way to proceed. At Kap Savary they found themselves in a violent current which they were barely able to stem with the ship's engine. They tried to work out to sea to find a way around the ice, but, Mikkelsen wrote (1933b:393),

> everywhere the pack was heavy, and icebergs came sailing down with the current to ground on the edge of a large shoal covered by an immense sheet of unbroken ice … our only possible chance of getting westwards was evidently to keep quite close to the almost perpendicular coast, where we experienced many difficulties from the strong current, the many icebergs and the drift which was often so violent as to cause the ice to close up ahead of us, where minutes before we had had open water or … to open up and become passable, where we had not at all thought it possible to be able to make any progress.

Finally they found shelter in a fjord just east of Kap Ravn. It was just there that the scientists found a significant and very distinct division between the fauna and flora of the north and the south. The enforced delay gave the opportunity to make a journey over the inland ice to investigate the geology of the Weidemann Bjerge, a great range receding into the distance far to the west. In this region was a hint that the basaltic structures of the north were to give way to "more interesting species of rock." The weather "remained the finest imaginable" during most of their ten-day stay, but close-packed ice prevented them leaving the anchorage.

The sea ice opened so that on August 2 they could at last proceed in the schooner, and beyond Kap Stephenson they found much open water, but strong winds and sleet lashed the coast and prevented any mapping on land or from the ship. While passing along the coast, Mikkelsen observed that since 1900 many of the small glaciers had wholly or partially retreated. Two large glaciers between Kap Rink and Kap Normann had completely disappeared and the land at the head of the bay was nearly bare of snow.

Søkongen was nearly forced ashore in the fjord by Kap J.A.D. Jensen. Mikkelsen put in there to seek shelter from the gale, snow, rain, and fog. There was a belt of ice within the entrance of the fjord, and beyond was open water, but the swell which offshore was inconsiderable became greatly magnified because of a funnel-effect within the fjord, setting the ice belt in violent motion. The vessel lost speed and began to drift shoreward with the ice. The easterly gale blew more ice into the fjord. The crew tried to turn the schooner toward open water. With the mass of very small ice pieces packed around, it was dangerous to use the propeller, but they dared not stop it and had to use full power to retain command of the ship. All hands, scientists and crew, had to force the bow around with poles against the ice.

> The ice pitched up and down along the sides of the vessel; the water roared and foamed round the fragments of ice and over the large ice-foots, on which we were frequently made to ride. Above us towered the land, dark and sinister; the wind came in violent gusts down the almost perpendicular mountain sides; it rained and was half dark, but all on board exerted themselves to the utmost ... after two hours of very hard work we again got into open water, without the vessel having suffered any damage worth mentioning (Mikkelsen 1933a:40).

The crew built another house at Mikis Fjord, and there they came upon ruins of a very old and large indigenous settlement. They found graves, meat depots, fox traps, tent rings, and ancient houses. The huts were excavated, and in some were human skeletons. The artefacts, many well preserved, indicated the site had been inhabited in the fifteenth century.

ICEBERG OFF THE
BLOSSEVILLE KYST
COURTESY ARCTIC
INSTITUTE,
DENMARK.

At Mikis Fjord the basaltic formations gave way to gabbro and gneiss formations giving a different character to the coast. Instead of rough and dark peaks, there were coloured mountains worn smooth by ice. The yellow-red slopes with dark basaltic intrusions lent a "more lively and friendly appearance."

While the work of house building proceeded in Mikis Fjord, the geologist Lawrence Wager and the cartographer Michael Spender worked in nearby Kangerdlugssuaq, the largest fjord between Scoresby Sund and Ammassalik, which Wager had visited on Watkins' expedition. At the beginning of August *Søkongen* moved into Kangerdlugssuaq and found a secure anchorage in Uttental Sund, named for Valdemar Uttental, the treasurer of Mikkelsen's Scoresby Sund Committee and the donor of a church to the Scoresby Sund colony. Kangerdlugssuaq reaches far inland away from the fogs and cold waters of the coast, but even so the vegetation was sparse; the greater part of the country was practically bare. The geology of the region does not readily form soil and there is little retention of moisture for plant growth, but the fjord and Uttental Sund are rich in sea life. Here for the first time along this coast Mikkelsen found walrus, and narwhals, fjord seals, and bearded seals were numerous – "we saw very great numbers of seal" (Mikkelsen 1933a:48). Surprising were the numbers of Greenland seals: "Once we counted from the ship at the same time three herds, each containing from fifty to one hundred animals." With the numbers of sea mammals in the region, a population of bears was not surprising. They found bear paths trodden along the passages among the several fjords around Kangerdlugssuaq. Sea birds were numerous.

Because hunting conditions seemed so favourable, Mikkelsen built two more houses in Uttental Sund, finishing the second on August 16. Inuit in years past had lived well in this region. Numerous formerly inhabited sites were found, but a disaster of some kind must have come upon those early people. In several huts the archaeologists found a number of skeletons; the inhabitants had met with sudden death of unknown cause.

Mikkelsen found peculiar weather conditions in this region. While they might enjoy calm, fine weather in Uttental Sund, just a short distance away in Kangerdlugssuaq the wind could be so violent as to prevent work and endanger the vessel itself amid the ice. On August 19 they could "not hold the *Søkongen* against the gale, which was now so violent that we drifted astern, the machine going full speed forward" (Mikkelsen 1933a:54).

At the head of the great fjord they found very little vegetation and there were no signs of bird or other animal life on the land, but in the sea mammals were still numerous. Near the head of Kangerdlugssuaq they came upon the Norwegian sealing vessel *Polaris* at anchor. Its people were building a house on shore, one of the Norwegian stations for the International Polar Year of 1932–33. "It seemed to us a curious place for a radio station, the chief object of which was the sending of meteorological reports, for the house was built in a small ravine with violent gusts from the mountains, whereas it was entirely calm right outside on the fjord" (Mikkelsen 1933a:60). The Norwegians had very few choices, in fact, for possible sites for their station in that steeply mountainous country.

Bad weather began on August 25 and continued through September 1 with practically unceasing gales and violent rain. Work on shore was impossible. After several days the very bad weather moderated and on September 2 the ship reached Lake Fjord, or more properly Tugtilik, where they built another house. This house would be used by the expedition of 1932–33 led by Watkins and after his death by John Rymill. Mikkelsen left coal, gasoline, and food to supplement the Watkins expedition's rather limited supplies. *Søkongen* reached Ammassalik, the end of their journey, two days later, and they arrived in Iceland on September 12. There Mikkelsen and the scientists left the vessel, which returned to its home port in West Greenland.

Ejnar Mikkelsen received the Gold Medal of the Royal Geographical Society in 1934, and in the same year, in recognition of his services, Mikkelsen was appointed Inspector for East Greenland, which post he held until his retirement in 1950. He remained active in East Greenland affairs for another twenty years, and became a principal founder of the Danish Arktisk Institut. He spent a year with his wife in Ammassalik in 1937, and his last visit to Scoresbysund was in 1964 when he was eighty-three years old. He was then made an honorary resident of the settlement. He was ninety-one when he died in 1971.

EJNAR MIKKELSEN
COURTESY ARCTIC INSTITUTE, DENMARK.

A Diversity of Expeditions and Interests

RYMILL AT TUGTILIK, 1932–33

After Gino Watkins returned from his expedition to East Greenland in 1931, he had hoped to take an expedition to Antarctica, but the world economic depression precluded any chance of raising enough funds to make that possible. Pan American Airways offered a modest grant if Watkins would continue to examine the possibilities of an air route over East Greenland. The airline was then just beginning its expansion of its overseas service and it hoped to develop a transatlantic service. Watkins accepted the offer and decided to establish a base in Lake Fjord, known as Tugtilik to the East Greenlanders, about 130 km (80 mi) north of Ammassalik. On his previous expedition Inuit had shown Watkins a lake 4 km (2.5 mi) long within a valley there, and he thought that it might offer the possibility of a flying boat base. Watkins was accompanied by three companions from his previous expedition, Spencer Chapman, Quintin Riley, and John Rymill. Toward the end of Watkins' 1931 expedition, Rymill with a companion had sledged across the ice sheet to the west coast. Watkins' objects in 1932 were to record weather conditions at Tugtilik for a year and to survey the vicinity as an extension of their earlier work. He hoped to extend the survey inland across the coastal mountain range to the edge of the inland ice sheet. He also hoped to climb Mont Forel, thought to be 3,350 m (11,000 ft) high, one of the highest mountains in Greenland. The expedition travelled to Greenland on the four-masted, steam-powered vessel *Gertrud Rask*, the annual supply ship to Ammas-salik. ,

Watkins' resources were very limited. Ejnar Mikkelsen offered to build one of his cabins in Tugtilik for the expedition's use, and Watkins planned to support his party by hunting as he had done on the boat journey in 1931. Tragically, Watkins was drowned while hunting in his kayak on August 20, only ten days after the party arrived at Tugtilik. The accident left the remaining three – Chapman, Riley, and Rymill – very limited in their ability to carry out the program. One man had to remain at the base to make the weather observations. At least one man had to spend considerable time hunting, and the third had to survey the area as best he could. Sledge travel in the winter was hindered by deep soft snow. Rymill noted (1936:368): "The snow became so deep that it was quite impossible to do any journeying other than short hunting trips until the beginning of February." Rymill and Chapman travelled over the sea ice to Ammas-salik in the middle of February to buy dogs for their spring journeys. The ice was unsafe and unpredictable and Rymill fell over his head through a crack in the ice. While camping on the sea ice they were caught in a bliz-zard and the ice began to break up. A crack appeared in the ice under their tent and, wrote Rymill (1936:369), "we spent a most uncomfortable night sitting fully dressed, one on each side of this crack." The wind subsided the next morning, and they were able to reach Ammassalik on February 22, sixteen days after they started.

After returning to their base with dogs, they started on their first survey trip and journeyed 65 km (40 mi) inland from the coast, passing mountains and over crevassed glaciers where the existing maps showed inland ice. From the top of a 2,100-m (7,000-ft) mountain, Rymill and Chapman found mountains and glaciers stretching west and north as far as they could see – another 65–80 km (40–50 mi). The glacier crevasses looked "very much worse" than those they had already crossed. Rymill had in fact fallen into one. "It is almost impossible for one man to pull another out of the type of crevasse we were meeting." With a party of only two they considered the risks were too great and decided to turn back, reaching their base on April 5. An early breakup of the pack ice further hindered their survey of the coast in the vicinity of Tugtilik, but they made a second journey inland, where they were able to extend the survey made in March, and returned to the base on May 26. They encountered heavy ice on a boat trip in June to Ammassalik and were held up at one point for ten days. Rymill wrote (1936:371):

> We were anchored in a bad place, but by blowing up a floe with dynamite we were able to work the boat behind some protruding rocks, where she would be safe from the ice. The bad weather continued, and as we were anchored under a cliff, we were in danger of being hit by falling stones. These stones are loosened by continuing thawing and freezing, and we could hear them falling all around us. By using some more dynamite we were able to work our way into a neighboring fjord where we found a good anchorage for the boat. We waited here for ten days until the ice opened up again.

They concluded their work in August by mapping the coast from Tugtilik to Sermiligâq ("a fjord with several glaciers") 92 km (57 mi) from Ammassalik, in all about 210 km (130 mi) of convoluted coast. They left Greenland on *Nordstjernen*, the schooner supporting Knud Rasmussen's Seventh Thule Expedition, on September 21, 1933.

Their expedition had been greatly handicapped by the loss of Watkins the leader – a quarter of their manpower, by difficult and dangerous sea-ice conditions for small boat travel along the coast, by unstable and very rough ice compounded by deep snow for sledge travel on the coast, by having less than the minimum number of people needed for safe travel on the inland ice, by severely crevassed and mountainous terrain on the inland journeys, by deep soft snow and frequent blizzards near their base, and by an early breakup of sea ice in the fjords. With all the difficulties, they achieved many of their main objectives – a nearly full year of meteorological observations and topographical mapping of the terrain near Tugtilik and 210 km (130 mi) of coast from Tugtilik toward Ammassalik.

John Rymill later led a very successful three-year expedition to Antarctica on which Riley, W.E. Hampton, and Alfred Stephenson, all veterans of Watkins' expeditions, served. Rymill was awarded the Polar Medal and the Founder's Medal of the Royal Geographical Society. He died in

1968 in an automobile accident near his birthplace of Old Penola Station in Australia, aged sixty-three.

BOYD AND NEW DISCOVERIES WITHIN THE GREAT FJORD, 1933

Louise Boyd returned to East Greenland in 1933, again chartering *Veslekari* and taking a scientific staff of five. The main objective was study "of certain elements of [the] remarkable scenery, particularly the fjords and glacial marginal features" (Boyd 1934:465). They planned to map small, critically selected areas in detail using photogrammetrical techniques then being developed by the American Geographical Society. "To the best of my knowledge," Boyd wrote (1934:465), "we were the first American expedition equipped to undertake ground photogrammetrical survey." They mapped five areas with the new techniques on this expedition.

Boyd had a sonic depthfinder installed on *Veslekari* so that they might examine the fjords in detail and obtain profiles of the North Atlantic Ocean between Norway and Greenland. Tests off the Norwegian coast showed that the machine could sound as deep as 2,200 m, or 1,200 fathoms (7,200 ft). Prior to this test, sounders that could be installed on vessels such as *Veslekari* had not reached depths greater than 1,375 m, or 750 fathoms.

Veslekari sailed from Norway on July 4, and after a stop of several days at Jan Mayen met drifting ice on July 12. The ship voyaged through 224 km (139 mi) of ice in about nineteen hours and reached Greenland thirty-six hours after leaving Jan Mayen. The ice-free water along the Greenland coast was several kilometres wide. The fjord region was now before them, Boyd wrote (1935:11), "a land where deep inlets cleave the coast and run back among the mountains as far as 120 miles (192 km.) from the outer skerries; where walls of rock, bizarre in form and brilliant in color, rise to heights of more than a mile above the calm waters of the fjords; where mighty glaciers come down from the inland ice cap to the fjord heads and spill over the valley walls."

Near the Norwegian radio station at Myggbukta, Boyd's party installed a self-recording tide gauge, one of two lent to the expedition by the U.S. Coast and Geodetic Survey. Lauge Koch arrived in a floatplane from his expedition ship, then stopped by ice off Franklin Ø, with information about ice conditions along the coast and in the fjords, which were still solidly plugged by very thick ice. Boyd's party spent the next few days along the outer coast, waiting for the fjords to clear, visiting Bontekoe and Arundel Øer, and carrying on a detailed physiographic survey of the valley in the vicinity of Myggbukta – Mosquito Bay. It was in this valley that Boyd the photographer "was unable to obtain a clear focus. I found that it was not the camera's fault, but that my lens was so covered with the massed bodies of mosquitoes that only by beating them off could I photograph my objective" (Boyd 1935:15).

They were able to enter Kejser Franz Joseph Fjord on July 23, landing at several points and finding ancient dwellings at Smedal. The farther west they went the narrower became the fjord "whose canyon-like walls increase in height, vividness of color, and beauty of form as one penetrates farther into its recesses. ... Andrée Land here dominates the western side of the fjord with a wall faced with bright and varicolored strata – among the most exquisitely tinted in the entire fjord region" (Boyd 1935:16).

The expedition set up the second automatic tide recorder in Blomster-bugt at the western end of Ymer Ø, and found that this part of the island supports an abundant plant and animal life. Herds of muskoxen and many Greenland hares roamed the hills. The hares are pure white, very large, and plentiful throughout the fjord region, although often too quick to be photographed.

The voyage in the fjord was interrupted by a radio call for help from the Norwegian vessel *Polarbjörn* which had run aground in Alpefjord 129 km (80 mi) to the south. *Veslekari* steamed all night at full speed, but then received another message that *Polarbjörn* had been refloated and all was well. Boyd sailed north again, entering Kempes Fjord and admiring the brilliant reddish hues of Geographical Society and Ymer Øer. The vessel pursued a zigzag course to obtain and record an echo-sound profile of the sounds and fjords. They found the bottom of Kejser Franz Joseph Fjord to be 762 m (2,500 ft) deep, while on each side mountains rose more than 1,830 m (6,000 ft) – nearly 2,745 m (9,000 ft) of sheer cliff. They contin-ued their physiographic studies in Isfjord.

Kjerulfs Fjord has no glacier, but within its 15-km (9-mi) length Boyd counted over 400 of the larger icebergs. The fjord appears to be a trap for icebergs drifted in from other sources. "These icebergs, majestic in height and size, give an impression of permanence and durability – a thought that is soon dispelled, however. A booming sound, reverberating through the fjord, foretells their doom. An instant later what had seemed so indestructible is now a shattered mass of broken ice" (Boyd 1934:469).

On the land inland from the head of Kjerulfs Fjord, Boyd measured Arctic willows that were 0.6–0.9 m (2–3 ft) tall, with the spread of their limbs many times greater than their height.

Beginning August 10, for several weeks they carried out their principal investigation on Frankels Land. Their route inland lay along Gregorydal, at the head of Kejser Franz Joseph Fjord, into the interior to the Mystery Lakes seen by James Wordie from Petermanns Bjerge in 1929. Boyd wrote (1935:34):

> Inanimate nature seemed almost alive in these valleys. Changes were continually taking place in the topography: rocks, large and small, single and in groups, constantly ripped down the steep mountain sides, forming deep troughs and rolling out on the valley floor. On the south wall, ice calved off from the hanging glaciers thousands of feet above us and spilled its fresh white substance over the varicolored rocks.

Along the way Boyd's party continued its detailed studies of remarkable features of the valley.

> On the north side of the valley the dry stream beds were ablaze with the autumn coloring of the bilberry, which resembles our blueberry and is delicious to eat, and of the crowberry with its dark-green foliage. Particularly brilliant were the fiery reds of the bearberry and the reds and yellows of the dwarf birch....
>
> Along the edges of the valley floor lay many old bleached reindeer horns; reindeer moss, of which I have seen but little anywhere in eastern Greenland, was also growing there. In a country now almost totally lacking this principal food for the

reindeer, it seemed astonishing to find so many of their horns and bones (Boyd 1935:34–36).

The last reindeer in East Greenland had been seen by Nathorst more than thirty years earlier.

Boyd's party reached the two Mystery Lakes on August 17 and found blocks of ice calving off Jaete Gletscher into the larger lake. Icebergs had calved into the lake when its shore lay at a higher level and were still stranded on dry land. How long they had been there was a mystery.

Boyd wrote (1935:36):

> Wind and sand to me were enemies. So fine was the sand in the Gregory and Mystery Lakes valleys that it permeated everything and did not even spare my photographic equipment. Regardless of all possible care, lenses and the innermost parts of the cameras fell its victims. Near the Mystery Lakes my large camera, even though the tripod was well braced with large stones, was suddenly hurled down a bank, necessitating repairs in camp that night.

Louise Boyd returned from Gregorydal to the ship on August 23. The next day they retrieved the tide recorder in Blomsterbugt, and on the following day fog shut in so thick that the vessel could not move. They collected the rest of the shore party returning from the lakes on the 26th, when the sunshine of summer had been replaced by fog and thick clouds. On September 1 the fog lifted and the surveyors and Boyd landed at the outer end of Kjerulfs Fjord. "Everywhere as far as one could see the autumn coloring was glorious. Its brilliant tints brought out patches of vegetation that earlier in the season had toned in indistinguishably with the rest of the landscape" (Boyd 1935:37).

The autumn colouring told them it was time to leave. As they left the head of Kejser Franz Joseph Fjord, they entered Geologfjord for an anchorage. "On both sides throughout its length of some twenty-three miles (37 km.) this fjord displays a greater quantity and variety of superbly colored strata than are to be seen for the same distance in any of the other fjords" (Boyd 1935:37). The next day, September 3, *Veslekari* went aground.

She refloated on September 4 after fifty-four tons of sea-water ballast, two motor boats, a rowboat, and more than three tons of fuel oil were taken out. Fifteen tons of coal had to be dumped. The vessel's refloating was assisted by a wire cable anchored to a small grounded iceberg 213 m (700 ft) away and wound in on the ship's winch. Once afloat, they entered Nordfjord and Moskusoksefjord, and when snow prevented further work they left Kejser Franz Joseph Fjord. Two gales and a blinding snowstorm met them near the outer coast; they awaited better weather at Myggbukta. On September 9, quite late in the season, they finally departed, meeting a narrow belt of ice that they crossed in about half an hour. They reached Norway's Lofoten Islands in four days, and were back in Ålesund on September 16 having spent sixty days in Greenland.

LINDSAY AND THE LONGEST SLEDGE JOURNEY, 1934

In the early 1930s the coast of East Greenland was generally mapped, but the western limits of much of East Greenland – where the valleys and mountains disappear under the inland ice sheet that covers most of Greenland – were unknown. In some places the inland ice comes down to the coast. Fridtjof Nansen in 1888 had been very fortunate in finding one such place near Colberger Heide where he could reach the inland ice directly from the coast and then make the first crossing of the ice sheet. H.G. Watkins had been similarly fortunate in 1930. J.P. Koch and Alfred Wegener in 1913 had reached the inland ice, but only after a substantial struggle across Storstrømmen and Dronning Louise Land. In other places the inland ice sheet reached the inner ends of the great fjords that were as much as 290 km (180 mi) inland from the coast. In most areas tens of kilometres of great mountains and valleys with badly crevassed glaciers lay between the coast and the inland Ice. It was very difficult to cross that land, as shown by James Wordie's efforts in 1926 to reach Petermanns Bjerge and John Rymill's efforts in 1933 to push inland from Tugtilik. Hardly anyone other than those few had attempted to penetrate overland into the interior.

Gino Watkins' small Gipsy Moth airplanes, the first to fly over East Greenland, had extended the range of sight west of the coast, and in 1930 Watkins and D'Aeth had photographed a great inland mountain range that had previously been seen only once. Flights by Knud Rasmussen and Lauge Koch in 1932 and 1933 had passed over and photographed some of the inland areas, but the westernmost limits of large areas were still unknown, and there were no astronomical positions on the land itself upon which a reliable map of the interior could be based.

Martin Lindsay decided that the way to approach the problem was from the west. If the mountainous land prohibited travelling inland from the east, he reasoned, then the inland ice offered a possible route from the west coast. Lindsay believed that he could cross the inland ice and then must inevitably come across the westernmost mountains of East Greenland as they emerged from the ice sheet. Lindsay's proposed route was not easy. It would require a sledge journey of over 970 km (600 mi) even before he reached the mountains of the east coast where his survey could begin. He would then face the task of surveying 560 km (350 mi) of country; altogether, a journey of over 1,600 km (1,000 mi) would be required. He did not get much encouragement in Britain for his proposal. The general opinion seemed to be that such a long unsupported sledge journey was impossible. The Royal Geographical Society refused his request for support. It was only because of a mistake in the British Foreign Office that Denmark gave Lindsay permission for the expedition. The merit of Lindsay's approach to the problem became clear in 1934 even as he was carrying it out. In that summer a French party and an Italian party each tried to approach the Blosseville Kyst and journey inland to map the interior. Neither was successful even in getting ashore.

Lindsay, a lieutenant with the Royal Scots Fusiliers, had been a surveyor with Watkins in 1930–31, and he had sledged across the ice cap from Watkins' base to Ivigtut in Southwest Greenland with J.M. Scott and Alfred Stephenson. His companions for the new venture in 1934 were Andrew Croft, photographer and dog driver, and Lieutenant Arthur Godfrey of the Royal Engineers, surveyor. Lindsay sent Croft to Greenland in the autumn of 1933 to buy dogs, to learn to drive them, and to lay a one-ton cache of supplies at the edge of the ice sheet. Lindsay and Godfrey followed in the spring of 1934, but their ship was delayed three weeks before arriving in West Greenland. Their approach to the ice sheet therefore was made difficult and miserable by the thaw of snow and ice. It ensnared their dogs and sledges on bare stony ground, on hard rough ice, and in morasses of melted snow and slush on the edge of the ice sheet. On June 10, after a difficult struggle to overcome those difficulties, they started across the inland ice. Lindsay wrote (1935a:398):

> The following week was the worst any of us had ever experienced. Always wet to the skin, we had to relay our heavy loads through morasses often waist deep, a process extremely exhausting to men and dogs.... The ridges between the swamps were seamed with crevasses, in which we had the misfortune to lose five dogs.... We experienced great difficulty in persuading the dogs to wade or swim the streams. They would cower shivering on the banks until one less timid than the rest could be induced to lead the way.

By June 18 Lindsay, Godfrey, and Croft were beyond the thaw zone and for the next two weeks they enjoyed fast travelling. As they approached the east coast the travelling became more difficult and they began to experience bad weather. On July 12–15 a blizzard confined them to their tent. "We experienced a slight foretaste of the really bad weather that was to be our fate for the second half of the journey." Once they could travel again, they were in a state of excited uncertainty because they could not know when they might expect to find land emerging from the ice. If they had known, they would not have been there; it was their job to find out. Lindsay wrote (1935b:205) of July 20: "The next few hours were amongst the most memorable of my life." The first land they came upon was a typical Alpine formation. "No sailor has ever made a more welcome land-fall" (Lindsay 1935a:399). Croft wrote (Lindsay 1935b:205):

> During this never-to-be-forgotten time peaks appeared over the horizon with thrilling rapidity, both to our left and right fronts, and straight ahead a long span of land mostly covered by ice and snow. It was an awe-inspiring and grand sight after the past few weeks of barren wilderness; each rise we crossed the more peaks we saw, and towards the end of the night's journey the long absent sun came vaguely through the heavy clouds and twinkled on these glorious sights.

When Lindsay, Croft, and Godfrey sighted land on the east coast they had travelled 1,050 km (650 mi), including relays, from the west coast. It had taken them almost five weeks to cross the ice sheet. They were west of the innermost reaches of Scoresby Sund. Ahead of them on their route to the southwest, behind the Blosseville Kyst and the Kangerdlugssuaq country that had frustrated John Rymill, lay 560 km (350 mi) of uncharted mountain country, the longest piece of still uncharted territory in the Arctic. Lindsay would carry his survey down as far as Mont Forel, one of the highest mountains in East Greenland. Lindsay's final destination, Watkins' base in 1930–31, was 887 km (550 mi) away.

Mont Forel had been discovered by the Swiss glaciologist and mountaineer Alfred de Quervain in 1912. He and three other skiers and mountaineers crossed the ice cap from Disko Bugt to Ammassalik as part of a study of the "balance sheet" – the gains and losses of snow – of the inland ice. The Swiss travelled with three sledges and twenty-five dogs making the crossing in little more than a month. It was a well-planned expedition that had few adventures and accomplished a series of detailed and significant observations of the ice sheet. Their closest approach to Mont Forel was 113 km (70 mi).

Mont Forel had been surveyed in 1931 by Alfred Stephenson, travelling from Watkins' base camp with E.W. Bingham and Lawrence Wager. The journey to the mountain took Stephenson's party sixteen days and covered 284 km (176 mi). Stephenson and Wager climbed to within 213 m (700 ft) of the top, but were prevented from reaching the summit by the steep slopes of the ice dome that caps the mountain. They had reached 3,170 m (10,400 ft), the highest point reached at that time in the Arctic and 244 m (800 ft) higher than Petermanns Bjerge, climbed by Wordie's party two years earlier. On their return Stephenson's party were able to survey much of the terrain from Mont Forel to Watkins' base.

Lindsay's route to Mont Forel in 1934 lay across a series of hills and valleys of ice caused by the lay of the land under the ice. Lindsay wrote (1935a:400): "One of these eminences will always remain in our memories. Having climbed somewhat laboriously to the top from the ice-cap side we were confronted by a magnificent vista of mountains to the south, south-east, and south-west. Range upon range stretched before us; peak after snow-clad peak stabbed a cloudless sky."

But clear weather essential for the survey was rare. Only three days out of eleven were clear in that northern part of their survey. One day the weather was overcast as they approached an ice ridge, but, wrote Lindsay (1935b:215–16),

> then the sun peeped out from under the blanket of clouds and cast the most glorious light all around, tingeing everything with reddish gold.... We went over the crest and reached the summit quite suddenly, to be confronted by a truly magnificent panorama. It was a view that none of us will ever forget, and the abruptness of it almost took one's breath away.... To the South was a superb vista of ranges stretching as far as one could see. They all appeared to be typical basalt piles showing the characteristic step structure, and with the flows lying horizontal. Most of them were pyramidal in shape, looking fantastically Egyptian and curiously out of place. In the distance there were many lovely ice-peaks and one great mountain mass which ... caused us considerable excitement.

That great mountain mass would prove, after agonizing uncertainty, to be the peak whose geographical position they had come so far to determine.

Slowly they made their way southwest, mapping and photographing the mountains and collecting geological specimens where possible. It was hard going. "The crossing had taken far more out of us than we had realized at the time ... we were in a wretched state of permanent fatigue" (Lindsay 1935a:401). Lindsay gave Godfrey great praise for the painstaking manner in which he carried on the survey. "Only those people who have themselves attempted similar work in the face of cold, hunger, and at times almost overpowering fatigue, can properly appreciate his work" (1935a:401). Lindsay credited Croft with keeping the dogs at work when they were thoroughly worn out and bored with hauling the sledges. The dogs had by then been in their harnesses nearly three months and would spend fifteen weeks altogether in harness. "That we managed to keep them going in the face of greatest reluctance on their part was entirely due to the brilliant driving of Croft.... There are probably not more than half a dozen men in the world who could have driven those dogs at that stage of the journey. Without Croft's driving our transport system would have collapsed, and we would have had difficulty in completing the journey" (Lindsay 1935a:401).

Early in August they had a splendid view of the great mountain mass. They called it The Monarch. The Danes named it Gunnbjørnsfjeld. At 3693 m (12,200 ft), it is the highest in Greenland and in the Arctic. "In front of us was The Monarch massif, rising sheer on the far side of the Glacier. The sun, now very low in the heavens at midnight, shone on it and clothed it with a golden sheen, and the Glacier itself was crimson. The whole panorama was soaked in beauty and none of us will ever forget it" (Lindsay 1935b:233).

For the first time since Amdrup had seen it from Nordre Aputiteq in 1900 and Watkins had photographed it from the air in 1930, the mountain's position was established by a proper land survey. Lindsay had great hopes that his expedition would be able to do so; its accomplishment was a proud moment for him, but the mountain's position was determined only with difficulty. Lindsay was convinced at the first sighting that it was the highest mountain, but Godfrey's initial computations indicated that it was not, and Lindsay was crushed. Only days later did Godfrey find a mistake in his figures, and all rejoiced in the result. Lindsay wrote of their hopes to locate Gunnbjørnsfjeld: "it carried us forward when life was difficult; it fed us and kept us warm.... With a climax followed by two anti-climaxes and then one last smashing climax, it burnt through our feelings like an electric needle, causing us in turn all the pains of exultation, bitterness, despair, merriment and then once more, and finally, exultation" (Lindsay 1935b:224).

Quite unexpectedly, because the inland ice had been thought to extend unbroken almost to the sea coast immediately south of Kangerdlugssuaq, they discovered a new range of mountains with alpine features that rose to over 3,050 m (10,000 ft) and stretched for 113 km (70 mi) toward the south. The new range was later named the Kronprins Frederik Bjerge. When about 32 km (20 mi) north of Mont Forel, Lindsay's expedition reached an elevation of 3,290 m (10,800 ft), the highest altitude of the inland ice of Greenland.

They arrived at their destination, Watkins' base in 1930–31, on September 5. They had travelled 1,920 km (1,200 mi), and for 1,760 km

(1,100 mi) they had been entirely self-supporting without assisting parties or pre-arranged food depots or game from the land. This was certainly one of the longest self-supported sledge journeys ever undertaken.

They had accomplished their purposes, a survey of the inland mountains from 70° N to Mont Forel at about 67° N, and measurements of the altitudes of a large section of the inland ice. They had pinpointed the location of Gunnbjørnsfjeld. They had obtained photographic panoramas of the newly discovered mountain ranges to aid the construction of a map. In spite of the consistently bad weather they had obtained ten astronomical fixes of their positions along the survey route. They had occupied an additional thirty survey stations from which they had taken bearings to the new land. They had maintained a detailed meteorological log throughout the journey.

Inuit took them by boat from Watkins' base to Ammassalik about 48 km (30 mi) away, and a Scottish fishing vessel took them on board on September 15 just before the pack ice closed in. If the vessel had been a half day later, they would have had to remain for the winter. Lindsay, Croft, and Godfrey reached Aberdeen three weeks later.

Andrew Croft and Arthur Godfrey later served with distinction in other Arctic work. Martin Lindsay was awarded a Gold Medal by the French Geographical Society and was recognized by the Royal Belgian Society and the Royal Swedish Society for Geography and Anthropology for the work of his expedition. He was later elected to Parliament and knighted. Sir Martin Lindsay, CBE, DSO, died at age seventy-five in 1981.

COURTAULD'S TRAVELS IN RASMUSSEN LAND, 1935

Augustine Courtauld had been part of Wordie's expedition of 1926 and that of 1929 when they had climbed Petermanns Bjerge, then thought to be the highest mountain in Greenland. Courtauld had also been with the Watkins expedition in 1930–31 when Watkins, flying over the coast, had seen mountains far inland that he thought exceeded 3,660 m (12,000 ft) in height. Martin Lindsay approached the mountains in 1934 by sledging over the ice sheet from the west coast, and Lindsay's party was able to fix the position of the mountains. In 1934, also, French and Italian expeditions had planned to cross the coastal ranges to climb the mountains, but neither was successful in reaching the coast.

Courtauld and Lawrence Wager planned a joint expedition in 1935 for the dual purpose of climbing the mountains and studying the geology of the region. They had the benefit of the aerial photographs and maps made by Knud Rasmussen's Seventh Thule Expedition in 1932 and 1933. Courtauld's climbing party would return to England at the end of the summer. Wager's party would spend the winter. Wager was an experienced mountaineer as well as a geologist with Arctic experience. In 1933 he had participated in a Mount Everest expedition.

Courtauld's party included three Danes, Ebbe Munck and the archaeologists Helge Larsen and Eigil Knuth, and four wives of English participants. The wives' "presence on board proved pleasant and useful" (Courtauld 1936:196).

Courtauld and Wager chartered *Quest*, the vessel that Watkins had used. They left Aberdeen on July 4 and encountered the ice pack on July 15. From the edge of the pack the coastal mountains could be seen clearly, but the ship soon got into a "tight belt of small floes with a large number of great icebergs around us.... Toward evening we lost manuevering power owing to the ice being pressed around the ship so closely that the propeller could not be moved" (Courtauld 1936:196). The strong southerly current drifted them helplessly toward a line of icebergs, one of which was found by measurement to be 66 m (216 ft) high. The crew tried dynamite to free the ship, to no avail. When it appeared that they would be carried onto the icebergs, preparations were made to abandon the vessel. The current carried the vessel around and past two potentially lethal bergs, one of which they cleared by a few metres and the other by half the ship's length. By evening of the following day, in thick fog, they reached an anchorage behind Kap Dan. At Ammassalik they took on board two Inuit families, totalling fourteen people, who were to spend the winter with Wager's party. Courtauld noted (1936:197) that "there were fourteen of ourselves, fourteen crew, fourteen Eskimo, and fourteen dogs." *Quest* steamed north for two days inside the coastal islands. Then they met thick and closely packed ice with no open water next to the land. The next day they were able to reach Lake Fjord, or Tugtilik, and the day after that, still in fog, they steamed out and were caught by the pack and carried 19 km (12 mi) offshore. For eight days they were held in the pack in perfect weather – blue sky, bright sun, and no wind. They succeeded in reaching Kangerdlugssuaq, but it took two days to cross the fjord, where they landed the Inuit and the archaeologists. Open water enabled the vessel to reach Irminger Fjord. They had hoped to reach farther along the coast where there seemed to be a possible route inland to the mountains. Because the ice that delayed them appeared unlikely to change and the season was getting late, they decided they must make an attempt to reach the mountains from Irminger Fjord, even though that entailed an overland journey of 160 km (100 mi) each way. A preliminary reconnaissance, in bad weather, found a possible sledge route inland, and on August 7 they started, the main party of six men, with a supporting party of three, and with three Norwegians from the crew assisting. They had two sledges, which they hauled, and food for four weeks. The Norwegians, not equipped for camping, turned back at the end of the first day. The next day the weather became fair and remained so almost continuously for the rest of the journey. For a week their route lay west of the Sorgenfri ("Sorrow-free") Gletscher, across snow fields – "the snow was soft and like a mixture of sand and glue" (Courtauld 1936:199), over small glaciers, along ridges, and through mountain passes, dragging and relaying their sledges. They had to get beyond the badly crevassed zone of the Sorgenfri Gletscher and to a point where they could cross the Christian IV's Gletscher, which lay between them and the mountains. From a pass of 1,006 m (3,300 ft) they could see in the northwest "the magnificent southern face of the Watkins Mountain. The wall of this range ... made a wonderful contrast to the sharp spires of the Kangerdlugssuaq peaks, and Wager, who knows the Himalaya, thought it the most impressive mountain wall he had ever seen" (Courtauld 1936:200). The supporting party turned back as they approached the Christian IV's Gletscher. Courtauld's and Wager's party negotiated a complex and difficult system of crevasses and reached the big glacier. On a rocky point by the ice edge Wager found fine impressions of fossil plants. Christian IV's Gletscher is one of the largest true glaciers in the world, 177 km (110 mi) long and 11–24 km (7–15 mi) wide between high mountain walls. They had feared that it would have crevasses too wide to cross, but the glacier surface proved to be smooth and level. "The only thing that worried us was the excessive glare from the level expanse of snow" (Courtauld 1936:201–2). They crossed it in two days and were then at an altitude of 1,493 m (4,900 ft) and within striking distance of the summit of Watkinsbjerge. They began the ascent at 4:30 the next morning and by noon were at 2,900 m (9,500 ft), where they left two tents and provisions. "Of the weariness of that ascent I can say nothing of interest" (Courtauld 1936:202). Late in the day they reached the summit and found it to be 3,719 m (12,200 ft) high (corrected in later years to 3,693 m or 12,116 ft). They took photographs and made observations, and Ebbe Munck hoisted the Danish flag on a ski stick. Thus was climbed the highest mountain – Gunnbjørnsfjeld – in Greenland and the Arctic. "As we slowly worked our way down the summit ridge the sun set, leaving in the north-west a sky of green and orange. The air was now completely still while the shadow of the earth came overhead like an azure shutter, turning the shadows to a deep blue against the pale snow" (Courtauld 1936:202). On the following day half the party climbed an adjacent peak. "The sharpness of the summit … made observations somewhat difficult owing to the small space, almost all of which was required for the instrument itself" (Courtauld 1936:203). In camp that night, far from the coast, they were visited by three pure white ivory gulls. The party spent a few days making observations and collections in the vicinity of the Watkinsbjerge, and then returned to the coast on August 22. *Quest* had returned to that pickup point a half hour before them.

While the climbing party was away, *Quest* landed the Danish archaeologists, Larsen and Knuth, on Skærgaard Halvø next to Kangerdlugssuaq, where they excavated the larger of two Inuit settlements consisting of seven house ruins, tent rings, graves, and meat depots. These were the ruins that Lieutenant Amdrup had discovered on his great small-boat journey along the coast thirty-five years earlier. The other site consisted of two house ruins. An excavated grave contained a woman's outfit of dishes, scoops, and knives. Another contained a body wearing a woman's ornaments, a necklace of 139 bear teeth, thirteen ornamental bodkins, a so-called winged needlecase, a thimble-guard, and a wooden scoop. Helge Larsen wrote (Courtauld 1936:211) that "few places in Greenland have given so many and such good grave-finds as Kangerdlugssuaq; the Eskimo of this region have been very careful of their dead." Numerous hunting implements and domestic tools were found in the house ruins. In all, more than a thousand implements were recovered.

The early people of Kangerdlugssuaq apparently belonged to the Inugsuk culture that had been identified earlier in West Greenland and had arrived in the Ammassalik area from the south in the latter part of the fourteenth century. Larsen estimated that they had arrived at Kangerdlugssuaq during the latter half of the fifteenth century. Larsen in 1931–32 had found remains of the Inugsuk people mixed with Thule people 740 km (460 mi) farther north at Dødemandsbugten on Clavering Ø.

Helge Larsen and Eigil Knuth found that the houses over the years had been subdivided into smaller and more easily heated compartments. Larsen believed that the houses indicated a slowly decreasing population, originally consisting of only a few hundred souls, that became extinct probably early in the nineteenth century. He felt that starvation was an unlikely explanation because of the abundance of game in the region. Larsen found seals to be "extremely abundant" in 1935. An epidemic also was not consistent with the evident slow decline of the population. He felt that births in this small population simply could not keep up with the mortality, a likely part of the dangerous life of the adult hunters. Larsen believed that "murder and revenge for bloodshed were of everyday occurrence" (Courtauld 1936:211), as they had been in the Ammassalik district, and also contributed to this dangerous life.

Courtauld's party left the coast of Greenland in memorable conditions. He wrote (1936:204–5):

> Once clear of the Kangerdlugssuaq ice and the bergs off Kap Edvard Holm, the water got more open the farther out we got.
>
> In such perfect conditions the evening was one of rare beauty for Greenland.... At sunset the lights were most beautiful. All the floes became a very pale rose while the water between was the palest green. To the west was the dark line of the coast mountains, the sky yellow and gold behind. The air was quite still with no sound.... During the [next] day, as the coastal mountains sank below the horizon, the Watkins Range climbed up out of the sea until by evening we could make out

all the high tops. Again we watched a perfect Greenland sunset: the sea, the ice, and the distant mountains all became coloured with the most delicate shades of mauve, pink, primrose and green. In the twilight mirage changed the distant icebergs into all the fantastic shapes so well known to travellers in these parts. By next morning we had passed the magic ring into the fog and grey sky of the North Atlantic.

They arrived at Aberdeen on September 9.

WAGER AND A STUDY OF KANGERDLUGSSUAQ, 1935–36

While Augustine Courtauld and his party were travelling inland in Rasmussen Land and climbing the Watkinsbjerge, *Quest* landed supplies with William Deer and P.B. Chambers, members of Lawrence Wager's party, who were to build a house on Home Bugt off Uttental Sund, adjacent to Kangerdlugssuaq, near the two houses built by Ejnar Mikkelsen in 1932. The houses would shelter Lawrence Wager's party for the coming winter. Wager had been geologist with Watkins in 1930–31 and with Mikkelsen in 1932. He also accompanied Jean Charcot on *Pourquoi-pas?* in 1934 when Charcot attempted, in vain because of heavy ice, to reach the Blosseville Kyst. Wager was anxious to return to Kangerdlugssuaq, a region of great geological interest. Courtauld had invited him to join Courtauld's mountain climbing party, an invitation Wager quickly accepted.

Wager's wintering party consisted of seven Europeans and fourteen East Greenlanders. Wager and his botanist brother, H.G. Wager, were accompanied by their wives. Deer was the second geologist, E.C. Fountaine was the doctor, mountaineer, and surveyor, and Chambers was general assistant and zoological collector. The fourteen Inuit were family and dependents of Enoch and Hansi, two outstanding hunters from the Ammassalik district.

The party was well established for the winter by the first week of September when the botanical and geological work began. The weather in September was nearly perfect for the work. Although a violent foehn wind could be heard on several occasions in the nearby main fjord, nothing of

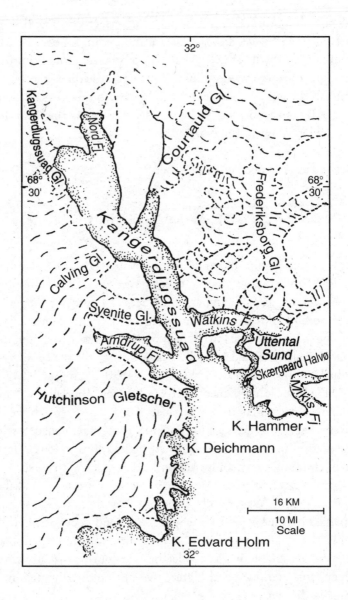

KANGERDLUGSSUAQ

it could be felt near their base in Uttental Sund, just as Ejnar Mikkelsen had experienced in 1932. The detailed geological work ended early in October when snow fell and covered the land. The expedition then turned to finding a route inland onto the ice sheet by which they hoped to make journeys in the spring all around the Kangerdlugssuaq area. Maps made from the air photographs of the Seventh Thule Expedition in 1933 were of great help in finding a possible route. Chambers and Fountaine set off with backpacks up the Frederiksborg Gletscher, but found it hopeless because of severe crevassing. In mid-October Chambers and Fountaine set off again, joined by Lawrence Wager and Deer, to try a different route. They crossed fjord ice to climb the face of a valley glacier and camped less than a kilometre above its face. "That evening there was a prolonged roar of falling and moving ice lasting many times as long as that from a disintegrating iceberg. In the morning we found that the fjord-ice over which we had sledged had been broken up by the falling away of a quarter mile of the glacier front where we had climbed on to it" (Wager 1937:398). They proceeded on and by the sixth day they had found a route inland.

Until the main fjord froze in January, travel beyond Uttental Sund was impractical. They spent November and December making a map of the base area and training dogs for the spring journeys. Depot laying in preparation for long spring journeys began in early January, but was made difficult by cold and darkness. One such journey took six weeks to lay a dump of 455 kg (1,000 lbs) at 1,341 m (4,400 ft) altitude on a glacier about 65 km (40 mi) from base. At the end of January Deer and Hansi sledged to the head of Kangerdlugssuaq, where they found that the house used by three Norwegians in 1932–33 had been completely demolished, apparently by the wind, in spite of having a concrete foundation and a 1.5-m (5-ft) wall of turf around it.

Lawrence Wager and Fountaine started for the inland ice sheet on March 5. Their travel was seriously slowed by the friction of the snow surface such that in seven days they were able to cover only 29 km (18 mi). From an advanced depot they were able to make two journeys among the mountains, covering 580 km (360 mi) in five weeks. At times in thick mist and snow, their lead dog, Piniksok, held them on a steady course, corrected only occasionally by reference to the compass. While the lowest temperature at the base was –29°–30° C (–20°–22° F), Wager and Fountaine on this journey experienced –47.2° C (–53° F).

Chambers, Deer, and H.G. Wager made a second spring journey beginning April 25. They crossed the fjord and travelled among the mountains west of Kangerdlugssuaq. This journey was hindered by snow and mist which made it dangerous to work among the crevassed glaciers among the mountains. A depot of food upon which they depended was buried and lost under 2.4–3 m (8–10 ft) of new snow. Its loss cut short the trip. They estimated the total snowfall at 4.6–6 m (15–20 ft). They returned to the base on May 13.

A number of journeys, up to eighteen days, were made from the head of the fjord down to Kap Deichmann at its southwestern corner to investigate the geology on the western shore of the Kangerdlugssuaq region. The most important geological work of the expedition lay within 65 km (40 mi) of the base. Thus in early March Deer and Hansi worked among the mountains at the head of Amdrup Fjord, at the end of March Deer and H.G. Wager investigated the mountains inland from Kap Deichmann, at the end of April Fountaine and L.R. Wager worked in the vicinity of Amdrup Fjord, and in early May Fountaine, Hansi, L.R. Wager, and the Greenlander Jacko went off to the head of Kangerdlugssuaq. Fountaine wished to measure the speed of the glacier, perhaps the fastest in East Greenland. They found the fjord ice much broken and forced into undulations by the glacier's forward motion through the winter. They found only the remains of a food dump put down and covered by heavy stones by the Watkins expedition in 1930. Most likely a huge wave produced by the formation of an iceberg from the glacier had dispersed the cache. In late July H.G. Wager and his wife and Chambers travelled in the vicinity of the Sorgenfri Gletscher collecting plants and insects. The party was in the field for eighteen days

Fountaine and Deer departed on June 1 for a second long inland journey. They had a bad start when they both broke through the sea ice and fell up to their necks in icy cold water. Fountaine wrote (Wager 1937:409): "Fortunately only the back of the sledge had broken through, the dogs and the front remaining on firmer ice; after some difficulty we ourselves were able to get out on the ice and eventually picked our way delicately to shore, where we camped and dried our clothes and equipment in the sun."

Climbing a glacier to the ice sheet, they had a minimum temperature of –27° C (-15° F), "which seemed rather low for the time of the year." On a nunatak at the edge of the ice sheet they found a broken ice-axe left by Martin Lindsay in 1934. They then travelled for twenty days across the Kangerdlugssuaq Basin around the head of the great glacier and fjord. On the last day of June they climbed Panorama Bjerge "and enjoyed a superb view of the coastal mountains, from what we believed was Mount Forel in the south to the Watkins Mountains 100 miles [162 km] away to the north-east" (Fontaine in Wager 1937:410). Their view spanned nearly 355 km (220 mi). They then travelled south along the west side of the glacier and fjord, where they met L.R. Wager and Chambers on July 14. Fountaine and Deer had travelled 725 km (450 mi) on their six-week journey.

The Inuit who had spent the year with Wager in Kangerdlugssuaq lived well. Hansi kept a record of animals killed: 410 seals, including 22 of the large bearded seals, 28 bears, and 40 narwhals.

Lawrence Wager had made arrangements to be collected in the summer of 1936 by a Norwegian sealing vessel, but was prepared to stay for a second winter if sea ice conditions made it impossible for a sealer to reach the base. Ice conditions were so favourable in 1936 that the sealer *Selis* appeared at the base on July 29, two weeks before it was expected. Because H.G. Wager's party was still in the field, the captain of *Selis* agreed to return on August 17, and on August 19 the Europeans and the Inuit were on board and on their way to Ammassalik. Wager's party landed in Iceland on August 24 and arrived in England early in September.

The expedition had achieved a very comprehensive investigation of the Kangerdlugssuaq region, and The Royal Scottish Geographical Society awarded its Gold Medal to Lawrence Wager for the excellence of the work.

This was not the last of Greenland for Lawrence Wager. He returned to the Kangerdlugssuaq region with W.A. Deer for the summer of 1953 when they found that retreat of the glaciers since 1935 had exposed many new areas of rock for study. After Wager's death in 1965 Deer returned once again to the same area in 1966 to continue the work begun by Wager in 1930 on the Watkins expedition.

DIVERSIFIED INTEREST AND ACTIVITY.

In the early and mid-1930s there was growing interest in East Greenland – in addition to that of the Danes, Norwegians, and British. In 1930 Alfred Wegener led an ambitious German expedition that was a continuation of his study of the ice sheet with J.P. Koch in 1912–13. Three stations were established, on the west coast, in the interior of the inland ice, and on the east coast. The eastern station was on the western shore of Jameson Land in the interior of Scoresby Sund, as close to the eastern edge of the ice sheet as the small party could get. Three men recorded the weather there for nearly nine months.

Part of the increased activity by several nations was a result of the Second International Polar Year of 1932–33. The French established an observatory at Scoresbysund, where they made meteorological measurements, including upper-air radio-sonde trials, and where they kept auroral records. The French equipped their station with an automobile, the second in East Greenland after that of Mylius-Erichsen's expedition, apparently to service a substation about 4 km (2.5 mi) away. Wind slowed construction of the substation. After completion it was completely blown down on November 11, 1932, but was rebuilt and operational in a month.

The Dutch established a Polar Year station at Ammassalik. They included cosmic radiation, magnetism, and ionospheric measurements in their program. Their auroral photographs were coordinated with those of the French at Scoresbysund.

Jean Charcot had led two expeditions to the Antarctic before World War I. He had his vessel *Pourquoi-pas?*, a very strong and handsome steam-powered, square-rigged bark, especially built for the second expedition. After the war he continued voyages into the Arctic. He first visited East Greenland in 1925 when he visited the newly established colony at Scoresbysund. Charcot returned to East Greenland every year, except 1927, until his death in September 1936. Charcot principally made hydrographic studies of the waters of East Greenland, and in most years Charcot also visited Scoresbysund. He transported various small expeditions, incidental to his primary oceanographic studies, on several occasions. In 1932–34 the vessel transported and supported the French Polar

Year station at Scoresbysund, and in 1934–35 Charcot supported a French anthropological expedition at Ammassalik.

Charcot, then approaching seventy years of age, set out for Greenland once again in 1936 with *Pourquoi-pas?*. Ice conditions were unusually favourable. After a stop at Ammassalik, Charcot went into Scoresby Sund for geological work on Milne Ø. As they returned from Greenland there was an explosion in the engine room and the vessel went into Iceland for repairs. They departed Iceland on September 15 for Copenhagen, where Charcot was to receive the Gold Medal of the Royal Society of Denmark. Three hours after departure the vessel ran into a storm that increased in violence during the night. The foremast was broken and the radio antenna was carried away. Because of the strength of the wind, the ship could not reach shelter in Reykjavik and so tried to steam offshore to safety. *Pourquoi-pas?* was driven onshore in the darkness and struck rocks. She began to sink at once. Only one member of the crew survived. A diver later found that the wreck was broken in four pieces. The bodies of Jean Charcot and his companions were recovered and given a national funeral in France.

BOYD – BAD ICE YEARS AND GOOD, 1937, 1938

Louise Boyd's expedition of 1937 was again on the Norwegian vessel *Veslekari* and with two geologists, a botanist, a surveyor, and a radio operator. The scientific focus of the voyage was the geological characteristics of glacial recession and the associated plant communities. The echo sounding work in 1933 had proved to be of such value that Boyd added a hydrographer to the staff with the intent of making ocean soundings a principal objective. The hydrographer would also be responsible for current, tidal, and magnetic observations.

Boyd intended to travel as far north along the east coast as ice would permit, but recognizing the uncertainties of ice conditions she planned for an alternative of returning to the region of the great fjords to continue her work there.

Boyd went out of her way to visit for a day Bjørnøya about halfway between northern Norway and Svalbard. As the expedition left the island it got a taste of the kind of season it would be. A strong southeast gale sent rough seas sweeping over the deck of *Veslekari*. Even in the mess room, water often knee-deep surged around the legs of the party. Boyd's usual visit to Jan Mayen was likewise marked by a storm. The vessel met the East Greenland ice on July 12. "So difficult did we find the ice, however, that it was not until July 25 that we finally reached the coast and landed" (Boyd 1948:11). The weather in the ice was bad with much rain and fog, contrary to clear conditions usually found in close pack ice. They landed at the southeast point of Clavering Ø, where large ice floes, some 7.6 m (25 ft) high, pressed against the shore. There they found a cabin with the French flag flying. Members of Count Gaston Micard's expedition had wintered in Loch Fine on *Quest* and were waiting at the cabin for the ice to clear so they could return to Europe. Count Micard would be back in East Greenland the next year.

We shall not encounter *Quest* again, but she was a famous old vessel (Erskine and Kjaer 1998) and she deserves a note here before we leave her. She was built in Norway in 1917 as a wooden sealer and was named *Foca 1*. *Foca 1* was of 125 tons, 39 m (111 ft) long, beam 7 m (23 ft), and with a draft of 2.75 m (9 ft) forward and 4.3 m (14 ft) aft. The bow was solid oak sheathed with iron. The vessel was originally fitted with 125 h.p. steam engine and ketch-rigged with sails. She became famous when Sir Ernest Shackleton bought her, renamed her *Quest*, and took her to the Antarctic for his last expedition in 1921–22. Shackleton died of heart failure on the vessel at South Georgia. After her return from that expedition *Quest* was bought by a Norwegian company for use again as a sealer. In 1928 she was engaged in a search for the Italian dirigible *Italia* wrecked when returning from the North Pole. In 1930 and 1935, as we saw, she took Watkins' and Courtauld's expeditions to East Greenland. The *Quest* continued as a sealing vessel until 1962, when on May 5 she sank in the ice north of Belle Isle between the coasts of Newfoundland and Labrador. No lives were lost. She had sailed both polar seas for forty-five years.

Veslekari, with Louise Boyd's 1937 expedition on board, steamed into Young Sund north of Clavering Ø, where the scientists began their work in Lerbugt. While they were ashore Boyd went on with the ship to the head of Tyroler Fjord, first explored by Julius Payer in 1869. Mountains 1,067–1,219 m (3,500–4,000 ft) high rose on each side of the narrow waterway.

Boyd brought up the scientists and the party spent several days at the head of Tyroler Fjord.

Their work was interrupted, as it had been in 1933, by a call from *Polarbjörn*, fast aground for three days at Zackenberg Bugt in Young Sund. The ship had grounded near her bow when the echo-sounder located amidships was showing adequate water under the keel. It took eight hours for *Veslekari* to float *Polarbjörn*. Boyd left Young Sund on August 4, and, convinced that dense ice would preclude a voyage north along the coast, she decided to return to Kejser Franz Joseph Fjord. En route they met very heavy ice off Hold with Hope. "We had to wind our way slowly and with much pushing through ice floes, some of which were heavy and closely compacted." They were stopped by thick ice off Home Forland and later found the radio station, Myggbukta, at Mackenzie Bugt blocked with firm ice. By perseverance the vessel found open water in Foster Bugt and entered Kejser Franz Joseph Fjord. Boyd wrote (1948:24): "This was my third visit, but repeated visits increase rather than diminish the thrill that one experiences at the grandeur of this fjord, the magnificence of its towering walls and snow-covered mountain borders with summits rising to 7,000 to 11,000 feet [2,134–3,537 m]. The brilliant coloring of the walls, whether seen in dull light or full sun, has a beauty and vividness quite beyond imagination."

They stopped briefly at the mouth of Geologfjord and anchored in Blomsterbugt, where everywhere there was much more snow on the mountains than in 1933. They went on to land at Renbugt and then anchored off Riddarborgen, from whence they took motor dories to the Nordenskiöld Gletscher at the head of Kejser Franz Joseph Fjord.

On August 9 the scientific party landed at the head of Kjerulfs Fjord for a four-day investigation. Their camp was at the head of Agassiz Dal. The floor of the east-west part of the valley is filled with glaciers, and the mountains rise almost perpendicularly to 1,830–2,164 m.(6,000–7,000 ft) or more. The ship moved out of the fjord and anchored on the south side of Ymer Ø. Two days of very bad weather followed during which no one could go ashore or the vessel move from its anchorage. On August 17 they visited the Danish radio station at Ella Ø. They entered Kempes Fjord and Rhedins Fjord on August 18, but clouds and fog precluded any useful scientific work except echo-sounding. Bad weather continued as they went farther south in Kong Oscar Fjord and when they anchored in Alpefjord. They found an anchorage at the northwest end of Narvhal Sund, where the geologists were able to do some work on the larger of two glaciers.

Because of the bad weather and the amount of pack ice drifting far into the fjords, portending an early winter, the captain of *Veslekari* on August 23 ordered that they finish their work and depart for the outer coast. They spent one more day ashore at Blomsterbugt. They found thick, tight ice in Foster Bugt and were unable to break through to the open sea. The ice squeezed the ship, but she was freed by the use of 2 kg (5 lbs) of dynamite attached to poles and thrust into small openings under the ice close to the ship. Their only option was to retreat by way of Sofia Sund between Ymer and Traill Øer into Kong Oscar Fjord. They worked for eleven hours on August 26 to get through the ice to the entrance to Sofia Sund through which they were able to reach Kong Oscar Fjord without difficulty. In the fjord itself there was much thick ice; many of the floes were 4.6 m (15 ft) above the water. There followed two days of hard work to get the ship through. They were out of the ice by 2:00 a.m. on August 29. Boyd returned to Norway on September 19 by way of Spitsbergen.

Because of the very bad ice conditions of 1937, Louise Boyd had been unable to voyage very far north along the coast as she had hoped. She tried again in 1938. Her expedition included a hydrographer, a surveyor, a geologist, and a radio expert. They sighted the Greenland coast off Shannon Ø on July 25. Two miles of ice separated them from Lille Pendulum Ø and Bass Rock, so they moored *Veslekari* to the ice and walked to Bass Rock. The two wooden cabins built in 1901 and occupied by Ejnar Mikkelsen and Iver Iversen in 1911–12 still held stores of pemmican in perfect condition. On the 26th, after working through heavy floes, they anchored at the radio station at Eskimonæs on Clavering Ø. Moving on, they entered Copeland Fjord on the west side of Clavering Ø and spent two days in Granta Fjord, discovered by James Wordie, with an "exceptionally rich flora, and, as in all such places along this part of the coast and in the fjord region, there were many musk oxen" (Boyd 1948:54). On July 30 *Polarbjörn*, which had anchored nearby, requested help for their radio. Boyd's radio operator needed eight hours to repair it. The next day they began the effort to voyage as far north as possible. After working through tight ice off Wollaston Forland, *Veslekari* made good progress past Shannon Ø to the southern end of Store Koldewey. Open water permitted easy passage to the northern end of Germania Land, but ice completely blocked Skær-fjorden. They were stopped at the northern end of Ile de France at about 77°50' N. Securing the ship to the edge of the fast ice, Boyd's party went ashore. It was the farthest north landing that had then been made from a ship on the east coast of Greenland. All of this outer coast, from Store Koldewey to Ile de France, is low and unbroken by inlets or harbours. It offers no refuge from ice pressing upon the land. The captain urged that they depart later that day, August 3, to avoid being caught in the south-drifting ice fields. They were able to land at Danmarkshavn, one of the best harbours in East Greenland, where Mylius-Erichsen's expedition had spent two winters. Unlike the huts at Bass Rock, the house at Danmarkshavn was in bad condition and little usable material remained. Boyd's party found many muskoxen and hares enjoying the good vegetation in the valleys near by. By August 10 the ice in Dove Bugt opened to permit them to enter Mørkefjord. Returning to Danmarkshavn, they met Count Eigil Knuth's ship *Gamma* and Count Gaston Micard's *En Avant*, both expeditions spent the following winter in the vicinity. Boyd returned south along the east coast of Store Koldewey. From a peak on the island Boyd could see that the southern end of Dove Bugt was ice-free, therefore they entered and ran into Bessel Fjord, a long narrow fjord running 55 km (34 mi) due west. "The walls are in many places, especially on the north side, nearly vertical. Here are to be found some of the most colorful and striking bandings that I have seen in any of the East Greenland fjords" (Boyd 1948:72). The head of the fjord broadened into low, level ground on which were two hunters' cabins and numerous muskoxen grazing on rich vegetation.

Boyd's expedition corrected the map of small islands in the northern end of Dove Bugt, and at Godfred Hansen Ø they met the Danish ship *Gustav Holm*, which was unloading materials for a new hunting station. In three weeks *Veslekari* had been able to get into every part of Dove Bugt. Farther south, entering Ardencaple Fjord first explored by the Danmark Expedition in 1908, Boyd wrote (1948:77) that "the colorings and bandings of Ardencaple Fjord, particularly those at the western end, are among the finest and most brilliant to be found anywhere on the entire east coast of Greenland.... The cliffs, which in places rise to 5,000 feet [1524 m] and more, are covered with them [the colored bands] for many miles. The brilliant coloring continues in Brede Fjord."

Glaciers of all kinds and descriptions covered the walls of Smallefjord, an inner branch of Ardencaple Fjord, completely dominating the fjord.

Boyd took her departure for Norway from the southeast corner of Shannon Ø on August 27 and met no serious ice. *Veslekari* arrived back in Tromsø on September 8 by way of Adventfjorden in Spitsbergen. This was the last of Louise Boyd's expeditions to Greenland.

The two major reports of Louise Boyd's expeditions to Greenland, published by the American Geographical Society, contained seventeen scientific reports by participants. The publication of the second volume, reporting her 1937 and 1938 voyages, was delayed until after World War II so that the many photographs and information therein could not aid the Germans in their efforts to establish weather stations in East Greenland. She took tens of thousands of photographs of the Arctic regions, all deposited with the society. Louise Boyd was made an Honorary Fellow and received the Callum Geographical Medal of the American Geographical Society. She was a Chevalier of the Legion of Honor of France and received the Medal of King Christian X of Denmark and the Andrée Plaque of the Swedish Academy of Anthropology and Geography. She received honorary degrees from the Universities of California and Alaska and from Mills College, and she was an honorary member of the California Academy of Sciences. Louise Boyd died in 1972. "Thus ended the long life of a woman as remarkable for her social and cultural stature as for her impact on polar exploration and on the lives of many man and women of science" (Wood and Washburn 1973:279).

Exploration Completed, Society Transformed

KNUTH FOLLOWS MYLIUS-ERICHSEN, 1938–39

Count Eigil Knuth and Ebbe Munck conceived their expedition to Northeast Greenland while on Augustine Courtauld's expedition to Rasmussen Land in 1935. Munck was one of the party that climbed Gunnsbjørnsfjeld and Knuth excavated archaeological sites with Helge Larsen. Knuth readily admitted that his and Munck's love of East Greenland was in part the reason for their proposal for their own expedition, but they also felt that their generation had an obligation to continue the work of previous generations in exploring Greenland and maintaining Denmark's claim of sovereignty to the world's largest island. Knuth wrote (1942:24): "Hardly had the men of one generation concluded their work before a fresh party was ready to step in, and this tradition must be continued."

Eigil Knuth and Ebbe Munck organized the year-long expedition in fewer than six months. They were precipitated to the effort in part by a report that Ivan Papanin of the Russian scientific station named North Pole One, drifting on an ice floe out of the Arctic Ocean, had sighted new land between Svalbard and Northeast Greenland. The report stimulated interest in several countries. The feeling in Denmark was that since the discovery must lie closer to Greenland, it was important that Danes be the first to confirm and explore the discovery. It was this report that Lauge Koch investigated and found to be groundless with his flight in the spring of 1938 from Spitsbergen to Peary Land, but that objective had been only a secondary purpose for Knuth and Munck. Their primary efforts would be the scientific investigation of the coast of East Greenland from Danmarkshavn north to Peary Land. It had not been examined since the work of Mylius-Erichsen and the Danmark Expedition in 1906–8, and seen since only by Mikkelsen and Iversen on their desperate journey of 1910 and from aircraft by Lauge Koch in 1933.

Eigil Knuth was the largest financial contributor to the expedition. His long life was dedicated to the exploration of the Paleo-Eskimo and Inuit cultures of Greenland. He began his work in 1932. He returned whenever he could for sixty years; he spent his ninety-first summer in Northeast Greenland.

Knuth and Munck acquired *Gamma*, a 28.5 m (93.5 ft) wooden three-masted schooner and had her re-powered and strengthened and ice sheathed. Such a vessel of their own would make them independent of charter restrictions in working their way through pack ice. The Royal Danish Army Flying Corps lent them for the summer a de Havilland Tiger Moth aircraft on floats and a pilot, Captain Michael Hansen, who had never before flown a seaplane.

The small party had a strong scientific staff with much Arctic experience. Eigil Nielsen, geologist, had spent three winters on the east coast of Greenland, at Eskimonæs, 1932–33 and 1936–37, and at Scoresbysund, 1937–38. Paul Gelting, botanist, had wintered in East Greenland at Eskimonæs, 1931–32, and had spent three summers travelling the coast from Scoresby Sund to Wollaston Forland. Alwin Pedersen, zoologist, had wintered at Scoresbysund with Ejnar Mikkelsen's colonizing expedition of 1924–25, and in 1927–29 again at Scoresbysund, and in 1931–33 on Clavering Ø and Hochstetter Forland with Lauge Koch's expedition. Kurt Bek was a wireless operator for the Royal Danish Army Flying Corps. Svend Sølver was meteorologist, geologist, and cartographer. He had spent the year of 1933–34 at the magnetic observatory at Godhavn in West Greenland. The Danes were assisted by three West Greenlanders expert in the handling of dog teams: Ove Rossbach from Rodebay, Disko Bugt, Sakæus Sandgreen from Akunak, Disko Bugt , and Eli Kristiansen from Jacobshavn, now Ilulissat.

Eigil Knuth had not intended to winter himself on the expedition because he had planned work at Ammassalik. It was not possible to find an archaeologist, however, and so the Danish National Museum persuaded Knuth to fill that role. Knuth was trained as a sculptor, but he had participated in archaeological work in West Greenland in 1932 and 1934 under Aage Roussell and in East Greenland in 1935 with Helge Larsen. He had sledged across the Greenland ice sheet with a French expedition in 1936 and had spent the winter of 1936–37 at Ammassalik.

In addition to the pilot, Michael Hansen, there were three other summer members of the expedition: Ebbe Munck, whose principal role was to look after expedition affairs in Denmark; Aage Gitz-Johansen, an artist who had visited Greenland four times and had wintered on the west and east coasts; and Flemming Andersen, a zoologist on his first Greenland expedition.

The objectives of the scientific work were:

- *Archaeology:* a determination of the northern limit of the southern Eskimo culture, and the immigration road of the northwestern culture
- *Botany:* a floristic investigation of the region to make a statistical analysis of the vegetation and study the biology and ecology of plants in various places, to make an investigation of the annual variations of temperatures within the vegetation of various types and at the root level about 10 cm below the surface, to measure depths and durations of snow cover, to measure hydrogen-ion concentrations (soil acidity), and collect mosses and lichens.
- *Geology:* a study by Eigil Nielsen of Permo-Carboniferous strata of Mallemukbjerg near Ingolf Fjord, and an investigation of the northern parts of the East Greenland geosyncline and its boundary with the North Greenland geosyncline reportedly near Danmark Fjord. With the addition of Svend Sølver, bedrock geology was included in the studies as well as local map-making, observations of northern lights, and increased meteorological observations, all of which Sølver undertook.
- *Meteorological observations* to be extended for several years; the chief of the Danish Meteorological Office wrote Knuth that the program would "mean an exceedingly valuable addition to our knowledge of the weather conditions in this part of Greenland."

- *Zoology:* Alwin Pedersen, already very experienced in the animal life of East Greenland, asked to join the expedition. He acted as a semi-independent investigator with the purpose of continuing his studies on the biology and occurrence of muskoxen. He also planned to make collections of mammals and birds for the Zoological Museum of Copenhagen University, and to investigate the causes of declines of land mammals of Northeast Greenland in recent years.

Gamma, loaded with seventy-two dogs from West Greenland, reached the ice edge on August 3 and turned north looking for access to the coast. The passage was hindered by fog as well as by ice, and the airplane could fly, looking for passages for *Gamma* through the ice, only on August 8 and 10. On the latter date the pilot found how "extremely difficult" it was from the air to find the small ship amidst the ice, and how important it was to take careful bearings before flying far away from it. On August 12 the ship reached Danmarkshavn, where they met the Norwegian vessels *Veslekari* with Louise Boyd's summer expedition and *Ringsæl*, renamed *En Avant*, with the expedition of co-leaders Count Gaston Micard and Willie Knutsen that would spend the winter at their station Micardbu on the coast of Germania Land. On August 13 the pilot Michael Hansen flew north as far as Kap Amelie. Ice as far as could be seen prevented further progress with *Gamma*, and therefore they sailed westward into Dove Bugt to await better ice conditions. While hunting walruses there, the propeller of *Gamma* was slightly damaged. A repair required the ship to be grounded at low tide. The expedition therefore decided to build its wintering house in Dove Bugt. A suitable site was found at the mouth of Mørkefjord, where there was rich vegetation, plentiful salmon, a good building site, and ancient Eskimo sites. By August 22 the wintering party with all its supplies was landed, Knuth had flown north to become familiar with the general terrain around the station and with sledging routes north in the following spring, and the ship moved to a site for repair of the propeller which was easily accomplished. *Gamma* passed beyond the ice on August 31 and arrived in Copenhagen on September 10.

Erection of the house and installation of radio equipment and meteorological instruments kept the wintering party busy into September.

For ten days after the ship left they enjoyed the finest weather imaginable: brilliant sunshine and calm weather from morning to night. But a gale, snow, and frost in September made a chore of all the jobs needed to complete their preparations. In October, with decreasing temperatures and daylight, they undertook the chore of sledging supplies for depots northward along the coast in anticipation of the long journeys planned for the spring. The autumn journeys were delayed to the middle of the month by a thaw that spoiled the snow and sledging surfaces. Two parties, nevertheless, laid large depots near Gamma Ø near 78° N. The sun disappeared at the end of October, not to rise again until February 13, 105 days later.

Gelting and Ove were away for ten days under bright moonlight early in November on a botanical reconnaissance into Dove Bugt, and Knuth and Sølver undertook another depot-laying journey from November 9 to 24. On their return they visited the French-Norwegian station at Micardbu. There they arranged a cooperative program of photographing northern lights. Simultaneous photographs, made possible by radio communications, from three locations, Mørkefjord, Micardbu, and *En Avant* wintering at Store Koldewey would indicate by triangulation the height and location in the sky of the auroral displays.

Gelting and Eli made a four-day botanical reconnaissance in January, and Nielsen and Ove laid another depot north of the station. February brought in violent snowstorms and more intense cold; Nielsen recorded –56° C [–68.8° F] on February 8 on his depot journey. In the summer and early autumn muskoxen had been common near the station (Knuth had seen ninety-two at one spot not far away), but had disappeared with the sun. In late winter they were found to have spent the winter on high plateaus – 600–700 m (1,968–2,296 ft) – where the wind swept the land relatively free from snow and kept the ground and vegetation uncovered.

Long depot journeys to the north were undertaken in March. The main journeys themselves began early in April and lasted into late June. While the sledgers were away, Gelting and Pedersen, together and separately, made several trips throughout Dove Bugt. Meanwhile Bek continued the meteorological observations at the station.

Eigil Nielsen and Ove Rossbach were away on their long journey from April 1 to June 13 and reached as far as Kap Prins Knud at 81°30' N, a round trip of 2,350 km (1,458 mi). They encountered an ever-changing mix of dense fog, blowing snow, violent blizzards, and very heavy going, and splendid weather and good travelling. Often on the way north they had to relay the heavy loads, tripling the distances that had to be covered. At one point Nielsen's sledge fell into a crevasse. It took several hours of work to recover it. Nielsen began his geological work on April 23, when they reached Mallemukbjerg beyond 80° N. Thereafter he frequently spent hours working among the mountains. On May 2 they turned into Ingolf Fjord, leaving a storm behind them and finding pleasant weather within. They hoped to find an inland passage – a short-cut – through the mountains of Kronprins Christian Land to the great Danmark Fjord. They found that Ingolf Fjord branched in several directions, but bare ground made it impossible to continue with sledges inland beyond the fjord. They returned to the outer coast and travelled north around Nordostrundingen on Flade Isblink, the easternmost point of Greenland, and on to the present site of Station Nord, established in 1952. This was their farthest point of travel. A typical diary entry of Nielsen read (Knuth 1942:100):

> Night 17–18 May. Went up the mountains and then drove across the glacier. As the glacier was very rough and one of Ove's sledge runners was very weak, we had to drive very cautiously. Passed Nakkehoved and continued westward. At a distance of 15–29 km [9–18 mi] from Nakkehoved a low forland was seen below the inland ice with a very irregular shoreline. In the northward continuation of a small cape of this land (Kap Prins Knud) there was a small island, which we visited. The open Wandels Hav forced us westward into an area of deep snow, where we camped. Ove looked ill.

On their return southward they met Knuth and Eli on Amdrup Land with whom they "had some drams." Aside from some gales, fog, snow, and wearisome sledging west of Schnauder Ø, their return via the French-Norwegian station at Micardbu to Mørkefjord was uneventful. They had shot five large bears and a muskox along the way, the meat essential for the dogs on the long journey.

Svend Sølver and Zachæus Sandgreen set out with one sledge and ten dogs on April 7 and returned on June 12, travelling a total distance of

1,110 km (688 mi). They found the expected mix of sledging conditions, from bad and fatiguing going to good travelling, winds that blew their tent down, thick snow, dense fog that kept them in camp, and very clear weather with excellent visibility. Twice in two days their only sledge, with all their supplies, fell into water-filled cracks in the ice covered with thin snow. They shot three bears in a six-day period early in June.

Sølver and Zachæus did not attempt to travel as far north as Nielsen and Ove, but did sledge north of Lambert Land and farther inland looking for particular bedrock conditions. Sølver recorded (Knuth 1942:105) a typical day. "May 6. Not till 11.45 a.m. did it clear so much that we could continue westward along the coast. At last, as a change from the constant migmatite, the first quartzite appeared, whose transitions to the migmatite I examined. Very slow and laborious progress all day. Travelling time 8 hours."

Eigil Knuth and Eli Kristiansen started out on April 9 with two sledges and fourteen dogs. They returned to Mørkefjord June 27, having travelled 1,710 km (1,062 mi). On the way north, while looking for Eskimo or Inuit remains, Knuth fell into the water through a patch of thin ice covered with deep snow. He soon got out but lost his "splendid new Mauser rifle" to the bottom. Eli and Knuth grappled for an hour to retrieve the rifle but in vain; the rifle was lost forever.

> May 18. Rose at midnight, when the weather was clearing. Temperatures 9.5° C below zero. Climbed a mountain to get a view of the land. Started at 4 a.m. across Dværgfjorden and camped at 5.30 a.m. on Sophus Müllers Næs, where I found the house ruin and half an hour later began digging it out. Temperature at 2 p.m. 1.5° C below zero. Turned in at 9 p.m.
>
> May 19. Rose at midnight. Temperature 2.5° C below zero. Windy and overcast with squalls of snow. Worked in the place till 10 p.m. (Knuth 1942:117–18).

The next day, May 20, as Knuth dug in house ruins, Eli became ill. At 80°53' N, just north of Ingolf Fjord, on May 21 Knuth turned back, the decision forced by Eli's illness and by foggy weather. They met Nielsen and Ove on the way south, passed "a great many" seals in Ingolf Fjord, and spent four days at Eskimonæsset, an archaeological site found by the Danmark Expedition. Knuth dug the ruins there, and Eli was worse. Eli remained ill for the next twenty days as they travelled south. Knuth paused from time to time to excavate ruins while Eli rested. During the journey south Eli slowly recovered and by June 10 he felt fully recovered. They rounded Kap Amelie, and in Penthievres Fjord they killed three muskoxen. Travel now was over thawing snow, so they were often in slush and water and travel was slow and tedious. They spent a day at Micardbu and sledged on to Danmarkshavn, where there were many eider ducks, geese, Arctic gulls, ringed plovers, and nesting terns. There they killed three muskoxen. They reached Mørkefjord two days later over melting snow and ice.

July and early August were filled with scientific work in the vicinity of the station and in Dove Bugt. Sølver mapped the area and Knuth excavated several sites. On a boat trip into the head of Mørkefjord, Gelting made a botanical reconnaissance, Knuth looked for Inuit ruins, and the geologists Nielsen and Sølver walked overland back to the station, examining the terrain along the way. Knuth then excavated in southern Dove Bugt for several days.

On August 16, 1939, *Gustav Holm* arrived at Mørkefjord with four new men to man the station for the next year. Knuth and Ebbe Munck intended that the station should be occupied for several years to provide a long record of meteorological observations and to support further scientific work. As the ship left Scoresbysund, its last stop in East Greenland, for Denmark they learned that Germany had invaded Poland, the beginning of World War II. In spite of the war, the Mørkefjord station was manned by a few people into 1942 when the Danes at Mørkefjord became part of the famous Greenland Sledge Patrol.

WAR IN EAST GREENLAND

Eigil Knuth was able to place four men to continue the work of his station at Mørkefjord for the winter of 1939–40. They were relieved by three Danes, transported by *Veslekari* resupplying Norwegian hunters, in the summer of 1940. The three Danes were Ib Poulsen, Kurt Olsen, and Marius Jensen. Poulsen and Jensen had had previous Arctic experience,

Poulsen as chief radio operator at Eskimonæs for four years and Jensen as a hunter and trapper in 1938–39. The Mørkefjord station was manned by Poulsen, Olsen, and Jensen until the summer of 1942. At that time, because of the war, the Governor of North Greenland, Eske Brun, ordered all the Danes and Norwegians in Northeast Greenland to assemble at Eskimonæs on Clavering Ø or at Scoresbysund. His intent was to establish a sledge patrol which would travel throughout the country to detect any German activity in the area. Because regular weather reports from Greenland were important for the Germans, it was expected that they would try to establish weather stations in East Greenland. In fact, they had tried in 1940 and 1941 (Selinger 2001).

The Germans occupied Denmark and Norway in the spring of 1940 and took advantage of their positions in those countries to try to establish weather stations, as supposed Norwegian or Danish hunting stations, on the East Greenland coast. In August 1940 the Norwegian sealing vessel *Furenak* was sent with four Danes to establish a hunting camp at Kap Biot at Fleming Fjord, just south of Kong Oscar Fjord. Shortly after the Danes were landed and *Furenak* departed, the Norwegian patrol vessel *Fridtjof Nansen* arrived with British Royal Marines on board. The Norwegian captain protested that the Danes were violating the international court decision of 1933 that set aside certain districts for Norwegian hunters. Inspection of the Danes' equipment by the captain and the Royal Marines strongly suggested that the camp was a covert German operation. The meteorological and radio equipment were German, there was far more equipment than was normal for hunting camps, and one of the Danes was suspected to be and later was found to be a Nazi sympathizer. The Norwegians and Royal Marines destroyed the camp and removed the Danes to Iceland, where three of them joined the Allied cause. It appears that the reason *Fridtjof Nansen* arrived so quickly at Kap Biot is because the Danish sympathizer with the Germans had encountered Ebbe Munck, Eigil Knuth's partner, in Sweden while en route to join *Furenak*. He mentioned that he was going to East Greenland. Munck evidently so advised the Norwegians in exile in Scotland, who directed their patrol vessel to investigate.

The Germans tried again in 1941. They sent the Norwegian sealer *Buskö* with supplies for a new station, Jonsbú on Hochstetter Forland,

and to resupply other Norwegian hunting stations. The U.S. Coast Guard Cutter *Northland* was at that time on the coast, and while visiting the Danish station at Ella Ø her officers were told that an unknown vessel was farther north. *Northland* went north, found *Buskö* off Hold with Hope on September 9 and took her in charge. By inspection of the ship's papers and cargo the Coast Guard officers determined it to be a German covert operation. *Buskö* was sent to Boston, Massachusetts. *Northland* then found the station at Jonsbú, and upon inspection the Coast Guard determined it to be part of the German operation. The personnel were removed and the station destroyed. This was the last German attempt to establish a covert weather station in East Greenland.

These operations by Norway, Great Britain, and the United States were all on the edge on international law. Neither the Norwegians nor the British were at war with Denmark (even though Denmark was under a German "protectorate") when *Fridtjof Nansen* destroyed the Kap Biot station. The United States was not at war with Germany or Norway or Denmark when the officers of *Northland* seized *Buskö* and closed the Jonsbú station. Further, all these actions were taken within the territorial waters of Denmark. Just before *Buskö* was seized, President Roosevelt had declared that Greenland lay within the western hemisphere and the zone of protection of the Allied powers, which gave some justification to the Coast Guard action.

Eske Brun in 1942 called for volunteers from among the few inhabitants of Northeast Greenland to form the Sledge Patrol. This action also would raise a legal eyebrow. Brun, a civil administrator of the Danish government which was under the "protection" of Germany, in fact and without any authority to do so created a quasi-military force, composed of civilians, clearly directed against a country with whom his country was not at war.

In the whole area there was a total of twenty-six Danish and Norwegian hunters and weather observers and radio operators. From the volunteers for the Sledge Patrol Brun chose fifteen and made the station at Eskimonæs their headquarters because it was near the centre of the region to be patrolled. Ib Poulsen was appointed the chief of the patrol. Kurt Olsen, Marius Jensen, Eli Knudsen, Peter Nielsen, and the Norwegian Henry Rudi were also members of the patrol. Other members were at

Scoresbysund. In early March 1943, while patrolling with two Inuit toward Sabine Ø, Marius Jensen, very much to his surprise, came upon Germans at a Danish hunting camp at Germaniahavn, where Captain Koldewey had wintered. The Germans had established a weather station on Sabine Ø in the summer of 1942. Jensen and his companions immediately retreated to a hut at Kap Wynn, but they had been seen. The Germans, hoping to capture them and stop the news of German presence, followed and caught up with them. Jensen and the Inuit managed to escape in the darkness. (There was still darkness in late March.) They had to flee without their dog teams, without adequate clothing in the sub-zero weather, and without food. Jensen and the Inuit became separated, but all managed to walk 90 km (56 mi) to Eskimonæs. Jensen did it in thirty-four hours; the Inuit took somewhat longer.

Ib Poulsen, by radio, notified Eske Brun in West Greenland of the German presence. Then he sent Marius Jensen and Eli Knudsen north to locate Peter Nielsen and to bring him back to Eskimonæs. Nielsen had spent the winter alone trapping on Hochstetter Forland. Poulsen was afraid that Nielsen might encounter the Germans on his return, not knowing they were on Sabine Ø. Anticipating a German attack on Eskimonæs, Poulsen wanted as many of the Sledge Patrol as possible at his headquarters. With Jensen and Knudsen off to the north looking for Nielsen, the Europeans, Poulsen, Olsen, and Rudi, with two Inuit, took precautionary measures. The Germans arrived at night and in the confusion of the encounter the Germans fired tracer bullets from machine guns. The defenders had only hunting rifles and could not respond to the German firepower. Poulsen, Olsen, Rudi, and the Inuit fled into the darkness, the three Europeans without dog teams or adequate clothing. Poulsen became separated from Olsen and Rudi and the Inuit were separated from the Europeans. The Europeans retreated to a hunting camp 40 km (25 mi) away, where first Rudi and Olsen and later Poulsen, after Rudi and Olsen were gone, found a little food and some old cast-off clothing. Olsen managed to get off a message to Eske Brun with the last of the battery charge on an old radio. Then they all began a retreat south to the Danish station at Ella Ø. In spite of his poor equipment, Poulsen managed to walk to Ella Ø, 371 km (230 mi), in eleven days. He was the first of the five from Eskimonæs to arrive. The Inuit arrived a few days later.

ESKIMONÆS
COURTESY ARCTIC
INSTITUTE,
DENMARK.

In the meantime, Jensen and Knudsen had found Peter Nielsen. They began their journey south, but they did not follow Poulsen's orders for the route of their return, which was intended to keep them away from the Germans. Knudsen, travelling faster with his dog team and ahead of the others, ran into the Germans at Sabine Ø. He was shot to death as he attempted to escape. Jensen and Nielsen were captured. They were held captive for some days, but by subterfuge Nielsen managed to escape with his dog team and drove without stopping to Eskimonæs, where he found that the house had been deserted by the Danes and burned by the Germans. Nielsen immediately set out again, now for Ella Ø. Some days later he came upon Henry Rudi and Kurt Olsen laboriously trudging through the deep snows of Moskusoksefjord. The three, riding in turn on the sledge, reached Ella Ø a few days later. Shortly after, they left for Scoresbysund.

Now a strange thing happened. The German commander, an Austrian named Hermann Ritter, decided to make a reconnaissance northward from Sabine Ø. He knew that by now his station location would be known to the U.S. Army Air Corps, and he expected an attack. His purpose in going north was to find a place where the station might be relocated out of reach of U.S. bombers. He set off with Marius Jensen, still a captive, and Jensen's dog team. The two travelled together, captor and captive, for several weeks. In the meantime a German party set off to attack Ella Ø using the dog teams they had taken from the Danes. Eventually Lieutenant Ritter and Marius Jensen returned to the Norwegian house at Myggbukta. There Jensen managed to seize Ritter's rifle and revolver and reverse their roles. Jensen left Ritter alone in the cabin where, without a sledge or a rifle, Ritter was in effect a prisoner. Jensen raced his team 145 km (90 mi) to Ella Ø to warn of the impending German attack. When Jensen arrived and found the station empty, he did not set off for Scoresbysund following the others. He returned to Myggbukta and collected Ritter. His motive apparently was that he would not abandon the Austrian, with whom he had travelled peacefully in the north, to possible death alone. The two started off again for the south with Jensen the captor and Ritter the captive. Jensen knew the Germans were travelling to attack Ella Ø and so his goal was Scoresbysund 468 km (290 mi) away. It took him fifteen days to get there. Along the way Jensen took every possible precaution against Ritter once again reversing their rolls, but apparently Ritter was content to be captive. He was not German and he was not a Nazi, and he had reason to fear the Gestapo if he returned to Germany. He went along quietly to Scoresbysund. Later he was flown to captivity in the United States.

The German party did reach Ella Ø, where they did some damage, but they did not burn the Danish house. After their return to their station on Sabine Ø, U.S. bombers flying from Iceland attacked the German position. No one was injured or killed and not much damage was done. When the ice opened up later in the summer a German flying boat evacuated the nineteen people to Norway, all except one who was missing. That one, Doctor Rudolph Sensse, had set off by himself to try to find Lieutenant Ritter, whose capture by Jensen was not known to the Germans. Doctor Sensse had travelled toward Myggbukta, but melting ice and open water had cut him off from returning to his base. He managed to reach the hunting camp at Germaniahavn on Sabine Ø, where Marius Jensen had first encountered the Germans in March. There the U.S. Coast Guard found Sensse when its ship came in the summer to investigate the remains of the German camp.

The Germans had destroyed the Eskimonæs station, but in the summer the Danes, with the assistance of the U.S. Coast Guard and the supply vessel *Polarbjörn*, erected a new permanent weather station not far away at a site called Sandodden on Wollaston Forland. The Danes called the new station Daneborg.

The Germans made repeated attempts to establish weather stations in East Greenland. In their later attempts they tried to locate the stations as far north as possible, remote from the Sledge Patrol and beyond the range of the U.S. Army Air Corps Their expedition in 1943 was carried on board *Coburg*, which early in September and before the weathermen could be landed, became frozen into the ice about 20 km (12 mi) from Ile de France at latitude 77°30' N. The crew struggled to free the ship from the ice, and twice blasting materials were dropped to them from aircraft; blasting did not free the ship. By mid-October the ship had drifted south to 75°20' N, and there its drift ceased. It was then about 10 km (6 mi) offshore from the site of Ejnar Mikkelsen's winter house on Shannon Ø, its closest approach to land. The German headquarters in Norway was concerned that no landing had been achieved and proposed to fly out extra supplies with dogs and sledges to assist the weathermen in getting ashore and erecting their station. When the dogs were loaded on the aircraft, they became so unmanageable because of engine noise that they had to be taken off. The flight failed in its purpose because of bad weather. The weathermen did manage to drag supplies ashore, but they were unable to erect a house onshore. A few people remained aboard *Coburg*. Most of the weathermen and some of *Coburg*'s crew lived in tents set up within caves carved into snowdrifts. The personal experiences of Doctor E.G. Triloff were reported by Arnold Court (1949:111–14):

> They had tunnelled 12 m into a drift of hard snow 3 m deep which filled the shore end of a 40 m wide rock-walled gulley. Off the tunnel, 1.5 m high and 1 m wide, four rooms were excavated, each 2.5 m square and 1.8 m high, and tents were pitched in two of them, since all the lumber had drifted away in October. The other rooms were used for storage. A thick ice layer floored the tunnel-and-room system and firn-layer banding marked the walls. Only two ice axes and some aluminum avalanche tools, too light for digging, were available; excavated snow was dragged out on a piece of canvas. Eventually five such tunnel-and-cave systems contained seven tents housing 21 men. Except when weather permitted transporting supplies [from the ship], and during other essential tasks, the men spent all their time lying in their tents. They could not sit or stand because, to save fuel, the tent peaks were cut down, in the coldest weather, to only 1 m; new settlers always pitched tents high enough to stand in, but soon learned to prefer crowding to cold.... Only 3/4 liter of gasoline was allowed per tent per day, permitting only one warm meal and 'we could warm our hands only briefly after our weather observations. Yet, as long as we lived in the tent, the temperature never fell below –15° C (+5.0° F). We all became used to the cold in an unexpectedly short time and, after initial experiments, we habitually shed all our warm clothes when we entered our sleeping bags at night, and made entries in our logs with gloveless bare fingers without

effort when the temperature was a few degrees below freezing.' [The heat from the stoves] caused the cave roofs to sag so that they had to be trimmed off periodically – a very disagreeable task because it meant striking the tent, chopping, hauling out ice and snow, and repitching the tent.... During storms snow drifts in the tunnels had to be shovelled out continually, for later they might be impossible to remove. Besides, they restricted ventilation so that 'we awoke with headaches, matches were lighted with great difficulty, a candle burned with a weak flame, and one man fainted when he was about to leave the tent.' Once four men were almost asphyxiated by battery fumes because of a snow-clogged vent.

They broadcast weather reports through the winter, but the camp was found in April by the Danish patrol. One German officer was shot to death in the encounter with the Danes, but the station was not attacked by land or bombed. Early in June the Germans were evacuated by a large aircraft that landed on an ice runway. *Coburg*, still frozen in and damaged by the ice pack, was abandoned.

The Germans made two more attempts in the autumn of 1944. The U.S. Coast Guard cutter *Northland* intercepted one vessel, *Kehdingen*, in September off Store Koldewey. This vessel had been escorted into the ice by a submarine, *U-703*, which fired a torpedo at *Northland*. The torpedo struck an ice floe and did no damage, and the U-boat, hampered by the ice and unable to take any further action, withdrew. The Germans scuttled *Kehdingen* and surrendered to the Coast Guard. Upon the failure of this attempt, the Germans diverted a weather group intended for Zemlya Frantsa-Iosifa, north of the Soviet Union, to East Greenland. This second party landed on Lille Koldewey on October 1. They were quickly discovered by an aircraft from *Eastwind*, a new, powerful U.S. Coast Guard icebreaker. (*Eastwind*, incidentally, in that season voyaged as far as 80° N off Lambert Land, a record for this coast.) The German party was quickly captured, but their vessel, *Externsteine*, disappeared. Eleven days later it was discovered trying to escape the ice. Its crew surrendered after *Eastwind* fired at it. The captured German vessel was converted into a U.S. Coast Guard auxiliary vessel.

Even after these two failures the Germans planned a new effort to set up a Greenland weather station in the autumn of 1944. They hoped to place it in Kangerdlugssuaq, considered the best location for reporting the weather likely to affect conditions in Denmark Strait and north of Iceland. They planned to land four men and equipment in late November or early December by means of a long-range flying boat. Then, perhaps because of interservice rivalries, the Navy proposed to assign a submarine, *U-877*, for the project. The Navy then thought further about the probable ice and weather conditions so late in the year and possible jeopardy to the U-boat. In mid-November 1944, the submarine was ordered away on an Atlantic patrol. It was sunk by a Canadian naval vessel two days after Christmas. In the meantime, it became apparent that the available flying boat could not for technical reasons safely complete the job. Thus ended German efforts to establish weather stations in Greenland.

Weather information from Greenland was at least as important to the allies as to the Germans, and so the U.S. Army Air Corps with Coast Guard help established its own weather stations in East Greenland. They were in Prins Christian Sund; at Kap Cort Adelaer near Puisortoq; at Skjoldungen, a small Inuit settlement established in 1938 when 150 persons were persuaded to move to the hunting grounds there; at Comanche Bugt 140 km (87 mi) southwest of Ammassalik; at Ikateq, about 32 km (20 mi) north of Ammassalik; on Skærgaard Halvø, adjacent to Kangerdlugssuaq, where Lawrence Wager's party had wintered in 1935–36; and at Hvalros Bugt, very near the colony at Scoresbysund.

Ikateq ("shallow water" – implying flat land nearby) was one of the very few places on the southeastern coast that offered the chance of an aircraft landing strip. The U.S. Army Air Corps in the summer of 1942 built a 1,220 m (4,000-ft) gravel runway to be used chiefly for emergency landings for the many hundreds of aircraft passing across Greenland to Iceland and to Scotland. Six hundred U.S. servicemen manned the site in 1944. The runway at Ikateq was difficult to approach. There were high mountains north of the airstrip, and because of the surrounding mountains air turbulence could have been a major problem for aircraft approaching or leaving the airstrip. On two occasions avalanches destroyed the control tower. Snowfall was such that it was difficult to keep the strip clear in the winter

In addition to the weather station first established at Comanche Bugt in 1942, the Air Corps wanted a site on the east coast that could support overland rescue efforts for aircraft that were forced to land on the inland ice. Comanche Bugt was one of the very few locations along that coast that provided a relatively easy route from the shore to the ice sheet. It was in fact used to attempt the rescue of the crew of a B-17 bomber that crashed on the ice sheet a few kilometres inland from the head of Comanche Bugt. The maze of crevasses that surrounded the crash site were so treacherous that two of the would-be rescuers were lost in them. The weather station was closed in the autumn of 1942 after that accident. The B-17 crew were eventually rescued by aircraft landing nearby on the ice. So difficult were the circumstances, however, that nearly six months passed, in the middle of the winter of 1942–43, before all the survivors could be removed from the wreck site.

John T. Crowell was a master mariner who in the 1920s and 1930s had taken several sailing vessels to Greenland and the Canadian Arctic. Because of his Arctic experience, he was enrolled in the U.S. Army Air Corps in 1941 and put in charge of establishing several new stations in the Canadian Arctic and in East Greenland. Major Crowell re-established the station at Comanche Bugt in 1943 and established the station at Kap Cort Adelaer in 1943. Years later he recalled a remarkable observation of ice in the East Greenland Current:[1]

> Seamen have observed that the East Greenland Current, flowing out of the Arctic Ocean, generally "hugs" the East Greenland shore. As it is laden with vast amounts of heavy, multi-year Arctic sea ice and hundreds of large icebergs from Northeast Greenland glaciers, the East Greenland coast is often fringed with a broad band of ice of both kinds, extending many miles offshore. In late summer there is usually much melting of the sea ice and breaking up of the bergs as both are carried into generally milder temperatures by the current as it moves toward Cape Farewell.

---

1 These unpublished notes by Major Crowell are preserved in the Revere Memorial Library at Isle au Haut, Maine.

During World War II U.S. Forces were active in this region and in the summer and autumn of 1943 I was part of a unit that established two weather stations on the coast between Ammassalik and Prince Christian Sound. While two of our small ships were anchored in the harbor at Cape Adelaer we experienced an exceptionally heavy and sustained northeast storm with above average air temperatures. There was a broad band of old sea ice extending from shore to miles seaward. Also there were many very large icebergs scattered amongst the ice. We had worked our way through and/or between this mass of ice with difficulty upon our initial entry into this uncharted harbor. Deep water close inshore on this part of the coast allowed large bergs to drift in close to the entrance to our harbor.

Shortly after the storm abated I had occasion to leave the harbor on one of the ships. As we gained the open ocean we noted that most of the sea ice had disappeared, probably broken by the heavy seas and rapid melt. But there was a deep, powerful ground swell still on and we were amazed to see that the sea was covered with a blanket of small bits of ice mostly no larger than a man's fist, and many smaller, extending to the horizon. This tremendous expanse of broken ice was the residue of ice bergs that had broken up during the period of heavy seas and warm temperatures due to the departed storm.... Glacial ice (icebergs) has a "built-in" internal pressure, often "spalling" large sections, which sometimes within minutes will "explode" into fist-size and smaller. Such was the case here. Many of the scores of large icebergs that we had seen slowly drifting south between our harbor and the eastern horizon had evidently been destroyed.

But now the view from our deck was unusual. The surface of the ocean, closely covered with a blanket of small chunks of clear and close-packed ice, was an undulating sheet extending toward the offshore horizon. The engine was stopped while we pondered whether to proceed, and to our surprise, a strange, continuous tinkling sound was heard caused by the continued spalling or snapping apart of the small berg fragments. It was

rather a pleasant sound, somewhat like millions of tiny casta-
nets snapping.

We resumed our course on our way to Prince Christian
Sound and Tunugliarfik passing out of the blanket of small ice
in a few hours.

The weather station that Major Crowell re-established at Comanche Bugt
was located on Atterbury Dome, 351 m (1150 ft) high, just above the bay
named after the U.S. Coast Guard cutter *Comanche* from which the site
was surveyed in July 1942. Atterbury Dome was named for the captain of
Comanche. Wallace Hansen was an Army weather observer stationed at
Comanche Bugt. Many years later he wrote (1994:42–44):

> From Atterbury Dome the setting of the Ice Cap is a vista
> of untamed splendor, possibly one of the grandest views on
> Earth. When the weather is fair in coastal Greenland, visibility
> is limited only by the Earth's curvature. To the east and south-
> east the ice-choked Atlantic Ocean stretches to the far hori-
> zon. To the west is the Ice Cap itself, awesome in its grandeur,
> and from Atterbury Dome we saw its near two-mile height
> in one unbroken declivity, from its rolling crestline down to
> the sea.... At dawn for an hour or two or three, depending on
> the season of the year and hence the position of the sun, the
> entire sixty-mile-long scene is bathed in rosy alpenglow – the
> ice bergs, pack ice, rocks, and most of all the Ice Cap itself.
> Greenland's alpenglow is not a momentary thing glimpsed and
> gone like Alfred Lord Tennyson's faint flush of Monte Rosa
> ("How faintly flush'd, how phantom fair"). It lingers on and on
> as the rising Arctic sun skims low along the eastern horizon.
> Feasting my eyes from Atterbury Dome, I gaped in awe at its
> stark beauty, but it finally did fade, and in its place as the sun
> climbed its low arc into the crisp southern sky, the Ice Cap
> gleamed white as polished platinum.

The weather station at Comanche Bugt was closed in 1944.

KNUTH IN THE NORTHERNMOST LAND, 1947 ... 1995

Eigil Knuth and Ebbe Munck returned to East Greenland in 1947, as soon after World War II as the disruption of Europe permitted. The purpose of this expedition was a continuation of that of 1938–39 – that is, comprehensive exploration of the northernmost regions of the east coast. They planned a multi-year investigation of the geology, geography, biology, meteorology, and archaeology of Peary Land, which until then, as the expedition geographer Børge Fristrup wrote (1952:87), had "remained an impregnable fort, protected to the south by the inland ice and along the coasts by a belt of pack ice that to date no ship has been able to force [true, also, sixty years later]. Expeditions traveled by sledge starting from Thule or Danmarkshavn. The journeys were long and strenuous; a prolonged stay was out of the question; and it was impossible to make any sizable geological or archaeological collection."

Peary Land is about 43,443 km² (16,700 mi²) in area and is the largest ice-free region in Greenland. Only in 1938, when Lauge Koch flew over Peary Land from Spitsbergen, had any European seen its interior.

In the summer of 1947 a reconnaissance by Knuth and Munck laid the foundation for the main effort of the new expedition to this region. Two ships, *Godthaab* and *Gamma*, established a staging base at Zackenberg Bugt on Young Sund just north of Clavering Ø. From there a Catalina flying boat lent by the Royal Danish Navy would fly 870 km (540 mi) north looking for a wintering site in Peary Land. There was considerable skepticism in Denmark that open water for flying-boat landings and take-offs could be found in the region, but Knuth and Munck believed that open water might be found in shallow Jørgen Brønlund Fjord, named for the Greenlander who perished with Mylius-Erichsen, into which a large lake and several rivers were known to flow. There the flying boat might be able to land and establish the winter station. On July 27 the first reconnaissance flight found that, as expected, Independence Fjord was covered with unbroken winter ice that precluded landings, but that Brønlund Fjord was indeed open. Knuth led the first party of scientists to land on July 30. They remained in Peary Land for two weeks while two more flights brought up the first loads of wintering equipment.

The main expedition began in August 1948 when three Catalinas brought in thirty-eight tons of supplies, the eight winter personnel, and twenty dogs. The winter house was built at about 82°12' N, only 870 km (540 mi) from the North Pole, and continuous meteorological observations and reports to Denmark began soon after.

The Danes established their station in a remarkable but truly hostile and very windy land. Børge Fristrup wrote (1952:92): "The lowlands are decidedly a high-Arctic desert. All loose material is carried away by the wind; the sandstone is hollowed and ground into the most bizarre of forms; and even the hardest stone is polished and affected." Knuth, with the eye of a trained artist, wrote (1952c:4):

> Large and small, these stones all pointed their smooth polished surface towards the head of the fjord whence the wind came. Some were slowly 'eaten up' from one end to the other, some displayed their personality by retaining certain hard edges, and were gradually carved into unequalled masterpieces of abstract sculpture. At high levels one might as it were go to an exhibition, and for hours enjoy the richness of fantasy in the barren wastes.

About 16 km (10 mi) south of the station house is Christian Erichsen Gletscher, essentially a small, isolated ice cap covering 600 km^2(230 mi^2) with its top about 884 m (2,900 ft) above sea level. A substation with self-recording weather instruments was established there, and the geographers visited it regularly throughout the following two years. Often they climbed alone through the winter to the station in darkness and snowstorms, making twenty-five ascents in all and spending 125 days on the ice cap. On those occasions they made synoptic observations with those at the base. From measurements of snow accumulations and losses and from the positions of the ice margins which in places shrank 61 m (200 ft) in two years, they concluded that the ice cap–glacier is a mass of dead ice and there is no movement.

Sledge journeys began in the autumn of 1948 to lay depots for the spring work. The autumn journeys were not completed until the end of October, long after the sun had disappeared for the year. The sunless winter was made more difficult by gales making continuous outside scientific work impossible. Knuth wrote (1952c:3–4) that the wind swept "from the head of the fjord over the unsheltered, barren plains of clay day and night. With sand-drift and driving snow, whose crystals in severe cold were as hard as the sand grains themselves, scoured the stones at will." Winds over 110 kmph (70 mph) with gusts of 150 kmph (95 mph) were frequent and prolonged the first winter, but less so in the second. Calms were rare. Knuth wrote (1952b:345) that "the maelstrom of drifting snow raged around and over the house for weeks on end, day after day without slackening its speed of 70 miles an hour. When it did stop it was only for the storm to fill its lungs for a yet stronger gust. The lulls became shorter and shorter, and even those of us who had experienced this kind of thing before felt it to be pretty tough." Fristrup wrote (1952:92): "The intense winter cold makes the earth crack, and the station was frequently shaken by frost fissuring." But indoors, meteorological and magnetic observations continued without interruption. Weather reports were transmitted to Copenhagen four times daily for two years.

Dog sledge journeys for archaeological and geological investigations began in the extreme cold of March 1949. In the two-year expedition, sledge journeys covered about 7,580 km (4,700 mi) across the length and breadth of Peary Land. Trips were made eastward along Independence Fjord to the outer coast and around Kap Eiler Rasmussen to B.C. Schley Fjord, and westward through Midsommer Sø, possibly the largest lake in Greenland, to J.P. Koch Fjord on the north coast. One party journeyed into the heart of Peary Land, sledging through Børglum Elv to Nordkrone, a massive peak over 1,737 m (5,700 ft) high. Knuth (1952c:8) called it

> the acropolis of Peary Land, not only like the sanctuary of Athens in form but, as we realized with wonder, adorned with a veritable forest of columns and ruined walls – but here the work of the wind ... [Nordkrone] is the soul of Peary Land. Isolated it lies in the heart of the country expressing all its vast solitude. With its rows of giant pillars, its glaciers snaking in heraldic designs at the foot, it bears witness to the two mighty powers that reign over Peary Land, the wind and the frost.

The region around Brønlund Fjord is part of the great plateau that extends across North Greenland. Fristrup wrote (1952:91): "It is built of early Cambrian sandstone and dolomite with frequent intrusions of diabase and dolerite which in many places show an unusually beautiful six-sided columnar structure." Diabase and dolerite are both igneous rocks formed by the solidification of molten material. On an island at the eastern end of Independence Fjord the columns are "especially beautiful and attain a height of 400 feet [122 m]" (Knuth 1952c:4). Overlying this formation are Ordovician and Silurian and more recent sediments. Fossilized molluscs and corals were found in the Cambrian, Ordovician and Silurian sediments, and fossil fish were found in Triassic sediments. Petrified wood and leaves, perhaps surprising in a high-Arctic setting, were found and thought to be of the Cretaceous or Cenozoic age. The geologist Johannes Troelsen found evidence of glaciation 550 million years ago. Near Brønlund Fjord signs of very recent (geologically) volcanic activity were present in the form of almost fifty small gravel cones capped with materials of volcanic origin.

Vegetation is extremely scarce outside the river valleys, and large areas are entirely without plant life. In favourable areas the vegetation and animal life, considering the far northern location and extreme climate of the area, are surprisingly rich and varied. Over three hundred plant species were found. Plants are able to flourish in areas with some moisture because Peary Land has more hours of sunlight from early April to early September than does Denmark in the whole year. Twenty-one bird species were seen, of which twelve were breeding. Ptarmigan in flocks of a hundred were commonly seen in the first year, and king eider ducks bred on islands in Brønlund Fjord. Wolves seen by Lauge Koch in 1921 had disappeared, as had reindeer, whose discarded antlers were found here and there. Only one polar bear was seen. In fact, it came to their camp in 1948 while they were building their winter house. The bear's stomach was empty save for one chocolate bar. Peary Land appears to be too far north for polar bears, perhaps because of a scarcity of seals in the perpetually ice-covered waters (except for shallow Brønlund Fjord). The biologist Palle Johnsen wrote (Winther et al., 1950:9) that "The abundance of musk-oxen was astonishing, particularly in the Wandel Dal and on Herlufsholm Strand."

Knuth knew from Knud Rasmussen's 1912 report of tent sites of early inhabitants of Peary Land. Knuth found fifteen sites with a total of eighty-four tent rings adjacent to Brønlund Fjord, evidently the most favourable locale of the region. In spite of a very careful search Knuth could find only very small flint tools in five or six of those rings. He wrote (1952a:25):

> It was very fortunate that the tent rings were chiefly distributed along the shores of Brønlunds Fjord where members of the expedition were confined all summer after the spring sled journeys were over. No other circumstances would have driven an archaeologist to continue his scratchings and rummagings in sterile-looking gravel exactly like the gravel outside the stone circles, when one day passed after another without brining forth the least bit of bone, wood, or artifact.
>
> But perseverance had its reward, now here, now there, in finds of a tiny flint flake with traces of fine retouching along the edge. In the course of two years these sparse, small finds amounted to quite a collection telling its own story: tiny blades of flint, knife blades, scrapers, one roughly manufactured adze blade, and small flint lamellar flakes or "microliths."

At the time Knuth concluded that those small tools were of the Paleo-Eskimo Cape Dorset Culture and estimated that the Dorset people had lived there five or six hundred years ago.

On the outer coast, 200 km (125 mi) from the base, Knuth found the wooden frame of an Inuit boat 10.6 m (35 ft) long. The boat was held together with lashings of whale baleen and big spikes of walrus ivory with barbed points. A small number of iron nails were also found in the boat. From this Knuth concluded that the boat could not be more than three hundred years old. He noted that it appears to be the only boat that has ever passed around the north coast of Greenland. The frame was nearly complete and in a remarkable state of preservation. About 100 m (328 ft) away and under 0.6 m (2 ft) of snow he found numerous tools of the Thule Culture, the fully developed Neo-Eskimo culture dependent upon marine mammals. The finds included a wooden paddle for the boat made of small pieces of wood carefully lashed together. The boat was taken to the National Museum in Copenhagen, where it was reassembled. Knuth estimated at the time that the Thule people had lived there perhaps two hundred and not more than three hundred years ago. The last of them were those twelve lonely souls Captain Clavering had met in 1823.

The carbon-14 method of determining the age of organic matter by measuring its natural radioactivity was just then being developed as Knuth made his discoveries in Peary Land and was not yet ready for practical applications. Knuth was later able to get a carbon-14 age measurement for the whale boat and found that it was 470±100 years old, not 200–300 years old. And no doubt to his astonishment, the carbon-14 method applied to organic matter in tent rings showed that the ages of his "Dorset" sites were not 500 or 600 years, but 3,000 to 4,000 years. They thus could not be Dorset, but were of much older cultures which Knuth named Independence I and II. They are the oldest sites ever found in Greenland.

In the summer of 1949 two Catalinas in sixteen flights resupplied the Peary Land station with twenty-seven tons of materials and brought in six new personnel. Seven people spent the second winter at the station, and Knuth was again the leader. He noted that during four summers, seventy-five people had set foot on Peary Land and almost seventy tons of equipment were landed in 962 flying hours. The distance flown was equal to five times around the world and without any mishap.

Knuth and the Greenlander Jens Geisler made the longest sledge journey of the expedition, travelling into Frederick E. Hyde Fjord and then through Nordpasset into O.B. Bøggild Fjord and on to Hazen Land on the north coast. In the process he made substantial revisions to the existing map. "The journey through Frederick E. Hyde Fjord was not only my greatest experience in Peary Land but revealed the most beautiful scenery I have ever seen in Greenland" (Knuth 1952c:8).

Knuth later recalled (1952c:7) "the wonderful day – the thought that we are not to experience it again is almost unbearable – on which we … set out" for a long dog-sledge journey through Independence Fjord. Knud Rasmussen had once said, "Give me winter and give me dogs and you can have the rest." Eigil Knuth had led the last expedition of discovery and exploration in Greenland on which extended journeys were made by dog sledge as the main means of transportation.

EIGIL KNUTH
COURTESY ARCTIC INSTITUTE, DENMARK.

The Peary Land Expedition was concluded in the summer of 1950 when the Catalinas evacuated all the people, but Knuth with a few assistants returned again and again over the years to North Greenland as circumstances permitted, thoroughly examining the archaeological remains around Independence Fjord and Danmark Fjord and along the coast of Northeast Greenland. In 1987, at age eighty-four, Eigil Knuth on Ile de France at 77° N made perhaps his most important discovery. In three seasons more than 400 ruins of early Dorset culture dating to about 2500 BP were excavated. Knuth said "the Ile de France is unique; the site is simply bulging with artefacts" (Hattersley-Smith 1996:373).

Count Knuth was made Knight of the Dannebrog and received the medal of that order. He also received the silver Danish Medal of Merit. He received medals from the Royal Geographical Society, Royal Scottish Geographical Society, and the Danish Greenland Society. He died in 1996, aged ninety-two.

SIMPSON IN DRONNING LOUISE LAND, 1952–54

Inland from Dove Bugt, beyond the great barrier-like glaciers Storstrømmen and L. Bistrupbree, lies an ice-free region called Dronning Louise Land. It was first seen by members of the Danmark Expedition of 1906–8, and J.P. Koch and Alfred Wegener wintered at its edge in 1912–13 before their journey with Icelandic ponies across the inland ice.

Dronning Louise Land is roughly 160 km (100 mi) from south to north and about 74 km (46 mi) from west to east. It is crossed from west to east by five branching glaciers fed by the inland ice. It is not a large piece of ice-free land by East Greenland standards, but it was almost the last to receive any scientific investigation, in part because it is difficult to reach. In 1910 Ejnar Mikkelsen's support party, led by Lieutenant Vilhelm Laub, had intended when it left Mikkelsen and Iversen on Storstrømmen to return to *Alabama* at Shannon Ø by travelling west around Dronning Louise Land and thereby carry out a reconnaissance survey. Very strong winds greatly impeded their travel and they had to abandon the attempt.

Commander C.J.W. Simpson of the British Royal Navy saw Dronning Louise Land in 1949 when he passed by on a flight from Zackenberg to resupply Count Eigil Knuth's expedition in Peary Land. The pilot told

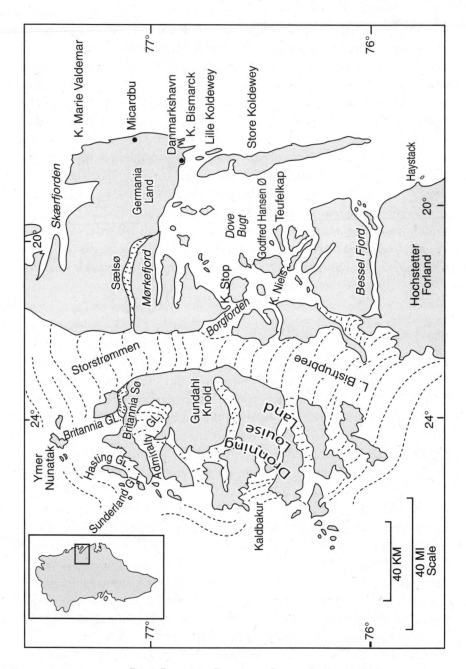

Dove Bugt and Dronning Louise Land

him that it was "virtually unknown" and was "one of the last major tracts of Greenland still waiting to be explored" (Simpson 1957:37).

Simpson believed in perpetuating the traditions of the Royal Navy in polar exploration, and the Admiralty had encouraged him. He had been given leave to visit the Arctic, and Ebbe Munck invited him to join the 1949 summer relief program of the Danish Peary Land Expedition. Simpson resolved to focus his efforts on the exploration of this remote Dronning Louise Land. In 1950 he was again invited to join the Danish program. With the cooperation of Count Knuth he was able to land at Knuth's Mørkefjord station of 1938–39 on Dove Bugt. Simpson walked to the head of the lake called Sælsø, where he could look at the edge of Storstrømmen, the formidable glacial barrier that had to be crossed to reach Dronning Louise Land. Simpson by this reconnaissance was trying to evaluate the magnitude of the problems of moving the necessary supplies overland from Dove Bugt, the nearest point of access by ship, to his chosen area for a survey of Dronning Louise Land.

On his return to England the objectives of Simpson's proposed expedition evolved from a relatively modest exploration of the ice-free land to include a substantially larger geophysical survey of the northern parts of the inland ice, with a wintering meteorological and glaciological station near the middle of Greenland's ice sheet. An undertaking of such magnitude meant that it would be nearly impossible to move sufficient supplies overland from the sea across the glacier to the ice-free land and then beyond onto the inland ice. Aircraft would have to be used if a landing site could be found for them.

In the following year, 1951, the British Coastal Command, using a Sunderland flying boat, landed Simpson and three companions on Sælsø. From there they walked across Storstrømmen, about 26–29 km (16–18 mi) wide. Simpson wrote (1957:56): "We met no crevasses; there was no excitement; it was just a weary, monotonous slog, up and down, up and down, wave upon frozen wave without end" (1957:57). Finally, after three days on the glacier, they set foot on Dronning Louise Land; "it was not an attractive place. All around stretched rolling, stony hills, dry, dusty, and almost devoid of life." But there they found an ice-free lake that would be suitable for flying-boat landings and takeoffs. Simpson called it Brittania Sø. They spent three weeks becoming familiar with the area, after which time they returned to England in the Sunderland, which returned to pick them up.

The main expedition began in 1952 when three Sunderlands, using Knuth's staging base at Zackenberg near Clavering Ø, carried supplies for two years into Brittania Sø, where Simpson's main base was established. While the main efforts of the expedition were now directed to the inland ice, the surveyors, Hans Jensen, Richard Brooke, and Keith Arnold, and the geologists, Douglas Peacock and Peter Wyllie, each with assistants, spent two years investigating Dronning Louise Land and Dove Bugt. Their jobs were to link the research that had been done in the north by the Danmark Expedition in 1906–8 with the work accomplished by others in the south; Dronning Louise Land was the unknown gap between those two previously studied regions. Glaciologists Hal Lister and Peter Taylor studied two of the glaciers, Britannia and Admiralty, that dissected the bare ground.

In the autumn of 1952 the scientists undertook their journeys by back-packing because there was not enough snow to travel by dog teams. They travelled along the glaciers in which they planted stakes to measure ice movements and the annual snow and ice gains and losses. The geologists examined the structure of the cliffs on either side of the glaciers. Hal Lister described (Simpson 1957:134) one camp site on Admiralty Gletscher: "The striking rock-colours of reds, browns and blacks were edged with snow that was rose-coloured in the fading sun. Iced lakes on the glacier looked beautifully blue, but were very slippery and, in the lakes that filled little basins at the foot of the valley walls, fallen stones looked ominously cold and imprisoned.... The whole atmosphere was of gaunt grandeur, terrific and awesome beneath the jagged, pinnacled cliffs."

Spring sledging for the geologists and surveyors began in March 1953, but because of low temperatures and strong winds flowing from the inland ice down the glaciers it was a painful month. "Constant headwinds gave us the brown marks of frostbite on our faces," wrote Angus Erskine (Simpson 1957:183). The weather kept them in one camp for eight days. Again the geologists worked down the glaciers flowing across the land and toward the south, but they found that they could not travel up the glaciers against the wind. Sledging conditions in March were very bad and they got little done. Conditions improved markedly in April, with continuous sunlight, less wind, and warmer temperatures.

The sledgers worked their way south up a long slope on the western border of Dronning Louise Land. Angus Erskine wrote (Simpson 1957:183): "At long last we reached the brow and looked southwards on a new panorama of Dronning Louise Land...The mountain peaks, that protruded in scattered profusion through the ice sheet in front of us formed a great massif to our left stretching into the sun spangled distance, were Alpine, sharp-topped and noble, far removed from the rounded hummocks near Brittania Sø." The highest peaks tower over the surrounding ice by about 915 m (3,000 ft).

May and June were productive months for the geologists who studied the cliffs along several of the transverse glaciers. They returned to the base after three months in the field. Peter Wyllie wrote (Simpson 1957:189):

> We let the dogs loose, and while they trotted busily around the Base, investigating all the smells ... there were smells for us too; smells of the soil and the flowers which were just beginning to appear; smells which assailed our unpractised senses like wafts of perfume. Sounds also seemed exaggerated to our dulled ears. Singing birds and buzzing bluebottles combined with the water trickling down the hillside to play us a symphony of summer, and before entering the Hut we walked around enjoying the forgotten smells, sounds and sights which greeted us every few yards. Life seemed perfect.

Meanwhile the surveyors, Hans Jensen and Richard Brooke, began their survey of Dove Bugt. Brooke wrote (Simpson 1957:192): "The Danmark Expedition in 1906–8 had started a triangulation of north-eastern Dove Bugt. It was our job to extend this triangulation to cover the whole of the bay, and later we hoped to connect it with the proposed triangulation of Dronning Louise Land." Jensen and Brooke had to sledge across Storstrømmen to reach Dove Bugt, a route which they knew from the expedition's experience was bad no matter where it was attempted. Several days of hard labour were required to cross the badly hummocked surface. Once across, the surveyors sledged to the southern end of Dove Bugt, where they began the survey. The work consisted in climbing to the tops of mountains, all of about 915 m (3,000 ft) in height, from whence they could sight their theodolite on conspicuous landmarks, build cairns as survey marks, and measure their angles. They carried their survey south as far as Bessel Fjord and then back into Dove Bugt. The mountain at Kap Niels had patches of hard snow at a steep angle that had to be traversed. On their descent they were separated. Jensen slipped and fell 91 m (300 ft) onto a hard rock outcrop. He died instantly, one of the very few fatalities suffered in the exploration of East Greenland. Brooke went for help and with the aid of Danes and expedition members at Danmarkshavn, they recovered Jensen's body and took it to the Danish station.

With the help of Angus Erskine, Brooke continued the survey out to Store Koldewey and then tied the survey to the points on the northern end of the bay where the Danmark Expedition had been at work.

The surveyors Brooke and Erskine confined their work in the fall of 1953 to the northern part of Dronning Louise Land, backpacking to their stations because the minimal snow again prohibited dogteam travel. They were away from the base for a month, until September 24. In this period their work was periodically interrupted by gales during which surveying from mountain tops was impossible. The geologists at that time worked in the areas around the nunataks to the north and northwest of the base and extended their work into October. Peter Wyllie wrote (Simpson 1957:272) that the work "when light and weather conditions are deteriorating rapidly, and working in constant winds at temperatures of 30 to 40 below freezing was miserable."

Two survey teams worked together in the spring of 1954 to tie the survey of Dove Bugt to that of Dronning Louise Land and to provide a "ground-truth" connection from sea level up to the geophysical surveys carried on across the inland ice by the rest of the expedition. Keith Arnold and Ron Moreton sledged down to Borgfjorden in Dove Bugt, where they took station on high ground. From there Arnold could sight across the narrowest part of Storstrømmen to a station on Gundahl Knold that Richard Brooke and Ted Jones occupied. By radio contact they made simultaneous, reciprocal observations of their stations. This was necessary to reduce to the minimum the unpredictable errors that would be caused by atmospheric refraction over the 16 km (10 mi) of glacial ice that was Storstrømmen. The job was done on April 13. Arnold and Moreton returned from Bjorgfjorden to reinforce the survey near the base so that the Danes could make maps from the aerial photographs they had taken. Brooke extended the survey into southern and southwestern Dronning Louise Land. Brooke wrote (Simpson 1957:313):

> Our first action was to climb Kaldbakur to have a look at the whole country.... It was the only place in the whole of the two years' survey where we needed to use a rope and moun- taineering technique. There was a very wonderful view from the top, especially looking towards the south, where there was an immense jumble of sharp, rocky peaks, altogether different from the more rounded and gentle forms of the rest of Dron- ning Louise Land.

On another summit they found a bamboo pole that had been left by J.P. Koch and Alfred Wegener when they climbed it forty years before. Brooke wrote (Simpson 1957:313) that "it gave us a big thrill to find this interesting relic: it somehow provided that link with humanity and previ- ous travellers that otherwise is so lacking in Dronning Louise Land." He presented the pole to the Danish Geodetic Institute.

The geologists had spent the month of March 1954, along the north side of Dove Bugt, and then journeyed, like the surveyors, to the southern parts of Dronning Louise Land where they spent many days among the high mountains to the southwest. On their return the geologists were often in company with the surveyors as both parties travelled northward along the inland ice at the western borders of the land. They travelled along Sunderland and Hastings Gletschers, named for the aircraft that supplied them; "a wonderful sledge route," wrote Brooke (Simpson 1957:315), "through some of the most beautiful scenery in Dronning Louise Land." Both parties returned to the base in June. Peter Wyllie said (Simpson 1957:319), "it was grand to be back with three months' sledging and over 1,000 miles [1600 km] behind us." The expedition base was evacuated on August 7, 1954.

EAST GREENLAND IN OUR TIME: MINING, AIR TRAVEL, WILDLIFE CONSERVATION, TOURISTS

Lauge Koch resumed his geological expeditions to East Greenland in 1947 with a small party and one ship. In the following summer he was able to acquire a Norseman aircraft on floats which greatly facilitated access to more remote regions. The discovery of metal deposits that year so stimulated the investigations that by 1949 two ships were assigned to the expedition, and Koch had ninety-seven scientists and support people in the field. In 1950 all personnel were flown to East Greenland by Icelandic flying boats. So successful were the aircraft in extending the season and saving transit time to and from Greenland that in the following year all transport was by aircraft and there was no expedition ship. Winter parties were discontinued after 1952, and in that year and in 1953 Koch extended the investigations to the lands north of 80° N. Helicopters were successfully introduced for mapping in 1954. Lauge Koch's last major expedition was in 1958, after forty-five years of nearly continuous Arctic research, interrupted only by World War II, since he first went to Greenland with Knud Rasmussen in 1913. He devoted his later years to a study of the scientific literature of Pre-Cambrian geology and he travelled widely to visit geologists. The narratives and results of his expeditions were published in over 20,000 pages in *Meddelelser om Grønland*. Additional reports appeared in other journals. He received many honours and twelve medals from various countries. The University of Basle and McGill University awarded him honorary doctoral degrees. Lauge Koch died in 1964, aged seventy-one.

As a result of the careful and extensive geological explorations over the years, a body of lead and zinc ore was found in 1948 near Mestersvig, an inlet near the southern end of Kong Oscar Fjord. Commercial mining began in 1951. The body was depleted by 1970, but by then about 58,000 tons of galena, the principal ore of lead, and 75,000 tons of sphaelerite, a zinc ore, were taken from the mine. An airfield was constructed at Mestersvig to facilitate the mining operations. The airfield became a principal port of entry into Northeast Greenland and made possible a great increase in small scientific parties and in mountaineering parties, attracted to the spectacular Staunning Alps, which were then able to reach the area conveniently from Europe and Iceland. The airfield at

Mestersvig was closed in 1985. It was replaced by an airfield closer to the village at Scoresbysund.

Mylius-Erichsen's base at Danmarkshavn was reoccupied in 1948 when the Danish government built a permanent weather and radio station. In 1950 the Sledge Patrol that Eske Brun had created during World War II was re-established. It is now called The Sirius Patrol, and it carries out long patrols with dog teams in the autumn and spring along the northeast coast. Station Nord was established for weather observations in 1952 close to the northeasternmost corner of Greenland. Aircraft from Thule, the U.S. Air Force base in Northwest Greenland, brought in the personnel and supplies for the station which can only be reached by air. No ship has ever reached that far north – except for the 500-year-old umiak that Count Eigil Knuth found in 1949 on Peary Land, not far from Nord. Nord was closed as a civilian-operated station in 1972, but reopened in 1975 and is operated by a year-round staff of five from the Danish Air Force. Station Nord is a base for scientific activities in that remote region. Eigil Knuth continued his archaeological research in and near Peary Land for over thirty years from a base at Kap Harald Moltke on Jørgen Brønlund Fjord supported by aircraft from Nord. For a time there was a weather station on the island of Nordre Aputiteq, where Amdrup and his party had found refuge from the ice on their small-boat journey in 1900.

In the early 1950s the venerable vessels *Gustav Holm* and *Godthaab*, which had played major roles in the investigations of East Greenland, were retired from service. *Gustav Holm* was built in 1893 at Elsinore, Denmark, and originally named *Grønland*. She was renamed *Gustav Holm* when the Greenland Administration bought her late in 1924 after the vessel, in spite of the wreck of her rudder by ice pressure, had successfully supported the establishment of the Scoresby Sund colony. She was sold out of Greenland service in 1952 and was bought by the Finns to serve as a mother ship for small fishing vessels. She then disappeared from Danish records. *Godthaab* was built in 1898 at Sandefjord, Norway, as a whaler, but was bought by the Danish Greenland Administration before she was completed. She was sold in the 1950s to the Faroe Islands to serve as a mother ship to the herring fisheries, and was again sold in 1974, apparently to be broken up for scrap. The two vessels were three-masted barkentines, not beautiful but immensely appealing to those interested in fine vessels. *Gustav Holm* was 44m (145 ft) long with a coal-fired, two-cylinder engine of 230 h.p. *Godthaab* was 35 m (115 ft) long with a two-cylinder engine of 240 h.p. Lauge Koch wrote (1955:251–52) that both vessels were exceptionally strong, and even in their old age were in good repair. "Both of them were well suited for ice navigation. The *Godthaab*, in particular, was capable of manouvering in ice-filled water, while the *Gustav Holm* was better suited to withstand the heavy pressure of ice hummocks." Koch noted that, in spite of their long service on the coasts of East Greenland and numerous small damages, only twice were they in serious difficulties. The first time was when *Godthaab* was struck by the gale in September 1929 which Lauge Koch described here. The second time was when *Gustav Holm* was caught in very severe ice pressure and driven aground at the Scoresby Sund colony in August 1937. That they gave faithful service until made obsolete and replaced by aircraft in the mid-twentieth century speaks so well for the men who built them and the men who sailed them.

The ice of the East Greenland Current remains as formidable as ever. In 1955 *Jopeter* was caught and damaged in the ice. The vessel had left Danmarkshavn with nineteen passengers and twenty-six crew on August 26, and for five days she struggled to break through the pack ice. The vessel became beset in the ice 14 km (9 mi) northeast of Store Koldewey. On September 4 a Danish Navy Catalina aircraft attempted to guide her out of the ice, but she was again beset. The next morning her propeller was broken off by an ice floe. Three ships went to her assistance. Passengers and some crew were transferred by helicopter to *Tottan* lying outside the ice. *Kista Dan* managed to come alongside *Jopeter* in an attempt to haul her free of the ice. *Kista Dan* herself became beset for a time, and by September 13 it was apparent that the ice was not likely to loosen enough to free *Jopeter*. The rest of her crew moved to *Kista Dan*, and *Jopeter* was abandoned in the ice. It was believed that she then sank, but nearly a year later an aircraft of Lauge Koch's expedition found her aground on a mudbank in Mountnorris Fjord on the east side of Traill Ø. Two vessels were sent from Norway to recover her. After *Jopeter* was pumped out, she was refloated without difficulty. Her cargo was transferred to one of the vessels, and she was towed to Norway by the other.

The venerable sealer *Polarbjörn* with twenty-three men on board was beset at the end of August 1957 in Foster Bugt after relieving Norwegian stations at Myggbukta and other locations. The port side was partly buckled and torn by the ice. Three ships in the vicinity could not reach her because of the ice. All on board *Polarbjörn* left and established a camp on the ice. The U.S. Air Force flew a helicopter in a cargo plane from Thule to Mestersvig, and on August 28 the helicopter began to evacuate the crew. The evacuation was completed on August 30. *Polarbjörn* was not as lucky as *Jopeter.* The veteran *Veslekari*, which had often assisted *Polarbjörn* in East Greenland, met a similar fate when sealing off Newfoundland in 1961. On the night of April 7 she was caught and crushed in the ice and sank after forty-three years of navigation in Arctic seas.

The Norwegians closed their radio station at Myggbukta in 1959, having operated it since 1922. In 1951 the United States had relinquished its rights to the wartime airfield at Ikateq, not far from Ammassalik. Operations at the airstrip were always difficult, and the military no longer had any interest in it. In 1958, when radar stations were built across the Arctic, a new airfield was built at an easier location at Kulusuk, 16 km (10 mi) east of Ammassalik, to serve the radar station at Kap Dan. The Danes operated the airfield, and when the radar station was closed in 1991, they continued the airfield, which by then provided a point of entry to East Greenland and easy access to the Ammassalik settlement for Danes on business, travelling East Greenlanders, and tourists who are accommodated at a small hotel in the colony.

The winter of 1953–54 in East Greenland brought deep snow cover and severe icing over grazing lands, and thousands of muskoxen died from starvation. The disaster caused great concern, but this was not the first occasion for discussions and proposals for the protection of wildlife in East Greenland. Just before World War I, French and German big game hunters had shot many polar bears in the pack ice. James Wordie in 1926 voiced concern for muskoxen, and during the 1930s the increasing competition between Danish and Norwegian hunters had been alarming. The zoologist Alwin Pedersen suggested in 1940 that the area between Shannon Ø and Ile de France should be designated a nature reserve. The catastrophe of 1953–54 lent urgency to the need for wildlife protection. By proclamation of the Danish government in 1956, protection was given to many species in Northeast Greenland: all species of geese, snowy owls, gyrfalcons, and walrus were given total protection. Only a few male muskoxen could be taken, and female and juvenile polar bears were totally protected. A National Park – in essence a wildlife preserve – for Northeast Greenland was proposed in 1966. After careful consultation with Greenlanders, the Danes designated the park in 1974 – "the world's largest and one of the world's most interesting nature reserve" (Vibe 1984:5). The park's southern boundary includes the inner half of Nordvestfjord in the far interior of Scoresby Sund. The western boundary runs northward to Petermann Gletscher in Northwest Greenland, and all the territory of northern and Northeast Greenland within those lines constitutes the park. It was estimated that in 1985 there were 15,000 muskoxen in East Greenland, all within the park. The reindeer that had disappeared by 1900 have not returned to East Greenland. Wolves were last seen in 1935 until a very few – less than a dozen – were again seen in 1984.

A most remarkable visitor to Greenland's east coast was Major H.W. Tilman, a veteran of the British Army of both world wars, a coffee grower in East Africa, and a Himalayan mountain climber. In his later years Tilman became an ocean voyager in rather small and usually ancient sailing yachts in search of remote mountains to climb. His voyages took him to both polar regions. In 1964 he and his climbing companions sailed in his famous *Mischief*, about 13.7 m (45 ft) long and not at all reinforced for encounters with the ice of the East Greenland Current, to Ammassalik with the intent of climbing mountains in the Skjoldungen region. The approach through the ice to Ammassalik that year was difficult, and *Mischief* had to be assisted by the local, small, ice-strengthened cargo vessel *Ejnar Mikkelsen*. In the passage through the ice *Mischief* was squeezed by two floes and suffered a serious leak. She had to be beached in Kong Oscar Havn, Ammassalik's harbor, and there the local Danish carpenter was able to replace and repair damaged planking sufficient for Tilman to get his vessel back to England.

In 1965 Tilman with a new crew tried again. He reached Ammassalik without difficulty and then sailed 280 km (175 mi) south, outside the pack ice, to Skjoldungen, much of the way in fog. There they enjoyed the climbing they had come for and then went on to Sehested Fjord, the next fjord to the south, where big floes and icebergs were "extremely numerous." After a climb in the fjord, Tilman passed on 50-odd km (31 mi) south for a visit at the weather station at Tingmiarmît before returning without incident to England.

Tilman lost *Mischief* at Jan Mayen in 1968, but acquired a similar vessel, *Seabreeze*, and tried to reach Scoresbysund in 1969. When within sight of Kap Brewster and at the edge of the ice his crew refused to go farther – Tilman called it "a polite mutiny"; he had to return to England with nothing accomplished.

Tilman tried for Scoresbysund once again in 1971, but met with such ice that "prudence prevailed." He bore away to the south for Ammassalik and Sehesteds Fjord. He reached Ammassalik in due course and without difficulty. The settlement, he noted (1974:37), had grown since his visit in 1965 – "a new wharf and warehouse at the harbour, more roads, more houses, and more shops ... now there are several privately-owned shops and even a coffee-bar complete with juke-box and fruit machine. The Greenlanders – the men at any rate – are happy-go-lucky, free spenders, and born gamblers; the fruit machine seemed to suffer accordingly, taking a hard and incessant pounding." Tilman and his companions managed some climbing in Sehested Fjord and returned home without much trouble.

Tilman sailed *Seabreeze* to Ammassalik in 1972 after once again trying without success to reach Scoresbysund. Off Kap Dan the engine failed and the vessel drifted in calm weather until overtaken by a gale that smashed her onto a skerry at the entrance to Sermilik Fjord. The crew took refuge on the islet about 23 m (70–80 ft) high. They were seen and rescued the next day by a passing boat. By then *Seabreeze* had slipped off the skerry so that only the top of the mast was above water. Later she disappeared entirely.

Tilman then acquired yet a third similar yacht, *Baroque*, in which he voyaged to West Greenland, Svalbard, and West Greenland again. In 1976 Tilman (he was then aged seventy-eight) had a most discouraging voyage in *Baroque* to East Greenland. He was considerably delayed by weather and ice but suffered no damage in reaching Ammassalik. Her crew made some local climbs, but on the day of their intended departure for home, Tilman's yacht went aground in the harbor and lay over on the falling tide. The boat took on water with the rising tide and her interior was soaked with a mixture of salt water and diesel oil. Tilman managed

to recover from this disaster, with the aid of the Danes and Greenlanders, and returned to Iceland where his crew left him. That was the end of
his Greenland voyagings. Major Tilman was later lost without a trace on
the small (and probably unsuitable) vessel of a friend while voyaging to
Antarctica.

Because of the population increase at Ammassalik after the Danes
established their station there in 1894, about 150 Greenlanders were
persuaded to move to Skjoldungen in 1938. W.A. Graah and Knud Rasmussen had both found this to be a very attractive location (except for
mosquitoes). The new settlement included a trading-company store, but
it apparently was not a long-term success. Skjoldungen was closed as a
permanent, year-round settlement in 1965. H.W. Tilman passed by in
August 1965, and saw only a few Greenlanders. He wrote (1966:182):
"There were the usual painted wood huts, quite a number of them, but I
thought it looked a fairly grim spot, stuck under some dark cliffs. As we
passed some children waved to us from the slightly dilapidated huts." By
mid-September the settlement was deserted. Apparently there were not
enough seals in the area to support the hunters, and so they were moved
back to the Ammassalik district, perhaps to return to Skjoldungen occasionally for summer hunting.

Ammassalik was always properly the name of a district, not of a
settlement, and with the evolution of home rule in Greenland in 1979
the town of Ammassalik became Tasiilaq (which means "something that
resembles a lake," referring to its nearly enclosed harbor) in the Ammassalik District. Scoresbysund, with a population of about 560 persons, was
given the name Ittoqqortoormiit. The new name of the settlement means
"the people living in big houses." Even with an air field not too far from Ittoqqortoormiit, and even with the big houses, it is the most remote settlement in Greenland, and relatively few visitors reach Ittoqqortoormiit.

"COMPULSORY CIVILIZATION"

In the eighteenth and nineteenth centuries and first half of the twentieth
century the Danes protected all the indigenous peoples of Greenland as
much as possible from outside influences by a paternalistic policy of strict
limits on foreign visitors and on imports and exports. This policy lasted

until the early 1950s, when it had became clear that World War II, with an influx of hundreds of U.S. servicemen and with all imported supplies coming from the United States, had made the Greenlanders very aware of the western world and its "astonishing new material culture and technology, until then totally alien to their world" (Robert-Lamblin 1986:147). The Danes realized that Greenland could no longer be isolated from the rest of the world. They then initiated a policy of gradual political, social, and economic assimilation of Greenlanders as "Northern Danes."

Greenland is perhaps unique among those parts of the world that had been colonized by western European powers in the seventeenth, eighteenth, and nineteenth centuries. Most such regions chose to become independent of the colonizers in the twentieth century, but in the late 1970s the people of Greenland voted to become a semi-autonomous province of Denmark, with a self-governing administrative structure and with representation in the Danish parliament. Tasiilaq and Ittoqqortoormiit each have their locally elected governing councils, administering their affairs with technical assistance from Danish specialists or Greenlanders trained in Denmark or West Greenland.

Life on the east coast had experienced a very slow transition following the establishment of the trading station and mission at Ammassalik in 1894 until 1950, and of astonishing rapidity after the 1950s, evolving from neo-stone-age pre-history to "westernization" in a little over sixty years. The demographer Joëlle Robert-Lamblin (1986) summarized the substantial studies that have been made of the changes experienced by the Ammassalimiut – the people of the Ammassalik region – and noted the critical developments that overturned the lives those people.

World War II was of course the first important turning point. The second decisive turning point began in the late 1950s and early 1960s after Denmark had made a decision to integrate Greenland into the western world. This involved:

- beginning in 1957, increasing concentration of the population into larger villages better equipped for trade and educational, medical, and religious services.
- an attempt to develop commercial fishing in 1957–58.

- the construction of a U.S. radar base and airfield at Kulusuk near Tasiilaq in 1957.
- the beginning of commercial aviation to East Greenland in the early 1960s.
- beginning in 1955, the modernization of Tasiilaq with a greatly increased Danish presence.

All of Greenland was undergoing "westernization" and integration with Denmark in the 1950s and 1960s, but West Greenland had been gradually exposed to such influences since 1721. East Greenland had been isolated from the rest of the world until 1894. The people of East Greenland then suddenly had access to benefits of westernization: elimination of serious famines, medical services, new tools and technologies, access to and travel in a wider world, European education, a much-less-hazardous lifestyle, increased population, and a social-services safety net. After the 1950s all the material amenities of modern life – refrigeration, telephones, washing machines, central heating, colour television – became available to East Greenlanders. "The adaptability of the Ammassalimiut is remarkable, particularly as regards anything to do with technology; but the social and psychological problems ... show how profoundly difficult it has been for them to apprehend a culture and society so entirely different from their own" (Robert-Lamblin 1986:123). East Greenlanders experienced the problems one must expect from exposure to an alien culture and such a profound and rapid transformation.. Epidemics, unemployment, social alienation, illegitimate births (now over 50 per cent), alcoholism, divorce, suicide, and crime became and remain serious problems.

Archaeological evidence suggests that when they were whale hunters, the ancient people of East Greenland lived in relatively large settlements, a concentration of hunters being necessary for successful whale hunts, and were fairly numerous. But with the decline of whales, the people had to turn to seal hunting, a resource subject to the uncertainties of migrations of some seal species and vulnerable, like whales, to increasing hunting offshore by Europeans. Seal hunting required that the Inuit become dispersed and nomadic, moving seasonally and often annually in search of game. But the resources of the sea were limited and "[i]n the late 19th century the balance between humans and natural resources became extremely precarious" (Robert-Lamblin 1986:19). It was in that state and just a year after a serious famine that they were found by Gustav Holm, who therefore planned for the establishment of the trading station in 1894.

As the availability of shops and social, medical, and educational services increased, people moved into Tasiilaq or the few smaller villages where such services were provided. Compulsory education for young people beginning in 1925 added to the trend, but the changes were relatively slow until the early 1950s. From 1955 to 1960 the average number of inhabitants per village increased 235 per cent. Housing became an acute problem. In earlier years highly-paid Danish carpenters were brought in at great expense to build houses for those few who could afford them or incurred debt for them. Later, much more affordable prefabricated houses, which East Greenlanders could assemble themselves, were introduced.

Now only a minor fraction of the population of the Ammassalik region are seal hunters. The last umiaks were used in 1966, and kayaks have been abandoned in favour of motorboats. Local resources can no longer support the greatly increased population, now seven times that of 1894. The Danes introduced a fishing industry for cod and halibut in the late 1950s, offering a diversified economy with wages. But the cod fishery is highly vulnerable to small temperature changes in the sea, and it is an uncertain economic activity in East Greenland. A number of people are now wage earners working for Danish contractors in construction of houses or facilities or in service activities. People are employed by the Danish trading company, by the hospital, by the utilities (water and electrical services), schools, local administration, and private enterprises (a hotel, shops, garbage collection, maintenance and repair services, tourist services). In the 1960s there were not enough jobs for all the people attracted to the villages and "the mass of the town-dwellers, particularly the young, were suffering cruelly from under-employment ... most of the town-dwelling East Greenlanders were reduced to idleness" (Robert-Lamblin 1986:116). The Danish authorities experimented with encouraging and assisting families to move seasonally away from the population centers into better hunting areas, and a number of families responded. But in general it was the same few families who migrated each year or every other year, and they were a very small part (0.5–5 per cent) of the population. The employment crisis was most serious in Tasiilaq and the larger villages. In the smaller villages, a much larger proportion of the people continue the hunting tradition, as they do in the Scoresby Sund region.

The Danish policy on the concentration or dispersion of the population was confusing. In 1938 it had encouraged the movement of people to Skjoldungen. In 1965 they were forcibly (Robert-Lamblin 1986:49) removed, mostly to a village near Tasiilaq. But then "[i]n 1966 the Danish authorities tried out an experiment to see if it was possible to encourage the Ammassalimiut to scatter out along the coast again."

The people of the Scoresby Sund region, Ittoqqortoormiit and two or three smaller villages, with much smaller populations than the Ammassalik region and much more remote and less accessible, have managed to avoid a number of the economic and social ills experienced in the Ammassalik region. Traditional hunting remains a major economic factor and foundation of diet in Scoresby Sund. Families still move out of the two or three villages in traditional hunting seasons. The hunters still use kayaks – but of plywood or fibre-glass now and not covered with seal skins.

The rate of population increase in East Greenland had been "spectacular" (Robert-Lamblin 1986:20) since 1894, at first largely because of better sanitation and hygiene and reduced infant mortality, and later because of greatly improved medical services. Population growth and migration to Tasiilaq and the villages threatened an unemployment crisis. Birth control efforts were introduced in 1969 in an attempt to stop the uncontrolled population explosion. The program quickly had effect; the birth rate in 1971 was half that of 1967. Employment opportunities have improved since then but employment problems still exist. The problem is exacerbated by the fact that younger people prefer town life, with all its diversions and amusements, and the possibility of wage-earning; they reject the more difficult and more hazardous hunting culture of their fathers.

Town dwellers and wage earners have largely adopted a western diet. The local natural resources are in fact insufficient to support the population. It is estimated that 80 per cent of foods in Tasiilaq are imported, a smaller percentage in the outlying villages, with an extraordinary consumption of sugar and starch products; "this led to catastrophic dental health conditions for the whole Ammassalik population.... Many young people are toothless or have dentures" (Robert-Lamblin 1986:124).

Under the old paternalistic policy, alcohol was forbidden to the people of Greenland. But when the new policy of assimilation and self-determination was introduced, the restrictions were removed. Alcoholism has become a serious problem – "a real social scourge ... leading to destitution, delinquency, crime, self-destructive tendencies and the rapid spread of venereal diseases" (Robert-Lamblin 1986:139). The per capita consumption of alcohol in all of Greenland is nearly twice that of Denmark, which is the highest in all of Scandinavia, and four times that of Iceland. Various schemes have been tried to reduce the consumption of spirits in East Greenland but without much success. An appreciable increase in suicide and crime such as robbery, assault, and homicide is mostly due to alcoholism.

Some privately funded social security assistance began in 1915 for the most vulnerable people. In the 1960s it became a regular government function administered by local authorities; old age and widows pensions, disability pensions, and family allowances. Support may also be provided in special cases for unemployment, for educational scholarships, and illegitimate children.

Epidemics have afflicted the Ammassalimiut in every decade since 1892. The small population of East Greenlanders had no immunities to western diseases often introduced with the arrival of ships in the summer. The common cold, influenza, whooping cough, measles, and other illnesses took their toll, but mortalities from epidemics have been greatly reduced since the mid-1950s.

The Danes have made great efforts to respond to the numerous problems that came with the responsibilities of colonization and assimilation of East Greenlanders into Danish society. The result has been numerous course changes in the uncharted waters of unprecedented social change. Joëlle Robert-Lamblin (1986:148) wrote:

> This small society, which before its contacts with the west managed its own existence and freely decided its own destiny, has all through the 20th century found itself on the receiving end of orders and counter-orders, the logic of which has most often escaped its understanding. First they were to preserve Eskimo traditions; then they were to become Northern Danes. At

one point they were to develop fishing at the expense of hunting, at the next they were expected to return to hunting. Now the population was to be concentrated in a few locations, now dispersed again. Some of the population was to be relocated to the west coast, then it was to remain in the east. Young people were encouraged to leave and integrate themselves in Danish society, then they were kept in the area. It was attempted to keep all the children, once born, alive by reducing mortality risks, and then reducing the number born by birth control or abortion. At first demands from the outside world for shark livers, seal blubber, fox pelts and sea mammal skins were to be met, later such efforts were stopped.

Robert-Lamblin (1986:149) concluded:

> In the past the Ammassalimiut have shown a great talent for adapting their technology, economy and demography to major changes such as converting from whaling to seal hunting and adapting to the scarcity of sea mammals after their over-exploitation by foreigners. Let us hope that the "compulsory civilization" (cf. Gessain 1969) to which they have been subjected for a century has not destroyed the extraordinary dynamism that has allowed them to survive in such climatic and ecological conditions.

Afterword

With relatively easy access from Iceland to the airfield at Kulusuk, Tasi-ilaq, with a population of about 1,700, has become something of a tour-ist centre. A tourist office, hotels, youth hostels, and tour operators and outfitters serve several thousand tourists a year. Wallace Hansen, one of the young U.S. soldiers who served for a year at Comanche Bugt during World War II, visited Tasiilaq with his wife. He wrote (1994:234) that "The Arctic has a magnetism that few visitors ever fully understand or overcome, especially long-time visitors. It eases its grip grudgingly, and it draws people back." The Hansens stayed at the "small, rather tidy" hotel and took a boat trip to the abandoned U.S. Army airstrip at Ikateq he had visited long before. No buildings remained. Hansen noted that everything worth salvaging had long since been removed. A dozen badly rusted army trucks, without engines, and hundreds of rusting oil drums littered the area.

Back at the village, Hansen watched the small, very sturdy, ice-rein-forced cargo vessel, *Ejnar Mikkelsen*, unload its cargo on the wharf. He noted (1994:249) the nature of modern East Greenland:

> Next to the wharf is the general store, carrying all manner of domestic and imported goods, ranging from canned Euro-pean delicacies to adult's and children's clothing, magazines and books, trail gear, nautical charts, and native carvings in ivory and stone.... Young women in bright blouses and flaring skirts, wearing tightly curled permanent waves and flaunting outrageously high-heeled boots, pored through the clothing racks. In thirty-three years the glaciers of East Greenland had retreated noticeably, but the Greenlanders had advanced con-siderably in terms of Western staples and luxuries.

Hansen recorded (1994:250) regrettable marks of civilization: "Litter is almost everywhere.... Cans and bottles stay where they land, but plastic bags are carried far and wide by the wind ... [but] We in the army littered Greenland a whole generation before the Greenlanders did." The Hansens took a walking tour across the tundra to a place called Blomsterdalen – "valley of flowers." They found that Blomsterdalen was well named.

> The ground was carpeted with flowers, mostly in rosettes or pincushion arrangements packed close to the ground in a mosaic of moss and sedges. Though short-stemmed, many of the flowers were large and showy.... Among the eyecatchers were fireweed, harebell, gentian, ranunculus, various yellow compositae, and cotton grass. A botanist would identify a lot more (Hansen 1994:246).

Hansen, the American soldier who had served in Greenland and had to return thirty-three years later, concluded his visit (1994:250–51).

> Our all-too-brief return to East Greenland was almost over ... then we were in the air, Kulusuk fell away, and we caught a last glimpse of the brooding coastal mountains stretching end-lessly to the north before they too disappeared in the mists. An old Danish expatriate, headed for home to Denmark for the last time, I judged, after years in East Greenland, asked if I would return again. "Of course," I replied, "and will you?"
> "Yes, of course," he nodded, and he lapsed into thoughtful quiet.

Glossary

archaean	pertaining to the oldest rocks of the Precambrian era.
basalt	a hard, dense, dark volcanic rock, often having a glassy appearance.
diabase	a dark-gray to black, fine-textured igneous rock.
dolerite	a coarse variety of basalt or diabase.
dolomite	a light-tinted – often gray, pink, or white – magnesia-rich mineral.
gabbro	any dark, coarse-grained igneous rock.
geosyncline	an extensive, usually linear, depression in the earth's crust in which a succession of sedimentary strata have accumulated.
gneiss	a banded or foliated metamorphic granite-like rock in which the minerals are arranged in layers.
igneous	formed by solidification from a molten or partially molten state.
kamiks	sealskin, waterproof boots worn by Inuit and Greenlanders.
magmatic	refers to the molten matter under the earth's crust, from which igneous rock is formed by cooling.
migmatite	a rock composed of metamorphic host rock with streaks or veins of a granitic rock.
nunatak	land completely surrounded by ice.
placoderm	fishes of the Devonian period that were covered with boney plates. They were ancestors of sharks.
plutonic	of deep igneous or magmatic origin.
quartzite	a metamorphic rock resulting from recrystallization of quartz sandstone.
schist	any of various medium- to coarse-grained metamorphic rocks composed of laminated, parallel layers of minerals.
tectonic	referring to structural deformation of the earth's crust.
theodolite	a surveying instrument with a small telescope for measurement of horizontal and vertical angles.
trilobite	any of numerous extinct arthropod species of the Paleozoic era, having a segmented exoskeleton divided by furrows or grooves into three longitudinal lobes.

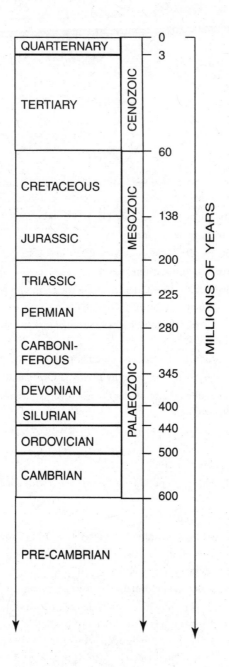

		MILLIONS OF YEARS
QUARTERNARY	CENOZOIC	0 — 3
TERTIARY	CENOZOIC	
		60
CRETACEOUS	MESOZOIC	
		138
JURASSIC	MESOZOIC	
		200
TRIASSIC		225
PERMIAN		280
CARBONI-FEROUS		345
DEVONIAN	PALAEOZOIC	400
SILURIAN		440
ORDOVICIAN		500
CAMBRIAN		600
PRE-CAMBRIAN		

THE AGES OF GEOLOGICAL ERAS AND PERIODS

Bibliography

Amdrup, G.C. 1902. Beretning om Kyst-expeditionen langs Grønlands Øst-kyst, 1900. *Meddelelser om Grønland* 27(4).

Amdrup, G. C. 1913. Report on the Danish Expedition to the northeast coast of Greenland 1906–1908. *Meddelelser om Grønland* 41(1).

Andreasen, C. 1998. NEWland: settlement patterns, social organization and economic strategies at a High Arctic polynya. 198–212. In J. Arneborg and H.C. Gulløv, eds., *Man, Culture and Environment in Ancient Greenland.* Copenhagen: The Danish National Museum and Danish Polar Center.

Anon. 1933. The legal status of eastern Greenland. *Geographical Journal* 82:151–56.

Anon. 1978. Kornerups Grønland: Andreas Kornerup, Sketches from Greenland. The Commission for Scientific Research in Greenland.

Apollonio, S. 2003. Letter to the editor. *Arctic* 56:205–6.

Bandi, H-G. 1964. *Eskimo Prehistory.* College, Alaska: University of Alaska Press.

Bobé, L. 1928. Early explorations of Greenland. 1–35. In M. Vahl, G.C. Amdrup, L. Bobé and Ad. S. Jensen, eds., *Greenland. Vol. 1. The Discovery of Greenland, Exploration and Nature of the Country.* Copenhagen and London: The Commission for the Direction of the Geological and Geographic Investigations in Greenland.

Boyd, L.A. 1932. Fiords of East Greenland. *Geographical Review* 22:529–61.

Boyd, L.A. 1934. Further explorations in East Greenland, 1933. *Geographical Review* 24:465–77.

Boyd, L.A. 1935. *The Fiord Region of East Greenland.* Special Publication No. 18. New York: The American Geographical Society.

Boyd, L.A. 1948. *The Coast of Northeast Greenland.* Special Publication No. 30. New York: The American Geographical Society.

Chapman, F.S. 1933. *Northern Lights: the official account of the British Arctic Air Route Expedition 1930–1931.* London: Chatto and Windus.

Clavering, D.C. 1830. Journal of a voyage to Spitsbergen and the east coast of Greenland, in His Majesty's Ship *Griper. Edinburgh New Philosophical Journal.* New Series. 9:1–30.

Court, A. 1949. Shipwrecked German weathermen winter in ice caves on Shannon Island, Northeast Greenland. *Arctic* 2:108–117.

Courtauld, A. 1936. A journey in Rasmussen Land. *Geographical Journal* 88:193–215.

Dahl, K.R. 1925. *The "Teddy" Expedition Among the Ice Floes of Greenland*. New York and London: D. Appleton and Company.

Elling, H. 1996. The Independence I and the Old Nuulliit cultures in relation to the Saqqaq culture. 191–98. In B. Grønnow, ed., *The Palaeo-Eskimo Cultures of Greenland*. Copenhagen: Danish Polar Center.

Erskine, A.B., and K-G. Kjaer. 1998. The polar ship *Quest*. Polar Record 34:129–42.

Freuchen, P. 1915. General observations as to the natural conditions in the country traversed by the expedition. *Meddelelser om Grønland* 51:341–70.

Fristrup, B. 1952. Danish expedition to Peary Land, 1947–1950. *Geographical Review* 42:87–97.

Gabel-Jørgensen, C.C.A. 1935. Dr. Knud Rasmussen's contributions to the exploration of the south-east coast of Greenland, 1931–1933. *Geographical Journal* 86:32–53.

Gabel-Jørgensen, C.C.A. 1940. Report on the expedition. *Meddelelser om Grønland* 106(1).

Gad, F. 1971. *The History of Greenland*. Vol. 1: *Earliest Times to 1700*. Montreal: McGill-Queen's University Press.

Gessain, R. 1996. Ammassalik ou la civilisation obligatoire. Paris: Flammarion.

Giaever, J. 1958. *In the Land of the Musk-ox*. London: Jarrolds Publishers (London) Ltd.

Graah, W.A. 1837. *Narrative of an Expedition to the East Coast of Greenland*. Transl. by G.G. Macdougall. London: John W. Parker.

Gulløv, H.C. 2000. On depopulation – a case study from South East Greenland. 43–54. In M. Appelt, J. Berglund, and H.C. Gulløv, eds., *Identities and Cultural Contacts in the Arctic*. Copenhagen: Danish National Museum and Danish Polar Center.

Hansen, W. 1994. *Greenland's Icy Fury*. College Station, Texas: Texas A&M University Press.

Hattersley-Smith, G. 1996. Count Eigil Knuth [obit.] *Polar Record* 32:373–74.

Hayes, J.G. 1934. *The Conquest of the North Pole*. New York: The Macmillan Company.

Hegemann, F. 1993. Journal of Captain Friedrich Hegemann of the ship *Hansa* during the German expedition to East Greenland, 1869–1870. Transl. by W. Barr. *Polar Geography and Geology* 17:264–329.

Holm, G.F. 1914. Ethnological sketch of the Angmagssalik Eskimo. In W.C. Thalbitzer, The Ammassalik Eskimo. *Meddelelser om Grønland* 39(1).

Holm, G. F., and V. Garde. 1889. Beretning om Konebaads-expedition til Grønlands østkyst, 1883–85. *Meddelelser om Grønland* 9(2).

Horn, G. 1939. Recent Norwegian expeditions to south-east Greenland. *Norsk Geografisk Tidskrift* 7:196–205.

Howarth, D. 2001. *The Sledge Patrol*. New York: The Lyons Press.

Hydrographic Office 1943. *Sailing Directions for East Greenland and Iceland*. H.O. No. 75. Washington, D.C.: Government Printing Office.

Ingstad, H. 1937. *East of the Great Glacier.* New York: Alfred A. Knopf.

Ingstad, H. 1966. *Land Under the Polar Star.* New York: St. Martin's Press.

Kjaer, K-G., and M. Sefland. 2005. The Arctic ship *Veslekari. Polar Record* 41(216):57–65.

Knuth, E. 1942. Report on the expedition and on subsequent work at the Mørkefjord station. *Meddelelser om Grønland* 126 (1).

Knuth, E. 1952a. An outline of the archaeology of Peary Land. *Arctic* 5:17–33.

Knuth, E. 1952b. Exploring Unknown Greenland. *American Scandinavian Review* 40:338–350.

Knuth, E. 1952c. The Danish expedition to Peary Land. *Geographical Journal* 118:1–11.

Knuth, E. 1967. Archaeology of the muskox way. Contributions du Centre d'Etudes arctiques et Finno-Scandinaves No. 5. Paris: Ecole Pratique des Hautes Etudes – Sorbonne, Sixieme section: sciences economiques et sociales. 70 pp. 8 plates.

Koch, L. 1923. Preliminary report on the results of the Danish Bicentenary Expedition to North Greenland. *Geographical Journal* 62:103–17.

Koch, L. 1924. North of Greenland. *Geographical Journal* 64:6–21.

Koch, L. 1926. Report on the Danish Bicentenary Jubilee Expedition North of Greenland 1920–23. *Meddelelser om Grønland* 70(1).

Koch, L. 1928. Two recent journeys on the coast of eastern Greenland. *Geographical Journal* 71:1–15.

Koch, L. 1930. The Danish expedition to East Greenland in 1929. *Meddelelser om Grønland* 74(10).

Koch, L. 1955. Report on the expeditions to central East Greenland 1926–39 conducted by Lauge Koch. *Meddelelser om Grønland* 143(1).

Koldewey, K. 1874. *The German Arctic Expedition of 1869–70, and Narrative of the Wreck of the "Hansa" in the Ice.* Trans. L. Mercer; ed. H.W. Bates. London: Sampson Low, Marston, Low, & Searle.

Larsen, H.E. 1934. Dødemandsbugten, an Eskimo settlement on Clavering Ø. *Meddelelser om Grønland* 102(1).

Lighthouse Press. 1998. *Sailing Directions Greenland and Iceland.* Annapolis, Md.

Lindsay, M. 1935a. The British Trans-Greenland Expedition, 1934. *Geographical Journal* 85:393–411. 86:235–52.

Lindsay, M. 1935b. *Sledge: The British Trans-Greenland Expedition, 1934.* London: Cassell and Co.

MacMillan, D.B. 1934. *How Peary Reached the Pole.* Boston and New York: Houghton Mifflin.

Malaurie, J. 1956. *The Last Kings of Thule.* London: George Allen & Unwin.

M'Clintock, F.L. 1860. *The Voyage of the 'Fox' in the arctic seas.* Boston: Ticknor and Fields.

Mecking, L. 1928. The polar regions: a regional geography. In W.L.G. Joerg, ed., *The Geography of the Polar Regions.* Special Publication No. 8. New York: American Geographical Society. Reprinted 1950.

Mikkelsen, E. 1913. *Lost in the Arctic, Being the Story of the Alabama Expedition, 1909–1912*. London: William Heinemann.

Mikkelsen, E. 1922. Report on the Expedition. *Meddelelser om Grønland* 52(1).

Mikkelsen, E. 1927. The colonization of eastern Greenland: Eskimo settlement on Scoresby Sound. *Geographical Review* 17:207–25.

Mikkelsen, E. 1933a. Report on the Expedition. *Meddelelser om Grønland* 104(1).

Mikkelsen, E. 1933b. The Blosseville Coast of East Greenland. *Geographical Journal* 81:385–403.

Nansen, F. 1890. *The First Crossing of Greenland*. Vol. 1. London: Longmans, Green, and Co.

Nathorst, A.G. 1899. The Swedish East Greenland Expedition. *Geographical Journal* 14:534–37.

Nathorst, A.G. 1901. On the map of King Oscar Fjord and Kaiser Franz Josef Fjord in north-eastern Greenland. *Geographical Journal* 17:48–63.

Nordenskjöld, O., and L. Mecking. 1928. *The Geography of the Polar Regions*. Special Publication No. 8. New York: American Geographical Society.

Odess, D., S. Loring, and W.W. Fitzhugh. 2000. Skraelings: first peoples of Helluland, Markland, and Vinland. In W.W. Fitzhugn and E.I. Ward, eds., *Vikings: the North Atlantic Saga*. Washington and London: Smithsonian Institution.

Peary, R.E. 1898. *Northward over the Great Ice*. New York: Frederick A. Stokes Co.

Peary, R.E. 1907. *Nearest the Pole*. London: Hutchinson & Co.

Pedersen, A. 1966. *Polar Animals*. New York: Taplinger Publishing Co.

Purchase, S. 1906. *Hakluytus Posthumus, or Purchas His Pilgrims Contayning a History of the World in Sea Voyages and Land Travels by Englishmen and Others*. Vol. 13. Glasgow: James MacLeHose and Sons.

Rasmussen, K. 1915. Report of the First Thule Expedition. 1912. *Meddelelser om Grønland* 51(8).

Rasmussen, K. 1932. South East Greenland: the Sixth Thule Expedition, 1931, from Cape Farewell to Angmassalik. *Geografiska Tidsskrift* 35:169–97.

Rasmussen, K, 1933a. Explorations in southeastern Greenland; preliminary report of the Sixth and Seventh Thule Expeditions. *Geographical Review* 23:385–93.

Rasmussen, K. 1933b. South-east Greenland. The seventh Thule expedition 1932. From Cape Farewell to Umivik. *Geografiska Tidsskrift* 36: 35–52.

Robert-Lamblin, J. 1986. Ammassalik, East Greenland – end or persistence of an isolate? Anthropological and demographic study on change. *Meddelelser om Grønland*, Man and Society 10.

[Ryder, C.H.] 1893. Lieutenant Ryder's East Greenland Expedition, 1891–92. *Geographical Journal* 1:43–46.

Ryder, C. 1895. Beretning om den østgrøndlandske Expedition 1891–92. *Meddelelser om Grønland* 17(1).

Rymill, J.R. 1936. The Tugtilik (Lake Fjord) country, East Greenland. *Geographical Journal* 83:364–80.

Schledermann, P. 1991. Ejnar Mikkelsen (1880–1971) [obit.]. *Arctic* 44:351–55.

Schledermann, P. 1996. *Voices in Stone.* Calgary: Arctic Institute of North America of The University of Calgary.

Scoresby, W., Jr. 1823. *Journal of a Voyage to the Northern Whale Fishery; including Researches and Discoveries on the Eastern Coast of West Greenland, made in the summer of 1822, in the ship Baffin of Liverpool.* Edinburgh: Archibald Constable and Co.

Selinger, F. 2001. *Von "Nanuk" bis "Eismitte." Meteorologischen Untersuchungen in der Arktis 1940–45.* Deutsches Schiffahrtsmuseum; Hamburg: Convent Verlag.

Simpson, C.J.W. 1955. The British North Greenland Expedition. *Geographical Journal* 121:274–89.

Simpson, C.J.W. 1957. *North Ice.* London: Hodder and Stoughton.

Smith, G.W. 1965. *The Eastern Greenland Case in Historical Perspective* by Oscar Svarlien. [book review]. *Arctic* 18:272–76.

Thalbitzer, W. 1914. Ethnographical collections from East Greenland (Angmassalik and Nualik) made by G. Holm, G. Amdrup and J. Petersen. In W.C. Thalbitzer, *The Ammassalik Eskimo. Meddelelser om Grønland* 39(2).

Tilman, H.W. 1966. *Mostly Mischief.* London: Hollis & Carter.

Tilman, H.W. 1971. *In Mischief's Wake.* London: Hollis & Carter.

Tilman, H.W. 1974. *Ice With Everything.* Sidney, B.C., Canada: Gray's Publishing.

Tilman, H.W. 1977. *Triumph and Tribulation.* Lymington, Hampshire, U.K.: Nautical Publishing Company.

Trolle, A. 1909. The Danish north-east Greenland expedition. *Geographical Journal* 33:40–61.

Vibe, C. 1984. The history and creation of the national park. *Greenland Newsletter* 4–5. Copenhagen: The Commission for Scientific Research in Greenland.

Wager, L.R. 1937. The Kangerdlugssuaq region of East Greenland. *Geographical Journal* 90:393–425.

Wandel, C.F. 1928. Scientific investigations in Greenland. In Vahl, M., G.C. Amdrup, L. Bobé, and A.D. Jensen, eds. *Greenland.* Copenhagen: C.A. Reitzel.

Winther, P.C., J. Troelsen, K. Holmen, P. Johansen, B. Fristrup, and E. Knuth. 1950. A preliminary account of the Danish Pearyland Expedition, 1948–9. *Arctic* 3:3–13.

Wood, W. and A.L. Washburn 1973. Louise Arner Boyd (1887–1972). *Geographical Review* 63:279–82.

Wordie, J.M. 1927. The Cambridge expedition to East Greenland in 1926. *Geographical Journal* 70:225–65.

Wordie, J.M. 1930. Cambridge East Greenland expedition, 1929: ascent of Petermann Peak. *Geographical Journal* 75:481–504.

Index